Belgium in the
Second World War

Jean-Michel Veranneman was a retired Belgian professional diplomat with a distinguished career and a keen sense and taste for history. He served in embassies in Germany, at the UN in New York, at the EU and at NATO in Brussels and as ambassador to Mozambique, Portugal, Israel, Brazil and the United Kingdom. When posted abroad the author noticed how little is known by the public outside Belgium about that country's involvement and role in the Second World War. His professional experience (he also served in the Belgian Army) and his fluency in several languages enabled him to consult sources and archives in many countries. As a result, this book aims to correct this, combating incomplete knowledge or simplifications sometimes caused by wartime expediency or propaganda with a balanced, factual and objective record. Jean-Michel sadly died in 2018.

Belgium in the Second World War

Jean-Michel Veranneman de Watervliet

Pen & Sword
MILITARY

First published in Great Britain in 2014
and republished in this format in 2021 by
PEN & SWORD MILITARY
an imprint of
Pen & Sword Books Ltd
Yorkshire – Philadelphia

ISBN 978-1-39901-141-9

Typeset by Concept, Huddersfield, West Yorkshire, HD4 5JL.
Printed and bound in the UK by CPI Group (UK) Ltd, Croydon CR0 4YY.

MIX
Paper from
responsible sources
FSC® C013604

Pen & Sword Books Limited incorporates the imprints of Atlas,
Archaeology, Aviation, Discovery, Family History, Fiction, History,
Maritime, Military, Military Classics, Politics, Select, Transport, True Crime,
Air World, Frontline Publishing, Leo Cooper, Remember When, Seaforth
Publishing, The Praetorian Press, Wharncliffe Local History, Wharncliffe
Transport, Wharncliffe True Crime and White Owl.

For a complete list of Pen & Sword titles please contact

PEN & SWORD BOOKS LIMITED
47 Church Street, Barnsley, South Yorkshire, S70 2AS, England
E-mail: enquiries@pen-and-sword.co.uk
Website: www.pen-and-sword.co.uk

Or
PEN AND SWORD BOOKS
1950 Lawrence Rd, Havertown, PA 19083, USA
E-mail: Uspen-and-sword@casematepublishers.com
Website: www.penandswordbooks.com

This book is dedicated to the memory of Raymond V. After the war he met Roger S. Both were Belgian but they had fought on different sides in the war, wearing different uniforms. Raymond's had been the British battledress, Roger's that of the Waffen SS. Both were in their twenties and both were motivated by idealism. One had served in Normandy, the other in Russia. The highly decorated Raymond V., having completed his law studies immediately after the war, defended Roger S. at his court martial. Roger S. was sentenced to death for high treason but was reprieved by Prince Charles, Regent of Belgium. Both these old soldiers died in their eighties, in their beds. Raymond V. was my father.

Contents

List of Plates

The main 120mm cupola of Fort Eben Emael.

A 75mm gun cupola at Eben Emael.

A fixed triple 75mm gun bunker at Eben Emael.

Inside a fixed 75mm emplacement.

The main entrance gate at Eben Emael.

Outside the main gate, one of several tin, dummy cupolas.

The strategically important Vroenhoven Bridge.

Early this century a completely new bridge was built at Vroenhoven but the Belgian army pillbox that had defended it in 1940 was preserved.

A sergeant and a squad of Chasseurs Ardennais pre-war, wearing their characteristic large green beret with boar's head cap insignia.

Chasseur Ardennais Dequand was, in civilian life, a cycling champion.

T13 and T15 light tanks were built in Belgium and equipped Chasseurs Ardennais and Cyclistes frontier troops.

King Leopold III inspecting a 47mm anti-tank gun crew.

The Renard R 31 armed reconnaissance plane was built in Belgium.

A few of the Fiat CR 42 Italian-built fighters acquired by Belgium on the eve of the war.

Belgian Fairey Battles.

The impact of German armour-piercing shots can be seen on this steel turret at Fort Battice.

All you could normally see of a retracted 75mm cupola.

Breech of a 75mm gun inside a turret of Fort Battice.

One of the thousands of Maxim machine guns received from Germany as reparations after the First World War.

One of the smaller generators at Fort Battice.

Part of Fort Tancrémont, outside Verviers.

One element of a Cointet barrier.

In the worst outrage committed by the Wehrmacht in Belgium, 86 civilians, their ages ranging from 16 to 89, were executed at Vinkt.

A group of Belgian RAF pilots congratulating their colleague Raymond 'Cheval' Lallemant on receiving the DFC.

The former Belgian embassy on 103 Eaton Square.

The plaque on 103 Eaton Square, commemorating the Belgians who volunteered here to serve in the Belgian armed forces in Britain.

The 'London Four', the Belgian government in exile.

Belgian Congolese troops entraining.

The Belgian ambassador to London in 1940, Baron Emile de Cartier de Marchienne.

The German military governor for Belgium and northern France, General von Falkenhausen.

Leopold III, King of the Belgians during the Second World War.

Lilian Baels.

The entrance to the sinister Fort Breendonk.

The torture chamber at Fort Breendonk.

The execution posts at Breendonk.

The gallows at Breendonk.

They chose the wrong side: Flemish SS parading through the streets of Antwerp behind a Wehrmacht officer.

Another who chose to collaborate: SS Lieutenant Colonel Léon Degrelle of the SS Sturmbrigade Wallonien received his Iron Cross First Class from the Führer.

The identity card of a Belgian Jewish woman, issued in 1935 and on which, during the occupation a Star of David and the word 'Jew' was stamped in both the languages spoken in Belgium.

Hergé, creator of the Tintin strips, went through an anti-Semitic phase.

The 'Hidden Children'. This moving drawing of a young Jew being protected by a Belgian was drawn by Israeli Belgian-born cartoonist Kishka for the cover of a book written by another Israeli of Belgian origin, Sylvain Brachfeld.

One of the most surprising exhibits to be seen at the Dossin Barracks – the Iron Cross awarded to German Jew Max Cohen for valour when he was in the German Army during the First World War.

Manneken Pis, the famous landmark statue in Brussels was adorned with makeshift British and American flags on 4 September 1944, the day the Allies entered the capital.

Two who fought on the right side: *Maréchal des Logis* Salman and *Cavalier* Desy of the Armoured Squadron, First Belgian Brigade, observe the enemy in Normandy from their Daimler Mark I.

Words of Thanks

The author would like to mention several historians who have inspired him. One of the best contemporary Belgian historians was Jean Van Welkenhuyzen, whose pioneering work has opened to the public many aspects that were previously unknown about Belgium in the Second World War. Like Van Welkenhuyzen, Jean Stengers of Brussels University (ULB), has left us too soon. The author had the privilege to be taught by him, as he was also by Professors John Bartier and Jacques Willequet. He was fortunate to be able to discuss the period and particular episodes with Professor Francis Balace of Liège University, Dr Chantal Kesteloot of the Centre d'Etudes de la Seconde Guerre Mondiale (CEGES) in Brussels and Prof. Van Goethem of the Dossin Barracks Memorial. Colonel Castermans, former CO of the Chasseurs Ardennais Regiment and a keen military historian read the chapters dealing with military operations, while Commander Douglas Stevenson USCG (Ret.) did the same for the paragraphs dealing with maritime aspects. Historians John Rogister and Sophie Hottat both kindly read the whole work while in progress. All made useful suggestions for corrections. Ana Carolina Lopes Ferreira da Silva drew the maps free of charge, while Pierre Lierneux of the Brussels Royal Army Museum and, again, Colonel Castermans, helped me with most of the pictures. Marie-Cécile Helleputte kindly donated most of her library on the Second World War, including several relevant books. To them and to a number of others the author would like to express his sincere gratitude, with a special thank you for his patient wife Maria.

Author's Note

At the publishers' prompting, the author has not interrupted the text with notes. They are cued by superscript number in the text and grouped together at the end of the main text. They usually refer to points that are of minor importance or are not directly part of the history of Belgium during the Second World War, but may be of interest to the reader.

Prelude: The attack on Fort Eben Emael

10 May 1940

At about 0030hrs[1] on 10 May 1940, Major Jottrand, the Commanding Officer of the big Belgian Fort Eben Emael,[2] situated about 20km north of Liège, was given an alert order, which he passed on to the garrison. Since the night before, a large number of the fort's men had been given home leave and this was the tenth alert. Many of his soldiers, believing this to be just another false alarm, were reluctant to leave their barracks outside the fort to man their posts inside it. But not long afterwards Jottrand, hearing anti-aircraft fire coming from Maastricht, immediately realized this time it was for real and gave orders to blow up the Kanne Bridge over the Albert Canal, which was his responsibility. This done, he also ordered the outside barracks to be destroyed so as to give the fort's guns on the southwest side an unobstructed field of fire and, as prearranged, to fire continuous and regularly spaced blanks from one of the cannons to recall some of the fort's men who were billeted in nearby Eben Emael village. Unfortunately, some of the men detailed to level the temporary barracks were just those supposed to man the AA machine guns on top of the fort, so they were thus delayed before they could get back to their posts.

At 0410hrs, several large, unmarked planes were observed circling and spiralling silently down towards the fort and at 0412hrs the first of nine Lufwaffe DFS 230 gliders, bringing the *Granit* (granite) group of *Fallschirmjägern* (paratroops), skid-landed on top of the fort amongst the cupolas. After months of repetitive and systematic training in secrecy in Hildesheim and the captured Czech forts, they had boarded their gliders in Ostheim field, near Cologne, at 0335hrs and had been towed in by Junkers 52s as far as the border, guided by a series of searchlights pointing the way to Eben Emael. Belgian *Canonnier* (Gunner) Rémy, after wondering at first whether the aircraft he was seeing were not Belgian planes in distress, finally opened fire on them just as one of the gliders crashlanded on another AA machine-gun nest. As the gliders landed, out scrambled German engineers/paratroopers who immediately proceeded to silence most of the big guns of the fort's cupolas, either placing single demolition charges inside the tubes or more lethally by placing the heavy 50kg hollow charges[3] they had brought for that purpose on the cupolas. Terrifying explosions rocked the gun turrets or blew deep cylindrical holes in the steel observation bells, obliterating the Belgian gunners or observers inside. Most periscopes were immediately shattered and several turret turntables disjointed when the turrets were lifted up to fire. Canonnier Furnelle was pulverized inside his observation clock just as he was reporting the landing of the curious noiseless planes close to him. Contrary to later popular belief German intelligence was not perfect as valuable effort was also wasted on dummy, tin cupolas.

More gliders brought the other three groups of *Fallschirmsturmabteilung Koch* (assault paratroop detachment): group *Stahl* (steel) at Veldwezelt Bridge, *Beton* (concrete) at Vroenhoven Bridge and *Eisen* (iron) at the Kanne Bridge over the strategic Albert Canal (see Map 1, page 6). As ordered Sergeant Pirenne blew the latter up as the Germans were close to storming it, but the two others were taken after a short, savage fight with flame throwers, and the demolition charges were defused. Most of the Belgian soldiers in the bunkers defending the bridges lost their lives.

After most of Fort Eben Emael's guns had been rendered useless, and several counterattacks both by part of the garrison and a platoon of Belgian Grenadiers located in the vicinity had failed, morale inside started to suffer from the constant deafening explosions that reverberated for hours inside the long galleries. Oberleutnant Witzig, in command of Granit but whose glider had broken its towing cable in flight, managed to find a replacement DFS 230 and joined his men. At some points the Germans blasted their way into the fort's turrets and sought refuge inside against fire from the other nearby Belgian forts – prearranged in case the enemy had gained the advantage. Inside a turret he had penetrated, a German NCO picked up a ringing telephone and slowly said, in English, 'The Germans are here', to be answered by a startled, 'Oh! mon Dieu!' *Feldwebel* (Sergeant) Arent entered cupola Maastricht 1 and descended the steel staircase leading to its magazine. He placed a 50kg hollow charge against the armoured door he found there barring his progress and retired up the stairs. In the confined space the charge completely blew away the heavy steel and concrete door from its locks and hinges and it smashed into a concrete wall behind, reducing to a pulp six Belgian soldiers who were at their posts behind it. The damage can still be seen today and is a poignant sight. The tremendous blast also deafened Feldwebel Arent, even tens of metres away, and destroyed the steel staircase, preventing him from going down again.

Unable to fire most of their guns, the garrison's morale had further deteriorated the next day, after a sleepless night, especially when a fire started among some calcium chloride that was kept to prevent the decay of corpses in case of a prolonged siege. White smoke engulfed some galleries of the fort and was taken to be poison gas, which was known to have been used recently by the Italians in Abyssinia.

On the second day of the fighting, 11 May, the *Fallschirmjägern* were joined at 1300hrs by land troops of the 4th Panzerdivision from 6th Armee under the command of *Generaloberst* (Colonel General) von Reichenau, who had come through the Netherlands, where some bridges had been taken by ruse, using Dutch uniforms. The bridges over the Meuse in Maastricht and the Albert Canal that had been blown up by Dutch or Belgian troops were immediately replaced by pontoon bridges and defended with abundant light flak.

German engineers of Pionier Battalion 51 also crossed the Albert Canal on rubber rafts under fire from the fort, lowered explosives against the casemates or used flamethrowers against them, whilst under intermittent fire from the other Belgian forts of Pontisse and Barchon.

In the morning of 11 May, Major Jottrand, after consulting his superiors in Liège by telephone, and seeing the plight of the fort becoming desperate, followed standing orders and called a meeting of Eben Emael's defence committee, the *Conseil de Défense*, composed of the senior officers. They agreed surrender should be offered as the Kanne Bridge, the only one under the fort's direct control, had been blown and practically all the fort guns had now been rendered useless. (The other two bridges over the Albert Canal at Veltwezelt and Vroenhoven, due to complicated command arrangements were not under the fort's control and Commandant Giddeloo, the officer responsible, was killed during a Stuka attack on his command post some kilometres north.) The wooden removable bridge at the fort's entrance was put back and Capitaine Vamecq, carrying a white flag and accompanied by a bugle sounding the cease-fire, made his way out to speak with the Germans. The bridge was left open and at this point a few panicking soldiers who happened to be near the entrance followed the parleying officer out, as the Germans ceased firing. Fort Eben Emael's surrender was accepted at 1215hrs, having held out for about a day and a half. Officers destroyed confidential papers and the garrison filed out. In the column of Belgian POWs that formed a little later a small girl could be seen, carried on the shoulders of Sergent Lecron. After the cease-fire

Lecron had rushed to his home in Eben Emael village, only to see that the Stukas had flattened it, killing his wife and three other children. The babe in arms was the only survivor. The Germans however did not allow her to be taken along and the child was later entrusted to a Belgian padre who took her to her grandfather. Both father and daughter survived the war.

Fort Eben Emael suffered twenty-three killed and about twice that number of wounded out of about 1,000 men. Today a plaque near the entrance lists those killed in action. The garrison was led into a captivity that would last five years for most. They were kept in isolation because they were deemed to know too much about new German tactics and weapons.

Heroic efforts were made over the next few days by Belgian and British Fairey Battles, as well as French Bréguet 693s, to destroy the captured bridges. These attacks only resulted in heavy loss of life, the Germans having immediately installed dozens of light 20mm flak guns – the planes flew straight into their accurate, murderous fire. Belgian Capitaine Glorie of 3ème Régiment d'Aéronautique was shot down in his Fairey Battle 'T70' at Vroenhoven Bridge on 11 May after he flew round for a quasi-suicidal second pass. He was killed and six planes out of nine in his *Escadrille* (Squadron) were shot down, their slow Battles being easy pickings for the German flak or the Luftwaffe Messerschmitt 109s waiting for them. Most crews were killed (five) or heavily wounded. Two RAF pilots won posthumous Victoria Crosses at Veldwezelt Bridge. A total of twenty-seven Belgian, British and French planes were shot down while attacking the Meuse/Albert Canal bridges.

The fact that Eben Emael only held out for a short period despite having been deemed impregnable, affected the morale of the rest of the Belgian Army. Eben Emael was not their finest hour. Some men fought bravely and died at their post, like Private Ancia, who volunteered to blow up a gallery and was killed in the explosion. Others shamefully panicked. Faulty strategic and tactical concepts and decisions by the Army staff were also to blame, like the fact that the garrison, composed of artillery men, was insufficiently trained for infantry-type fighting in sorties, and access to the gun turrets was obviously too easy. On the whole a long overland approach similar to what happened during the German attack on the forts of Liège in August 1914 had been anticipated, with plenty of time to lay mines and barbed wire, dig trenches and so on. But in fact there was a football field at the fort, giving the German photo reconnaissance planes clear indication that the area was not mined. (This had been allowed to keep the bored garrison in relatively good spirits.)

By contrast, about 400 Belgian soldiers died defending the Albert Canal bridges. Fort de Tancrémont, south of Liège, remarkably resisted from the 10th until 29 May – that is one day after the rest of the Belgian Army capitulated – and was granted the honours of war by the Germans, as was also the case for Fort Aubin-Neufchâteau and Fort de Loncin in August 1914. This contrast is typical of the conduct of the whole Belgian Army, indeed of all Western armies in these dark days of May 1940: some units fought gallantly; others made a poor show. The Germans at Eben Emael were highly motivated, propaganda-fed, tough soldiers. Later a Belgian veteran of the fort was to relate: 'We were citizens in uniform, defending our country and they were murderous characters, trained to kill.' Some German paratroopers of 1940 were former SA men, though there is no evidence these fought at Eben Emael. Two days after the attack Hitler himself presented nine of the officers involved, including Oberleutnant Witzig, with Knight's Crosses First or Second Class at Felsennest, his command post near Bonn. The other ranks were all promoted or otherwise rewarded with the exception of Private Grechza, who had replaced the water in his canteen with rum and was seen sitting, gloriously drunk, astride one of the big 120mm guns at Eben Emael as it swung back and forth. Group Eisen was the least successful, losing twenty-two men including its Commanding Officer Leutnant Schächter, and a further twenty wounded, only to see Kanne Bridge blown up. This however, was quickly replaced by a pontoon bridge.

Not many of the Eben Emael *Fallschirmjägern* survived the war, many being killed in Crete, where they took heavy losses. After this campaign, with the exceptions of Skorzeny's liberation of Mussolini at the Gran Sasso or the Battle of the Bulge, these elite Lufwaffe troops were never again used in airborne surprise raids.

Fort Eben Emael sits to this day, diamond shaped, its 66 hectares in the middle of the hilly terrain out of which it was cut, or rather dug, dotted with silent cupolas and shot-pocked square casemates (gun emplacements) in green pastures or woods. Several kilometres of unseen galleries and staircases link them underground, together with command posts, a hospital, generator rooms, sleeping quarters and so on.

It was built in the 1930s, just north of Liège, within sight of Maastricht at the Dutch–Belgian border, where the western surroundings of Maastricht form a bulge of Dutch territory on the western Belgian bank of the Meuse River. Incorporating lessons learned during the siege of the Liège forts in 1914, and together with the dozen other forts forming the *Position fortifiée de Liège*, the mission of its huge 120mm and 75mm retractable gun cupolas

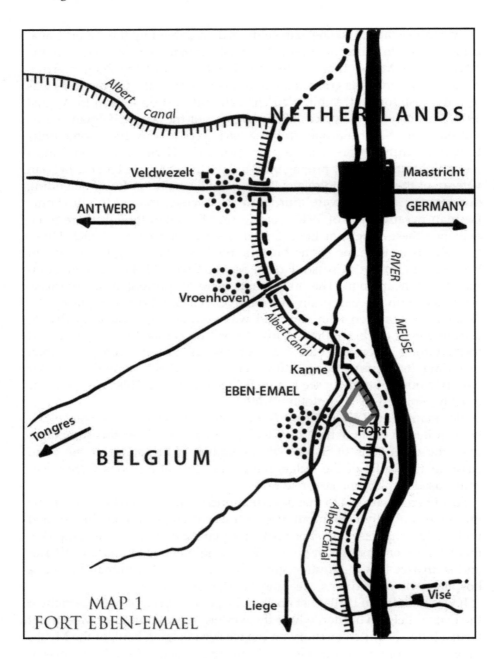

MAP 1
FORT EBEN-EMAEL

and numerous machine guns was to cover the bridge crossings over the Meuse in Maastricht and out of that Dutch city over the Albert Canal, which runs roughly parallel to the Dutch border and protects central Belgium. In the First World War Holland had remained neutral, but it was anticipated that in the next violation of Belgian neutrality this would not be the case.

The fort had acquired a reputation of impregnability (some newspaper articles called it the Gibraltar of the North) which the Belgian government had every reason to encourage, and it formed, with the Meuse River, from the French border to Namur and Liège and then on northwest along the newly dug Albert Canal, the first line of defence against a German invasion coming through the Dutch province of Limburg, which juts out a long way south between the German and Belgian borders. Eben Emael is situated close to where the two obstacles, the Meuse and the Albert Canal, meet. Thus it formed the easternmost hinge position of the first defensive line the Belgian Army was planning to hold against a German attack.

To make the Allies (France and Britain) believe that the German breakthrough in neutral Belgium and Holland was the genuine breakthrough (rather than the later Sedan to the Somme 'sicklecut' which was the real planned *Schwerpunkt* – where the main push would be made) it was essential to achieve three things. First they must take Eben Emael, then secure the Meuse/Albert Canal crossings, and finally lure the Allied force deep into Belgian territory (which for various reasons they wanted to do anyway), so that as many as possible of the French and British troops would be drawn into a trap – to be sprung when the Panzers reached Abbeville and the Somme estuary on 20 May 1940. To take Fort Eben Emael by simply bombing and shooting at it was feasible. That is how the other forts around Liège were dealt with, but at this point it would have expended too much time and heavy ammunition, so two new surprise weapons were used, apparently at Hitler's own prompting: glider transports and hollow charges, together with heavy, continuous Stuka bombing.

If the fall of Eben Emael (taken by surprise with new, hitherto unknown weapons) was bad news, it should be noted that the real catastrophe of the campaign was the fall of the key position of Sedan in France (taken with conventional means against an enemy that had ample warning), because it opened the whole Western Front to a turning and enveloping westward movement that was to lead to its eventual collapse.

The silent cupolas at Eben Emael still show the effects of the hollow charges, though they were partially cemented over by the Germans, who did not want their new weapon to be known. Only birdsong can now be heard where on a May dawn, the war in the West began with great noise, blood, suffering and destruction. Forts Eben Emael, Aubin Neufchâteau, as well as Battice and also Loncin, taken in August 1914 at the beginning of another war, and several others in the Liège area can be visited today.[4] A pleasant drive along the different bridges over the Albert Canal is also possible and several interesting monuments are to be seen close to them.

Introduction

At the date of writing, almost three-quarters of a century has passed since the outbreak of the Second World War. Many of the protagonists and certainly all those who held senior posts have passed away. It is now possible to try to dispassionately examine their feelings and situation, the decisions that were taken in the tragic days of the worst conflict the world has ever seen, the information on which those decisions were based, and the intentions that inspired them and their consequences. 'The historians of the future will judge!' is often heard whenever there is controversy. The fact that seven decades have now passed surely entitles us to count ourselves among those future historians.

In my previous career as a diplomat I often noticed how little is known outside its borders of the role Belgium played in the Second World War. Remarkably few books in English have been written about it. There are not many in any other language either, though a number have now been published in Belgium, in either French or Dutch, on particular aspects of the conflict. My intention has been to offer a factual, objective report of those momentous events, which left no family in my country unaffected (my own being no exception).

Also, with a few notable but relatively recent exceptions, not many books have been written about the Second World War or its most important developments that give an *overall* picture and they are too often based only on sources originating in one or other of the different belligerent countries. The tendency is rather to stick to what happened in this or that country (usually that of the author), and the sources tend to be monolingual. More often than not propaganda or some degree of mild nationalism is also present: our politicians and generals were all competent, our soldiers were courageous and victorious and behaved properly. The present book is indeed a relation only of what happened in Belgium and events concerning that country during those fateful years, but it also contrives to contribute to the bigger picture and draws on sources from all the affected countries.

Belgians know that they owe their freedom to the enormous sacrifices the British, Commonwealth and American troops made on their soil twice last century. Many, very many of the young English, Scottish, Irish boys and also young men from New South Wales, the Punjab, Manitoba or Wisconsin now rest forever in Belgian cemeteries. Their names are also read by visiting locals. The Belgian people have not forgotten them. If Belgium is attached to a closer integration of Europe it is in large part because it lived through two cruel and oppressive occupations, brought about through no fault of its own during two of the many wars between their neighbours which for centuries more often than not were fought on Belgian soil: at Sluys, Fontenoy, Seneffe, Ramillies, Oudenaerde, Malplaquet, Fleurus, Neerwinden, Waterloo, Ypres, Zeebrugge, Bastogne and many other places. European integration has the merit of having put an end to these wars.

Chapter 1

They knew it was coming: Belgium between the wars

Versailles

In 1918, when the Great War ended, the prestige of 'brave little Belgium', its army, its King Albert I and (Bavarian born) Queen Elisabeth, were extremely high. *King Albert's Book*, a volume put together by Rudyard Kipling to celebrate the courage of this small country and its monarch (as the subtitle says, 'A tribute to the Belgian King and people from representative men and women throughout the world') was to be seen on most British drawing-room tables. The King embarked on several visits to the former allies, including the US and Brazil, and everywhere Albert and Elisabeth were given rapturous welcomes. Monuments, statues and plaques were erected all over Europe and beyond. Schools, streets, hotels, mountain peaks, even dishes were named after them and when Albert died in a mountaineering accident in 1934, King George V gave the Belgian Army the privilege of being the only non-Commonwealth army to parade each year bearing its arms at the Cenotaph in Whitehall and then march to Horse Guards Parade – a tradition kept up every July since by a detachment, usually from the Belgian Navy.

A few Belgian politicians tried to ride that wave of popularity at Versailles and made claims, some reasonable, others on the whole unrealistic, like the annexation of the Grand Duchy of Luxembourg and of large chunks of neutral Holland, because it had allowed free passage to some of the retreating German troops in November 1918. Some 'loose cannons' in the Belgian Army and secret services even encouraged Rhineland separatism. It was agreed at Versailles though, that Belgium, which had suffered most from German occupation with total destruction of the Ypres area, the shooting of hundreds of innocent civilians and the carting away or outright destruction of industry, metals, coal mines etc. should have priority with regard to the German reparation payments. Luxembourg became permanently linked with Belgium in a customs and monetary union and two German speaking districts in the German border region, Eupen and Malmédy, were annexed. Belgium, whose colonial troops had helped to conquer German East Africa, defended by the famous von Lettow-Vorbeck, was also entrusted by the new League of Nations with the task of administering a part of it, those lands which later formed present-day Rwanda and Burundi.

Abandonment of neutrality

The neutrality which had been imposed on Belgium as a condition for its independence from the Netherlands in 1830 was now deemed obsolete by all and a military alliance with France, by far the largest military power at the time, the great victor of 1918, was thought to be necessary for fear of Germany. It was signed in 1920. In 1923, Belgian troops joined the French in the occupation of the Ruhr because reparation payments stipulated by the Versailles Treaty were not forthcoming.

One of the officers in the Belgian contingent was the author's grandfather, Major V., who had spent most of the four years of the previous war in the trenches.

The Locarno Pact

In 1925, most of the European countries came together at the Italian city of Locarno to negotiate a series of treaties that were later signed at the Foreign Office in London. Among other stipulations, the Locarno set of treaties guaranteed the integrity of Belgium's borders and its three large neighbours – Germany, Britain and France – were pledged to defend them, a guarantee repeated several times by all of them, including after the accession of Hitler to power.

Return to neutrality

In the late 1920s and early 1930s, reasons for Belgium to go back to neutrality began to emerge. These were both internal and external. Internally, there was the progress of the 'Flemish feeling' parties in Flanders, mainly VNV and DeVlag which, recalling the importance and glory of the Flemish merchant cities of the Middle Ages, considered the state of Belgium to have been an aberration created in 1830 by the French-speaking Walloons in southern Belgium and by the Flemish elites, who also spoke French. These nationalist Flemings advocated separatism, or at least better recognition of their culture and language. Their ideas, which had started to be voiced in the late nineteenth century, now built on the very different way the experience of the First World War – that is the occupation of Belgium and the terrible sacrifices the soldiers of the Belgian Army had endured in the trenches for four years – was seen by either the

French speakers and Flemings in whom it reinforced Belgian national feeling and patriotism, or, on the contrary a growing number of Flemings who saw things differently. This situation was partly due to some indisputable facts: Belgium was until the 1930s a predominantly French-speaking country: the Flemish/Dutch language[5] was spoken by few (some say it had almost disappeared except in the form of local dialects); courts usually heard cases in French in Flanders; and there was no access to secondary or higher education except in French, thus forcing young Flemings to study in another language than their own mother tongue. As a consequence the country was dominated by French speakers, including the Flemish elite. The new Flemish ideology was also based partly on a myth: Flemish soldiers had been killed in action, or even executed during the First World War because they could not understand the orders of their French-speaking officers.[6] The feeling of some if not many in Flanders was that Belgium, or rather the Belgian Flemish foot soldiers, who had actually been a majority (though not an overwhelming one – another myth) in the trenches, had been fighting someone else's war, that is the war of the French-speaking elite in Belgium, and that of France, against a fellow Germanic 'brother people'. A desire for a strong state-like autonomous entity became part and parcel of the Flemish nationalist movement, which was also pacifist, traditionalist and conservative, in a region where Catholicism and family bonds were strong. The lower Flemish Catholic clergy played an important role in the rise of Flemish national feeling during the nineteenth and twentieth centuries and sometimes described Paris, where anticlerical laws were passed at the turn of these two centuries and innocent Flemish girls serving as housemaids were said to have been perverted, as a modern Babylon. Among other demands concerning political rights and access to higher education in their own language, the Flemish nationalist parties lobbied for the liberation of Flemish politicians who had been jailed for collaboration during the first occupation (some were elected Members of the Belgian Parliament while still in detention) and the abandonment of the alliance with France.

The Vlaams Nationaal Verbond (VNV – Flemish National League) became, in the 1930s, by far the most important Flemish nationalist political movement. Led by Staf De Clercq, it received increasingly substantial monthly allowances from Nazi propaganda minister Goebbels but professed neutrality 'all round', thus not only against too close ties with France, but also it said, it would defend Flanders against Germany. Apart from the *Leider* (Leader or Guide), De Clercq, prominent VNV members of parliament were Gérard Romsée, Reimond Tollenaere and Hendrik Elias, about whom more later. Advocating a reunification with the Netherlands it tried to woo August Borms, the veteran collaborator of the First World War. After the Germans occupied Belgium, De Clercq and the VNV openly espoused the German creed and its publication became violently anti-Semitic, rejoicing in the deportation of the Jews. The *Leider*, De Clercq, became ill and died in October 1942 and his designated successor Tollenaere died fighting in SS uniform in Russia. During the occupation the influence of the VNV waned, in large part because the SS favoured and actively supported a rival Flemish nationalist group, DeVlag, led by Jef van de Wiele.

Verdinaso was led by Joris van Severen, a former Belgian Army officer who had fought in the First World War. Verdinaso is the acronym for Vereniging van Dietse Nationaal Solidaristen (Union of Dutch-speaking National Solidarists) – it advocated a mixture of social progress, Low Countries nationalism and, logically with this last, a (new) merger with Holland, from which Belgium had detached itself in 1830.

As in almost all European countries, parliamentary democracy came under fire in Belgium; it was rocked by scandals and extreme right parties also emerged which were not Flemish but Belgian nationalist, like Rex, led by the (later) *Obersturmbannführer* (Lieutenant Colonel) SS Léon Degrelle. Authoritarian and anti-parliamentary in nature, these parties sympathized to different degrees with Fascist Italy or Nazi Germany, from whom some received financial help. Flemish or Belgian nationalists also laid claim on recuperating cities in northern France like Lille, Arras, Dunkirk, Cambrai and Douai, which had been among the possessions of the Dukes of Burgundy and the Spanish Netherlands, and were annexed to France in the late seventeenth century by Louis XIV (see Chapter 3). The names of these places (Rijsel, Atrecht, Duinkerke, Kamerijk, Dowaai) and many smaller ones are of Flemish origin as are many local family names, folklore and traditions. A local Flemish dialect is still spoken in some of these places.

Other reasons to return to neutrality were of an international nature. They included the failure of the League of Nations to stop Italian, Japanese and later German military aggression, Hitler's withdrawal from the Covenant, the rearmament of Germany, the failure of France and Britain to react to Hitler's occupation of the Rhineland (which borders with Belgium), the policies of appeasement which they were seen to adopt, the fact that Chamberlain more than once offered to compensate Germany for its colonies in Africa lost at Versailles by handing over the Belgian Congo (and Portuguese Angola as well – Hitler refused) and so on.

France was now seen to seek an alliance with the hitherto ostracized Soviet Union – though threatening Germany's back was not at all likely to make that country less dangerous. The southern neighbour was affected by political instability and strife: in 1934, the extreme right rioted in the streets of Paris and a military coup staged by the *Comité social d'Action révolutionnaire*, aka 'the Cagoule' came close to materializing. In 1936, the Front Populaire government came to power and included communists, who were strongly antimilitaristic. Britain was seen to be allowing its military apparatus to fall behind in the 1930s and accepted partial naval parity with Germany in 1935. When it was felt more and more in Belgium that France and Britain were prepared to sacrifice the smaller countries and their overseas possessions (but not their own) to preserve peace at any cost, and war was felt to be inevitable anyway, a return to neutrality (after all, the Netherlands as well as Switzerland had been left unmolested in 1914–18) enjoyed growing support. Later events, like the *Anschluss* with Austria, when cheering crowds greeted the arrival of Hitler, or the shameful abandonment of Czechoslovakia at and after Munich, or the Norwegian fiasco (when Allied forces had to give way to the German invaders) were not of a nature to make Belgian public opinion change its mind, nor was the fact that when their 'official' ally Poland was crushed in September 1939, Britain and France did little about it apart from formally declaring war.

It should be said also that if relations with Britain remained correct, relations with France deteriorated somewhat in the 1930s because of the increasingly patronizing attitude of that country towards Belgium, and even the intention of at least some of its leaders to make its smaller neighbour a kind of vassal state, causing increasing mistrust in Brussels. Several public statements by French authorities did not help, even if well meant, as when Marshal Pétain declared, inaugurating a war monument in Belgium, that the country was 'the natural bulwark of France' or even worse, that 'the Belgians are the vanguard of Latin civilization facing Germany'. These declarations caused uproar in the Flemish press and consternation in the Brussels government. The annexation by Belgium of Eupen and Malmédy – part of Germany since Waterloo – which King Albert could not resist under pressure of the Belgian nationalists who wanted much more, was also felt by him, his son and many others to have been a poisoned gift by the Allies, because it created a point of friction with Germany which Belgium could have well done without. After

France declared war against Germany, but while Belgium was still neutral, the Belgian ambassador in Paris reported that General Weygand had told him the French General Staff had every intention of entering Belgium militarily even if Belgium opposed it.

By 1936, a quasi-general consensus had come about in Belgium to adopt, as King Léopold III's speech on 14 October 1936 put it, 'an exclusively and totally Belgian policy' – that is a return to neutrality, or more precisely what was officially called an independent policy, in the hope of escaping the next war. This caused consternation and anger in France and some French politicians who for some reason felt Léopold III to be more pro-German than his late father Albert I blamed it on him. 'C'est ce Boche de Léopold!' said French Foreign Minister Louis Barthou, when it was being discussed. King Léopold was certainly not pro-German and even less pro-Nazi. But he felt that the Allies, especially France, had been far too hard on Germany at Versailles, through exaggerated reparation demands denying its chances of rebuilding its economy and thereby upsetting the balance of power in Europe. Today, the Versailles Treaty is generally accepted by historians to have at least strongly contributed in sowing the seeds of Hitler's rise to power. In Belgium at the time, the actual reasoning behind the neutrality policy as expressed by socialist Foreign Minister Spaak, who had to defend it against a large part of his own socialist party, was that if war between Britain, France and Germany was inevitable anyway, Hitler's behaviour being an ever clearer indication of what was coming, if Belgium were neutral it stood a (small) chance of avoiding war, whereas this hope would be totally nonexistent if it was allied to France. And in that case the responsibility of the Belgian Government, had the country been drawn into a war it might have avoided, would have been crushing. With hindsight it is easy to criticize the Belgian neutrality policy, and many did and still do. It might have worked, but it didn't. Sweden and Switzerland managed to stay neutral; Belgium did not.

Another, often overlooked factor in all this was that the Maginot Line, a line of defence forts inspired by the unexpectedly important defensive role the Forts of Verdun had played in 1916, started at the Swiss border but stopped at Montmédy, east of Sedan, at the border of France with Luxembourg and Belgium – thus making an invasion of France through Belgium, as in 1914, even more tempting because it meant bypassing the Maginot Line. For that reason Belgium more than once insisted that it should be extended to the North Sea, which would have acted as a deterrent to a German invasion of its territory, but lack of funding meant that nothing came of this plan. In one case, the reason given in Paris was 'not wanting to offend the Belgians', which was of course a very weak argument indeed. In fact, British Secretary of State for War Hore Belisha proposed to extend the Maginot Line along the French–Belgian border but did not garner sufficient support.[7]

The Belgian government knew well enough that some voices in Britain, prominently that of Churchill, had condemned Munich and appeasement (as had some in France too), but at that time the man who would become the wartime British prime minister was a mere backbencher – he came to power on 10 May 1940, precisely the day Belgium was invaded.

Military build-up

To safeguard its newly asserted neutrality, Belgium had to build up a credible defence. The country whose inhabitants numbered fewer than 8 million in 1940, remarkably managed to field an army of more than 600,000 men in 22 divisions, though actual combatants must have been closer to 450,000. By comparison, the US Army in these pre-Pearl Harbor days numbered 189,000 men and the BEF's 11 divisions, gradually deployed in France after the declaration of war with Germany, were 300,000. France fielded 120 divisions and over a million men in the north-east of the country and was thus by far the senior partner in number and prestige, in the coalition that was formed on 10 May. These numbers exclude colonial troops overseas: in the case of the Belgian Congo there were another 15,000 men who did not engage in combat in Europe, unlike several French divisions which came from north or sub-Saharan Africa. The Dutch Army numbered about 280,000 men and Luxembourg's armed force about 1,000. On the other hand, Germany fielded 157 divisions, almost the same as the French, Belgian and British put together. The number of tanks on both sides was roughly equal but their principles of tactical use entirely different, as is well known.

Belgian Army uniforms, ranks, denomination of units and regulations were largely inspired by the French Army, as the Belgian forces had been trained after independence in 1830 by French and Belgian officers who had fought with Napoleon. Thus there were (and still are) *Régiments de Ligne* (or *Linie* for Flemish units), who were regular infantry, *Grenadiers, Carabiniers* – who were also infantry, and *Guides, Lanciers* and *Chasseurs à Cheval*, all cavalry. The Grenadiers and 12e de Ligne were the elite infantry regiments, the former being the unit in which members of the royal family usually served and the latter having strong links with the city of Liège. In the late 1930s some of the units became unilingual Dutch and gradually Dutch-speaking officers were appointed, though all officers above junior ranks had to be bilingual. Another infantry regiment, 4e Linie, kept traditional links with the city of Bruges, where it had long been garrisoned.

In 1940 the Belgian Army still basked in the glory of the 1914–18 campaign, when its relatively small force of 200,000 (117,000 of which were in the field army) had unexpectedly resisted the Kaiser's onslaught and had thrown a spanner in the Schlieffen plan for a European war, as revised by Von Moltke. This they did with the Liège forts slowing the German advance, and then by inflicting a bloody nose on some elite German cavalry units at the Battle of Halen (which General Guderian was later to use as an example in his book, *Achtung Panzer*) and, last but not least, by making a spirited, successful stand behind the small Yser River between Ypres and the North Sea, where they resisted repeated and very determined German attacks bent on taking the vital Channel ports just beyond them. In this way, the Belgian Army and its King/C-in-C clung on to the last bit of unoccupied Belgian territory, next to British lines which started at Ypres and went on into France and the Somme. The skilful Belgian retreat, followed by stiff resistance on the Yser in September and October 1914, won the French and British precious time, first to regroup for the Battle of the Marne and then to win the Race to the Sea. The Belgian front was stabilized for most of the next four years after the low ground in front of it was deliberately flooded. King Albert, mindful of the need to spare his soldiers' blood, refused to be drawn into massive attacks he did not believe in, like the Somme or Passchendaele. In 1918 he was given command of a large army group comprising British, French and American troops as well as his own, with whom he liberated a large part of the country. It is of interest that it was the Belgian Army which finally recaptured the small village of Passchendaele, so desperately fought for by British and Commonwealth troops in 1917, after it had been lost during the last great German offensive of 1918. One piece of advice King Albert gave his son Léopold was to see to it that the Belgian Army remained strong and that in wartime he should never leave it.

In the 1930s, when a new invasion from the east was identified as the main threat, the forts around Liège and Namur, which the Germans had taken with difficulty in 1914, were rebuilt and modernized and four new, bigger ones built, chief among them Eben Emael, to cover the Meuse valley north of Liège, where the German forces had been able to bypass the Liège forts in 1914.

A bitter and protracted debate took place as to whether the Belgian territory should be defended straight away at the border, which would have needed far more manpower than was available but was advocated mainly by the Walloons, who could not accept seeing a large part of eastern Belgium, bordering Germany, sacrificed. It was eventually decided that the serious defence would make use of natural obstacles like the Meuse, the Albert Canal, and successive river lines to the west of these. This made more sense, militarily. Lengthening the duration of compulsory military service, which the Socialist party first opposed on pacifist grounds, was also debated and the Socialists eventually gave way.

A new elite force was also created. Dixième de Ligne, a regiment that had given a good account of itself in the Great War, was largely expanded and transformed into two Chasseurs Ardennais Divisions and given new regimental colours by King Léopold in 1934, complete with the 10ème de Ligne battle honours. NCOs and other ranks were mostly locally recruited among the tough inhabitants of the Ardennes, a rugged part of the country bordering on Germany, as were some of the officers. Some men were drafted in from the newly acquired cantons of Eupen and Malmédy, and they spoke German. In order to enhance esprit de corps, the Chasseurs Ardennais were given distinctive, large green berets adorned with a wild boar's head as cap insignia. Their mission was to patrol the German and Luxembourg borders, to prepare the destructions aimed at slowing an invasion (not everybody shared the French Staff's view that the Ardennes were impassable) and then to rejoin the bulk of the army, since they were considered too valuable to sacrifice in a vain attempt to stop a strong German invasion.

Being so strong in numbers, the army was a serious drain on the country's economy, especially when many skilled workers (in fact about one in two young able-bodied men) were mobilized after September 1939, and it suffered from some serious defects. For one thing, as part of the emphasis on strict neutrality, its stance was strictly defensive. No guns that were in fixed emplacements were capable of reaching German territory.

The FN rifles and pistols, and Browning heavy and light machine guns (the famous BAR), provided by the ancient Liège small arms industry, were excellent and supplemented by thousands of older, heavy Maxim machine guns surrendered by Germany under the reparations agreements. The Belgian industry also manufactured an excellent small 47mm anti-tank gun whose shells penetrated the German Panzer I, II and Czech-manufactured Pz 38t mainly used in 1940. Some of these anti-tank guns were towed and others mounted on Belgian-built T13 and T15 tankettes, equivalent of the contemporary British Mk VI light tank. For transport there was an adequate number of Belgian-built lorries, and good motor-cycles also made in Belgium. Some troops used bicycles, a cheap and versatile way of patrolling difficult terrain using small rural pathways, and most of the artillery was horse-drawn as was also the case in the Wehrmacht.

Heavy armament and aircraft were another matter. Fortress artillery was of Belgian manufacture, made mainly by the Cockerill foundries in Liège and performed satisfactorily. If mobile artillery was good and plentiful, as was proven in May 1940, heavy tanks were felt by some ultra-neutralists in parliament to be 'offensive' weapons and only minimal numbers of British Vickers and French ACG1 were eventually procured. As for planes, the Belgian government only woke up during the Munich crisis of 1938 to the fact that their Fairey Foxes and Firefly biplanes, built under licence in Belgium ten years earlier were hopelessly obsolete, and the Gloster Gladiators only slightly less so. At that time Britain and France were themselves rapidly re-arming and only seventeen Hurricane Mk Is could be made available, along with sixteen Fairey Battle light bombers and a lone Spitfire Mk I. Casting further abroad forty Fiat CR 42 biplanes were also hurriedly bought in, but these proved no match in 1940 for the Messerschmitt 109 E. Brewster Buffaloes were also acquired in the US but only arrived, complete with Belgian roundels, in the port of Bordeaux just as France surrendered – some were cast straightaway into the harbour to prevent them from falling into German hands. There existed a Belgian aircraft industry and it produced the excellent Stampe and Vertongen trainers and the large parasol monoplane Renard R 31, an armed observation two-seater, the only military plane of Belgian manu-facture to see action in 1940. Alfred Renard, a Belgian engineer, also built a prototype single-engine monoplane fighter, the Renard R 36, which test pilots found to be at least as good if not superior to the Hurricane Mk I. The prototype crashed however and the purchase of Hurricanes and Fiats went ahead. During the Phoney War a few more RAF Hurricanes, forced down over Belgian airspace, were interned and some joined their Belgian brethren. Using so many different models of planes complicated training, overhaul, purchase and management of spare parts, and so on.

Even though neutrality was the official policy and the Belgian govern-ment went so far – to deprive the Germans of any pretext to invade – as to organize half-hearted manoeuvres on its southern (French) border, with under-strength and limited numbers of second-rate troops, staff talks were held in great secrecy between the three military establishments. If and as soon as Germany invaded Belgium, its government would appeal to the other Locarno guarantors, Britain and France, for help. At these secret talks military coordination and cooperation was agreed on – this had been badly lacking in similar circumstances in 1914. More concretely, the plan was that the Belgian Army, after an initial stand of a few days on the Albert Canal–Meuse line, would fall back on the Dyle River, roughly the Antwerp–Louvain–Namur line, there to be joined by the French and British troops, who would by then have had time to enter Belgium. The Belgians would have held the northern part of that line, with the BEF south of Louvain (Leuven in Dutch), then the French down to the French border (except around Namur itself, which would be held by Belgians), forming a continuous line to link with the Maginot Line at the point where the borders of Belgium, France and Luxembourg meet. A separate French Army Corps (7e Armée) under General Giraud, was to rush to Breda in southern Holland, in case that country was also invaded, to bolster its relatively small army (about ten divisions), since it was anticipated the Dutch would rapidly fall back on 'Vesting Holland', a national redoubt in the centre of the country, thereby exposing the northern flank of the defensive line in Belgium. On the whole the secret talks (not very secret, because there were leaks in Paris and thus the Belgians thought it wiser to keep some things to themselves) had their uses, but not all that was agreed would be implemented when the crunch came, as we shall see.

During and after the war, it was rumoured that a German construction firm had helped build Fort Eben Emael and that its plans had thus been in enemy hands. This was disproved,[8] but security was relatively lax. During the Phoney War, German, British and French attachés and undercover agents all snooped, photographed and listened. RAF and French Armée de l'Air photo reconnaissance flights were as frequent as the Luftwaffe ones.[9] Civilian spies too were crawling all over the country, including a British agent who came to prepare the sabotage of the big Antwerp oil tanks, posing as the cousin of HM Ambassador and staying with him. Though they had never met before, they duly addressed each other as 'My dear Cousin', even inside the embassy.

German Military Attaché General Baron Geyr von Schweppenburg remarked in his post-war memoirs that Belgian Defence Minister Albert Devèze was a chatterbox.

Warnings
If security was lax in Belgium, surprisingly enough it was no better in Nazi Germany. During the Olympic Games in Berlin in 1936, a German Army officer, Hans Oster, befriended Dutch Kolonel Bas, who was later

sent as military attaché to Berlin. *Oberst* (Colonel) Oster was the deputy of Admiral Canaris, head of the Abwehr, the German military counter-intelligence and espionage service. There were several other German information and counter-espionage services most closely linked to the Nazi Party or personally to Göring, Himmler or von Ribbentrop, who regularly deciphered the telegrams the Dutch and Belgian embassies in Berlin were sending to their capitals. This makes what follows almost unbelievable. Kolonel Bas worked closely with his Belgian counterpart in Berlin, Colonel Goethals and passed on to him any information he felt the Belgian government ought to know. An incredible twenty-six times between the months of September 1939 and May 1940, Oster gave Bas warnings that orders had been given to attack the Low Countries! This information Goethals dutifully passed on to Brussels, without revealing the source even in his coded telegrams, only mentioning it was trustworthy. The warnings were given time after time, only to see each attack cancelled by Hitler because of bad weather or other reasons. It seemed like crying wolf and the warnings, though genuine, were gradually given less and less credence, being judged in Brussels possibly to be a ruse to lure Belgium to call in the French and British troops prematurely (as we now know Hitler suspected Belgium might do), thus compromising the neutrality policy and giving the Reich a pretext to invade. Also the Venlo incident was well known, and inspired mistrust of anyone claiming to be German opposition.[10] The warnings, as was found on 10 May 1940, were nevertheless correct and undoubtedly constituted high treason by the German military behind them, who knew what they risked and were later to pay the ultimate price after the failed von Stauffenberg coup.

As if this was not enough, the German plans to invade Belgium literally fell from the sky on 10 January 1940. On that day a Messerschmitt 108 Taifun liaison plane, bearing Luftwaffe markings, crash landed at Mechelen aan de Maas, north of Maastricht, just inside Belgian territory and not far from the Meuse River which marks the border with Holland in that region.[11] Unhurt, two German majors clambered out and asked a local farmer where they were. When they heard to their consternation they were in Belgium, Major Reinberger at once started burning the papers he was carrying in his briefcase. The crash had been observed by Belgian soldiers nearby who were quickly on the scene, extinguished the fire and led both Germans to their small command post. The papers were put on the table. While Capitaine Rodrique started phoning to report what had happened, Reinberger suddenly grabbed the papers and threw them in the burning stove. Quick-thinking Rodrique put his hands into the stove (burning himself in the process) and once more recovered them. This time they made sure there could be no further attempt at destroying them. Belgian military intelligence collected the papers, which were found to be the detailed plans of what the Luftwaffe and its paratroopers were to do against Belgian objectives during the execution of *Fall Gelb*, the planned invasion of France via the Netherlands and Belgium. Major Reinberger, who had been tasked to take them from Münster to Cologne Headquarters, realizing he could no longer make it on time by road or rail because he had lingered too long at the Münster officers' mess, had unwisely and against orders for those carrying confidential papers, accepted Major Hoenmans' offer to take him in the liaison plane. In the winter fog Hoenmans had lost his way, run out of fuel and crossing a large river, thought it to be the Rhine, when in fact it was the Meuse.

The question was now for the Belgian general staff to decide whether the plans were genuine or a clever plant, again designed to draw Belgium into doing what the Germans wanted – that is, call in the Allied armies. Reinberger broke down completely and asked, but of course was refused, to be allowed to commit suicide. On top of it all, he said he also had a complicated private life and in his absence his wife might well find out he had been cheating on her. His despair seemed genuine enough and was an indication that the plans were real, but that of course could be faked. The fact that neither German was wounded was an indication to the contrary. The German military attaché in Brussels was allowed to visit and was left alone with the men. Belgian military intelligence had bugged the room and Reinberger proceeded to assure the attaché he had managed to destroy the plans, which was a lie but seemed indicative that the papers were real, as otherwise he most probably would have reported the opposite. Some senior Belgians like General Van Overstraeten, the King's military adviser, still had doubts but it was generally accepted the plans were real. They were indeed, and after the war General Guderian declared that they had been changed, and replaced by what was eventually carried out, mainly because they were thought to have been compromised. But since they were passed on (at least the gist) by Belgium to France and Britain, the Allies were reinforced in their belief that the main thrust was to come through central Belgium (which they very much wanted to occupy in a preventive move), rather than through Sedan as was eventually the case. The German plan at that time called for a two-pronged attack, one through Liège, overrunning Eben Emael and central Belgium and the other through Sedan. Hitler, who only half liked this scheme, in fact seized upon the Mechelen aan de Maas incident to scrap it and to transform the northern pincer into a mere feint, making the Sedan break-through the main thrust, as confirmed later by General Guderian.

In Belgium there were several reactions to the Mechelen aan de Maas incident. The world press immediately announced the crash landing but without mentioning the plans. Colonel Goethals, however, heard about them through his usual source in Berlin who added that as the plans were compromised, Hitler might well order the planned attack at once, before the Allies had time to change their dispositions accordingly. On reading his urgent report, Lieutenant General Van den Bergen, the Belgian Chief of General Staff, called for a general alert and also ordered the obstruc-tions facing the French border to be removed, so as to render the planned entry of French and British troops easier. This last decision however was considered premature in the light of the neutrality policy by his superiors, the monarch and government, and he was removed from his post, or so the official version went. In fact he was used as a scapegoat for the incred-ible imbroglio that followed.

King Léopold ordered a condensed version of the plans to be com-municated to the British and French, obviously in strict confidence, but not much credence seems to have been given them. In the light of this ulti-mate warning he also discreetly enquired with London about the guaran-tees of Belgium's independence, the absence of a separate peace with Germany, economic guarantees and the retaining of the Belgian Congo if Belgium allowed Allied troops in. This was done via Admiral Lord Keyes of Zeebrugge and Dover. Keyes, who had led the famous 1918 attacks to bottle up the submarine bases in Zeebrugge and Ostend, was a close per-sonal friend of both the late King Albert and of his son Léopold and would be seconded to him as a personal envoy when Germany invaded. Léopold did this however without consulting the Government, and Foreign Minister Spaak only heard of it when a (noncommittal and some-what aggressive) answer came from Paris via the Belgian embassy there – Whitehall naturally had consulted the French. The King found himself in an embarrassing position and Prime Minister Pierlot as well as Spaak remonstrated with him, saying that he had acted against at least the spirit of the Belgian Constitution that states that no act of the King is valid if not endorsed by a minister responsible before Parliament. Spaak, ever the sentimentalist, continued to bear some affection for Léopold and helped him out of this predicament. The controversial initiative by the King, using an emissary who, even though fully trustworthy was not Belgian and naturally was loyal to his own superiors, had another consequence.

The French GHQ, misinterpreting what the British told them, thought the longed-for invitation to enter Belgium was imminent and moved the allotted troops up to the border, only to cool their heels there and then, to their great disappointment, have to turn back. This caused added resentment in Paris where a kind of double game was suspected between the ministers – who, in good faith and not privy to the monarch's demarche – swore neutrality had not been abandoned, and the King who had in fact put out feelers as we have seen, even if more had been made of them than was justified. This would not help relations between French *Président du Conseil* (Prime Minister) Reynaud and King Léopold in May, when things came to a head. It also soured relations and caused mistrust between the King and Prime Minister Pierlot. Moreover, it was feared that the unnecessary French troop movements to the Belgian border would have been monitored by German spies, who would have noted the itineraries they used, what units (the better ones) would go to Belgium (this might have reinforced the reasons to adopt the vast encircling movement the Wehrmacht eventually used), and so on.

As a result of the Mechelen affair, several British officers in mufti were allowed eventually to make discreet visits to their future allotted positions south of Louvain on the planned Dyle Line (also known in Belgian literature as the KW Line, from the name of the two towns at each end, Koningshooikt, south east of Antwerp, and Wavre, south of Louvain) and renewed secret staff meetings were held. With the French however, the Belgian GHQ was more circumspect.

During the period leading to the invasion there were several other warnings. Princess Marie-José of Belgium, King Léopold's elder sister, had married the Crown Prince of Italy, Umberto of Savoy. She and even Italian Foreign Minister (and Mussolini's son-in-law) Ciano repeatedly warned the Belgian ambassador in Rome that his country was in the gravest danger of being invaded. So also did the Vatican through other channels. There again, the telegrams sent to Brussels by the Belgian Embassy in Rome were decoded by the German intelligence services, but not much seems to have been done about it in Berlin. Princess Marie-José was later to visit Hitler at Berchtesgaden and, among other subjects discussed, pleaded with him for the release of Belgian POWs. Quite baffled by her insistence, the Führer later called her the 'only man in the House of Savoy'. Her brother, King Léopold, had also asked her to try to find out how the 'impregnable' Fort Eben Emael had been so quickly taken. It was not a prudent move, because Propaganda Minister Goebbels saw too good a chance to miss and organized a much publicized visit to the spot. This was ironic because Marie-José loathed Mussolini and Fascism and had refused to join the Fascist ladies organization, only accepting to work as a nurse during the Abyssinian war. However, General Van Overstraeten accompanied her on the visit and the report of his findings was passed on, without his knowing via Switzerland to the British Intelligence Service by King Léopold. Later Commando operations like the British paratrooper attack of Pegasus Bridge on D-Day were along the same lines as the one against Eben Emael and the nearby bridges.

Chapter 2

Invasion: The Eighteen Days Campaign (10–28 May)

'Moi d'abord!'

On the morning of 10 May, German Ambassador in Brussels von Bülow Schwante asked to see Belgian Foreign Minister Spaak. Dressed in a morning coat, he was about to read out his prepared text (it had been waiting in his safe for many months by now) justifying the invasion, when Spaak cut him short, saying 'Moi d'abord!' ('Me first!') and told him that for the second time in twenty-five years the German Army had committed an act of criminal aggression against neutral and loyal Belgium. This time it was even more odious than in 1914, as no ultimatum, note or protestation had preceded it. Germany had thus violated its undertaking of 1937 to respect Belgian neutrality, renewed at the beginning of the (present) war. Spaak became very proud of his 'Moi d'abord!' and his words were to be repeated to him many times as a sign of appreciation or even jokingly.

Germany, but also Britain and France had indeed guaranteed (though somewhat reluctantly in the case of France) Belgian neutrality. As it was now being violated a formal appeal to the two other guarantors had to be made, so as to legally justify their prepared entrance into Belgian territory. This of course had been anticipated, prepared and rehearsed and Spaak at once asked to speak on the phone to the Belgian ambassadors in London and Paris. But to everybody's surprise the communications could not be set up, although the lines had been tested just the day before. Someone ran to the central Brussels telephone exchange to find out if they had been cut, but found that the clerks had taken refuge in the cellar, scared by the first bombs falling on the capital!

Eben Emael and resistance of the other forts

From the early hours of 10 May on, there was heavy fighting in Belgium. It felt the full weight of the XVI Panzerkorps (General Hoepner), belonging to von Reichenau's Sixth Army and supported by Kesselring's 2e Luft-flotte. The first violation of the border by land troops occurred at 0435hrs. The Belgian Army had been mobilized since the outbreak of the war in

September 1939[12] so could not claim to be caught by surprise. All main rail and road junctions, airfields and so on were heavily bombed or machine gunned, as were troop and refugee movements. Contrary to German claims, fleeing civilians would constantly and deliberately be attacked to hamper troop movements, in clear violation of the laws of war. Fighting was not to stop until 28 May, eighteen days later.

The Belgian troops tasked to defend the western bank of the Albert Canal, on both sides of Eben Emael gave a very spirited account of themselves. A company of T13 tankettes tried unsuccessfully to retake Veldwezelt Bridge and was destroyed. Two infantry regiments, 2e Grenadiers and 18e de Ligne were all but wiped out, in some cases having to fight against airborne enemy troops who had been landed behind their lines in gliders. The rows and rows of names engraved at the Vroenhoven Bridge monument lists the dead of 18e de Ligne. One of its companies being completely surrounded, an NCO asked Sous Lieutenant Ansquer to surrender. Seizing a BAR a furious Ansquer leapt out of his trench screaming: 'You will see how a Belgian officer surrenders!' and began firing, to be shot down by the enemy almost at once. When 2e Grenadiers ceased to exist as a fighting unit, a few surviving officers and men hid the regimental colours in a limestone cave and tried to 'exfiltrate' on foot to join the rest of the army. Few made it. The Germans became aware of artillery observers in Lanaken church tower and set it alight, burning alive the two Belgians.

In order to make their diversion in the Low Countries credible, the Germans had to send substantial forces into central Belgium. This they did and by noon of 11 May, the spearheads of Reichenau's hundreds of tanks, having used pontoon bridges built at Maastricht, were already at Tongeren (Tongres), 15km behind Eben Emael. It had been anticipated that the Belgian Army would hold the Albert Canal/Meuse lines for three or four days, so as to give the French and British Armies time to man the next line behind, the Dyle Line. A French cavalry corps provided with B1 bis, Somua and Hotchkiss tanks, under General Prioux, was to advance in the slightly hilly terrain north of Namur and stop the German Panzers who were expected to use this ideal tank country. They met indeed and battle was joined east of Gembloux. At Meerdorp a furious tank battle followed, perhaps the first in history. It can be considered a French victory as, skilfully deployed, the heavier French Somua tanks of the 2e and 3e Divisions Mécanisées Légères (DML) prevailed and stopped their opponents, but ultimately the German 3rd and 4th Panzer Divisions concentrated their more numerous light Panzer I and II as well as the excellent captured Czech (!) Pz 38t tanks in one mass attack and turned the French. Other French armoured units stopped for lack of fuel and became sitting ducks for the Germans.

On 12 May, seeing its position around Liège turned by the fall of Eben Emael and its surrounding area, the Belgian HQ gave orders for it to be evacuated and the troops manning it to withdraw to the KW/Dyle line. This was a very strong position that had been prepared for a long fight. If not turned later by the Sedan breakthrough it probably could have been held by the combined Belgian, British and French troops. Many pillboxes and small bunkers had been built along it, logistics prepared and artillery fire plans drawn. Gradually, between 10 and 14 May, the three armies took position in their allocated slots behind it. At Louvain, General Montgomery and his Belgian counterpart Général Pire found both had received orders to include the old university town in their line of defence. Montgomery, acting as a gentleman, just alternated his units with the Belgian ones and offered the Belgians his support, to the great fury of his superior, General Alan Brooke, who wanted the Brussels/Louvain highway under his sole control for his supply (and retreat) route – contrary to the discreet pre-war talks between staff officers, referred to earlier. Finally the Belgians budged and evacuated Louvain. Artillery observers from both armies climbed the same high factory building to start spotting. A local counterattack was successfully mounted by a mix of British and Belgian troops.

Relations between British and Belgian officers were on the whole good and usually were so with the French too, but some French officers behaved arrogantly. In La Roche-en-Ardenne, one Colonel de Lannurien decided that since the French Army was larger, it should command, even over Belgian troops in Belgium: 'Là où l'armée française parait, elle commande!' (Wherever the French Army appears, it is in command!) and with his handgun threatened Belgian Major Krémer of the Chasseurs Ardennais, who was tasked to destroy obstacles. Wiser council prevailed in the form of his own officers, who calmed him down. Worse even, General de la Laurencie had his Gendarmes take all Belgian soldiers seen in refugee columns, whether stragglers or in regular units, disarm them and put them to dig trenches for his own troops. This compromised the orderly retreat of some Belgian units and a potentially dangerous incident was resolved by the French military mission to the Belgian GHQ, the news having understandably caused uproar at the Belgian Divisional command concerned. Along the coast on the other hand, the French Navy sent units to Belgian ports and told their Belgian counterparts they would provide them with whatever they might want. Food supplies were also shipped from Britain.[13]

A conference was held at Casteau, near Mons, on 12 May. Present were King Léopold of the Belgians and his military adviser Général Van Overstraeten, the French Defence Minister Edouard Daladier with Generals Billotte and Georges and General Pownall deputizing for Lord Gort, C-in-C BEF. The unified command that had been so lacking in the First World War was decided upon, and Lord Gort and King Léopold, Commander-in-Chief of the Belgian Army, were placed under General Billotte's command, an arrangement for which the precedent of March 1918 existed, with General Foch in overall command. In both cases kings of the Belgians, heads of state, were subordinate to a French general, who in the case of Billotte was not even in overall command, being himself subordinate to General Georges and General Gamelin, the rather supine French C-in-C. Expediency took precedence over protocol. It was also decided to fight on the KW/Dyle Line. When driving back to his HQ at Fort Breendonk outside Brussels, King Léopold remarked to Van Overstraeten that he felt there was only limited faith in ultimate victory among the new allies of Belgium.

Meanwhile, after the fall of Eben Emael, the three other modern forts of the *Position Fortifiée de Liège*, Aubin-Neufchâteau, Battice and Tancrémont as well as Boncelles, an old refurbished fort of the First World War, put up a spirited resistance, often shooting at each other's tops on demand to dislodge German infantry. Between them tens of smaller bunkers or observation posts dotted the hilltops and had to be dealt with too. Constantly subject to furious artillery bombardments and Stuka attacks, these four forts were to hold out respectively until 21, 22, 29 and 16 May, after having had most of their cupolas and guns demolished, ammunition or supplies exhausted and large parts of the garrison put out of action. At Battice one single aircraft bomb, ricocheting into the entrance casemate, caused thirty-four dead. At Aubin-Neufchâteau and Tancrémont the Germans presented arms and saluted the garrisons when they finally filed out into captivity, officers leading. At Tancrémont on 28 May, German General Spang was offended when plucky Capitaine Devos seemed to doubt his officer's solemn word that the Belgian Army had surrendered and it took a Belgian colonel brought up the next day to convince him. Boncelles' commanding officer, Commandant Charlier was killed in action and Colonel d'Ardenne of Aubin-Neufchâteau had his sabre chivalrously returned to him by the German officer who had besieged him. It was later taken away from him on his way to captivity and then, in September, ceremoniously returned at his prisoner-of-war camp, Oflag VIIb. One cannot help thinking how things might have gone differently if Major Jottrand of Eben Emael and Capitaine Devos, whose much smaller and far less important fort held out for nineteen days, had been in each other's shoes ... But then the weapons used against them were different, and wholly predictable in the latter case. But then again, good officers prepare even for the unexpected.

'Wo sind die andern?' The Chasseurs Ardennais' brave stand

One of the Chasseurs Ardennais divisions plus a cavalry division and some engineers, commanded by General Keyaerts, were deployed in a large arc along the Belgian/German/Luxembourg border. As soon as the alert was given these well-trained and motivated soldiers blew up the bridges, collapsed the tunnels and felled trees or blew huge craters across all the key roads. Hundreds of prepared obstacles were created.

Furious fighting erupted around Martelange at the Luxembourg/ Belgian border, where the 1er Chasseurs Ardennais was attacked from four sides, including by 1st and 2nd Panzer Divisions and airborne troops from their back. A monument there now commemorates the Ardennais' courage.

At Bastogne, Caporal Cady calmly shot anti-tank bullets into the sighting slits of a Panzer approaching him until a machine gun burst killed him. 'J'li avo dit de nin si rind. Il n' si nin rindu!' his mother said in Walloon dialect when told. 'I told him not to surrender. He didn't!'

At Bodange, a crossroads behind Martelange, it was a German initiative that ironically slowed their own advance. The German command knew well that its progression through the Ardennes would be slowed by the Chasseurs Ardennais, so in order to speed up their own troops' advance before the French could come to reinforce the Belgians, about 100 light Fieseler Storch planes, which could land on very short strips, took 400 Luftwaffe paratroopers behind the Belgian lines at Nives, their orders being to fight their way eastwards towards Martelange to ease the 1st Panzer Division's progress. As elsewhere, the Chasseurs Ardennais were under orders not to get entangled in protracted battles, but to slow the enemy down and to withdraw when given the order. The German *Fallschirmjägers* (paratroopers) however cut any telephone lines they could find to create confusion, and when the pressure on the 1st regiment of Chasseurs Ardennais became too strong and Martelange was overrun, they were ordered to retreat in good order. But the 5th Company of Commandant Bricart could not be reached, and without orders to withdraw they bravely stood their ground entrenched in and around Bodange village, stopping the Panzer spearhead from 1000hrs till 1800hrs, when their ammunition ran out. At that time Bricart tried to make his way back but was shot down by machine-gun fire with several of his men. When the centre of Bodange, held by just a platoon, was eventually taken, the Germans were surprised to take only twenty-six unwounded prisoners. Frantically they manhandled them, screaming: 'Wo sind die andern?' ('Where are the rest of you?') In fact two platoons in Bodange itself had held off one whole division for six hours and the Germans had lost about a hundred men.

While the prisoners and wounded were being rounded up, a German soldier decided to try out one of the Belgian bicycles. Hurtling down a steep downhill street, unaware that braking was effected by back-pedalling, he crashed heavily against a wall and stayed lying there, to the great mirth of the Belgian prisoners watching.

At Chabrehez, three platoons of the 3eme Chasseurs Ardennais regiment, led by Second Lieutenants Gourmet, Cremer and Catin occupied well-located defensive positions near the crossing of a small river, and they too managed to stop the enemy, in this case General Major Erwin Rommel's 7th Panzer Division, for the whole of 10 May. Rommel himself, leading from the front, had spent the morning helping his men remove or avoid the obstacles in his way. At Chabrehez he organized an enveloping movement with three infantry companies and four tanks to conquer the Belgian position, which was reckoned to be manned by two companies at least. The German troops engaged and prevailed by 1730hrs, whilst the rest of the Panzer Division were stuck behind cooling their heels. Gourmet and Cremer were killed, the latter after he had surrendered. About thirty prisoners were taken, including Second Lieutenant Catin. The rest were either killed or wounded, though some managed to get back to the Belgian lines over the next few days. The 7th Panzer Division resumed its progress on 11 May at 0900hrs.

It was not the intention of the staff to leave the Chasseurs Ardennais indefinitely where they were until overwhelmed by superior forces, but rather to withdraw them to defensive lines along the Meuse. In most cases this is what occurred. Citing the resistance offered when small units stayed put, because they did not receive the order to retreat, some have said it was a wrong or at least premature decision.

The planeloads of German paratroopers at the Albert Canal and in the Ardennes and fake air-drops of rubber dolls all created a parachute psychosis – *'parachutite'* – and a lot of time and energy was wasted over the next weeks running after real and, more often, imaginary parachutists or fifth columnists. Contrary to the situation in the Netherlands, no serious reports confirm the use of the latter in Belgium except in the German-speaking Cantons, where Nazi sympathizers had long awaited this hour.

The troops engaged in the Ardennes now began to withdraw towards the Meuse River. The original plan was for them to cross that river at Huy, halfway between Namur and Liège, but the bridges there having prematurely been blown they went to Namur instead. Colonel Deschepper, Commanding Officer of 1er Chasseurs Ardennais, was killed by a Stuka bomb while reconnoitering the new positions of his troops.

Every army officer knows the timely blowing of bridges is a most delicate task. Too early and you prevent friendly troops from crossing. Too late and you allow the enemy to pass an important potential obstacle, or at least fail to slow him considerably. Hitler famously had an officer executed for failing to blow up the Remagen Bridge over the Rhine in 1944. At the Yvoir Bridge on the Meuse, Lieutenant De Wispelaere waited as long as possible because French troops were known to be still on the east bank. When two German armoured cars appeared he touched off the electrical fuse. As nothing happened he ran to a blockhouse to use the manual fuse and was killed himself while blowing up the bridge, just in time as the Germans were already crossing. One armoured car tumbled into the Meuse.

KW and Sedan

Most of the rivers in Belgium – the Meuse, Dyle, Scheldt, Lys (or Leie), and Yser – their valleys and associated canals, cross the territory in a south–north direction, and can thus be used as defensive lines against an invasion from the east. Withdrawal to the KW/Dyle line, as planned and where defensive works like bunkers had already been built, made good sense to all concerned. If it meant giving up a large part of Belgium and Liège, a major city, still it was shorter than the previous line, it protected central Belgium, including Brussels and Antwerp and the industrial centres of Hainault. The main supply dumps and hospitals were behind it and lots of roads and railroads led to it. It had been prepared in advance, observation posts, pillboxes and bunkers built and in many places Cointet obstacles erected.[14] These steel contraptions if strongly attached and kept under fire to prevent their removal could stop light tanks. To fight in Belgium rather than in their own country had also for the French the advantage of avoiding major destruction on their own territory, as had been the case in the previous war. If the three armies held ground next to each other they were, on paper at least, more than a match for the

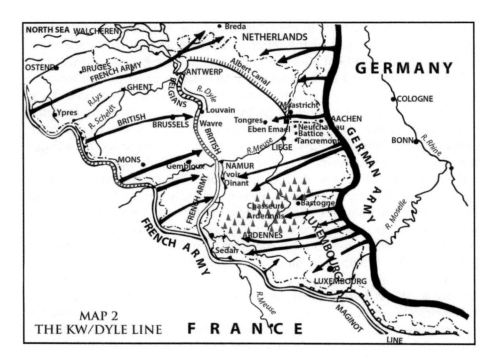

MAP 2
THE KW/DYLE LINE

Wehrmacht. Thus, a protracted halting battle on the KW/Dyle line was anticipated, until the Royal Navy blockade started strangling the German economy as it had in the First World War and the plentiful British and French colonial troops arrived, when numbers would tell. That was the plan. It went completely wrong because the French failed to anticipate a strong, tank-based German attack through the south of the Belgian Ardennes and Luxembourg, and put second-rate troops to defend the Sedan area gap, east of which the Maginot Line stops. Badly led, these troops when seriously attacked simply ran away, and the French C-in-C Gamelin had no reserves left to replace them, as he admitted to Churchill on 16 May. When the German tank spearheads were well on their way to the Somme estuary, it was realized that the French, British and Belgian troops were going to be surrounded in an enormous pocket in Belgium, cut off from their supplies and communications with Britain and the rest of France. Until 16 May the Belgian Army stood and fought on its slot of the KW/Dyle line and the German attacks were beaten back with skilful use of artillery, some with heavy losses.

When it became clear on the Allied side on that same day that the Sedan breakthrough was serious, it was decided to withdraw from the KW/Dyle

Line, on French orders, so as not to have all Allied positions in Belgium turned from the south. This was bad news for the Belgian Army for several reasons, although the Belgians could do nothing about it, certainly not hold that line on their own against the Germans. Withdrawal of the Belgian Army was executed between 16 and 19 May, to a line behind the KW/Dyle line along the Scheldt River, quite reluctantly as it meant giving up Brussels, the capital and Antwerp, the second largest city in the country. Moreover, the wounded in the large hospitals in these cities had to be evacuated, and most fuel, food, and ammunition dumps, including artillery shells had to be hastily transported or destroyed. Half of the small arms ammunition stocks were lost due to lack of adequate transport. Worse even, the routes the three armies would have to use to go to their new allotted positions intersected and since these roads were already under constant Stuka bombing and clogged with refugees, this made for giant traffic jams, forcing the Belgian engineers to build new bridges at some river or canal crossings. Railways were no better, as stations were also systematically bombed; at Gembloux a hospital train, clearly marked with red crosses, was hit with consequent heavy loss of life.

During the retreat a limited counterattack was mounted to recapture some bridges over the Scheldt River, and the dozen operational French-built AGC1 medium tanks the Belgian Army possessed were successfully used, though most were lost.

Brussels was declared 'open city', meaning it would not be defended, the Nuncio and Spanish and Italian ambassadors acting as go-betweens. On 17 May the first German reconnaissance troops entered the capital and engineers removed mines the British had left on the bridges crossing the city. The German flag was hoisted on all public buildings including the royal palaces. Next day two companies of Infanterie Regiment Nr 11 marched through the main streets of Brussels past General Joachim von Kortzfleisch, who then went to the famous town hall on the Grand Place to receive the city's official surrender from Burgomaster Joseph Vandemeulebroek, a well-known political figure at the time. It would have been a less unpleasant task for Mayor Vandemeulebroek had he known at the time that four years and four months later he would welcome Field Marshal Montgomery at the very same spot.

On that day too, Major Adair was retreating on the Brussels–Ninove road with the Grenadier Guards. In September 1944, General Adair, in command of the Guards Armoured Division would be taking that same road to be the first Allied General to enter Brussels.

Cooperation with the French Army and the BEF was not optimal. The complicated French command system did not help, as in fact two layers of French headquarters separated the Belgian GHQ from the French supreme commander General Gamelin, at Vincennes, the French GHQ outside Paris. Like Lord Gort, the Belgians were supposed to report to General Billotte, head of the French First Army group, who himself reported to General Georges, Commander-in-Chief of the North-East. On top of that there was mistrust between the British and the French who had, quite early, intercepted messages from Gort to London, discussing re-embarkation. Repeated British denials of more RAF squadrons to counter the overwhelming Luftwaffe air superiority, motivated by British worries about the defence of Britain itself, did not help either. Telecommunications were poor and when the Germans cut off the Allies in Belgium and northern France from the rest of France, the French in the north had to send their mail home via the Belgian GHQ, who sent it on to London by an undersea wire dating from the First World War, and from London it was sent to Paris! Generals could not be reached at their headquarters, appointments were missed – at an important meeting in Ypres, Lord Gort only showed up when it was over. To top it all, when Billotte was accidentally killed in a car crash on 22 May, his replacement General Blanchard was hardly ever heard of, even as things were going from bad to worse on the front.

As well as bad tactics like spreading out the tanks instead of concentrating them, bad relations and communications between Allies, bad planning and bad French generals at least in the Sedan area, bad French political leadership completely broke down when it was realized the Germans were nearing the sea and cutting off all the (best) troops in the north, numbering about 800,000 men! Prime Minister Reynaud and Defence Minister Daladier, never the best of friends, quarrelled openly and the President of the Republic Lebrun, had to convene a special meeting. It was decided to sack Gamelin and to send Reynaud to sound out the British to see if they could accept a separate peace,[15] which London and Paris were pledged never to make. On 26 May Reynaud duly flew to London, but incredibly failed to discuss the subject of his visit at all. Even worse he found out from Churchill that the British were withdrawing, but again incredibly said no word about it to the Belgians or even to his own people. In London, the new Churchill government came to power the day the fighting started. It was now taking a very different path from that of his predecessor, which at the time created uncertainty, as several members of the Chamberlain cabinet had stayed on. In Belgium as we shall see, the King, Commander-in-Chief of the army, was at loggerheads with his government. All this was far from ideal for waging war …

If politicians and generals bickered and in many cases failed, some of their troops fought valiantly. The British Guards only gave ground when ordered to do so and took serious losses. Near Asse, outside Brussels, the 15/19th Hussars fought a rearguard action in which twenty-two of their forty-eight Mk VIb tankettes were destroyed, and in one of them Major Cochrayne-Frith and all his crew perished. The survivors of that unit were absorbed into the 5th Inniskilling Dragoon Guards, of which King Léopold III was Colonel-in-Chief. It is a lasting legend that all French troops fought poorly in May and June 1940, but some units behaved heroically and suffered greatly, many officers being killed. The Moroccan *tirailleurs,* entrenched along the Brussels–Namur railway on 16 May, only gave up its embankments after bitter fighting.

The Dutch Army had been badly neglected during the pre-war years, in part because, unlike Belgium, the country had to support the cost of a large navy to protect Indonesia, or the Dutch East Indies as it was called at the time. Many of its thirteen divisions, under General Winkelman, were under strength and poorly equipped. Artillery was especially lacking. Some guns had been ordered from Krupp in Germany, but not surprisingly had not been delivered by the time the Wehrmacht attacked. The Dutch certainly did not have the means to defend a continuous line against the Germans and the plan was to fall back to successive national redoubts, first in central Holland, than around The Hague, Rotterdam and Amsterdam and finally in the islands of Zeeland (Walcheren and South Beveland), which could easily be supplied by sea, it was thought. This, however, would have exposed the Belgian northern flank of the KW/Dyle line and therefore it was planned to send a strong French force, under tough General Giraud, through western Belgium to the south of the Netherlands at Breda, to help the Dutch. This last plan was duly executed on 10 May (and its movements at the back of the Belgian Army caused some disruption), but the Dutch resistance collapsed quicker than expected and Giraud had to extricate himself back to Belgium across the Scheldt estuary.

The German onslaught on the neutral Netherlands, who had during the previous world war helped Germany up to a point,[16] was brutal and merciless. Several armoured trains laden with troops penetrated its territory (the Dutch managed to send one on a sidetrack), fake Dutch uniforms were used extensively and soldiers who had surrendered were used as human shields. An assault to capture Queen Wilhelmina and her government failed but floatplanes carrying troops landed near the strategic bridges over the Maas and Rhine rivers in the centre of the country and took them. From the first day heavy Luftwaffe bombardments on the Dutch airfields and also on the cities affected morale, and General Winkelman had to withdraw. When the redoubt around the major Dutch cities was about to fall, Queen Wilhelmina boarded HMS *Hereward*, a British destroyer, at the Hook of Holland and asked to be taken to the Zeeland redoubt to make a last stand there, emulating King Albert I of the Belgians in 1914. The captain of the *Hereward* took her to Harwich instead, apparently because he was unsure about mines on the approaches to Flushing (Vlissingen) in Zeeland. Once in Britain, the Queen (without even a nightdress, because she had not anticipated going abroad) was taken to London, to be met by King George VI at Victoria Station. Once this was announced, it affected the morale of the Dutch troops still fighting, and this together with a particularly savage bombing of Rotterdam, which could well have been followed by similar attacks against other cities, led Winkelman to lay down arms on 15 May. The Dutch surrender freed a substantial number of German troops to fight the Belgians, French and British.

It is interesting to note that unlike the Belgian surrender in a similar hopeless situation but after eighteen days of fighting, the Dutch surrender after only five days of resistance was not then and has hardly since been criticized.[17]

Most of the Dutch Air Force was destroyed on the ground including the modern Fokker G1s, but many of the fine warships escaped to Britain to fight another day, including in the bombardments of the Normandy beaches on D Day. So did a large part of the merchant vessel fleet.

The meeting at Ypres on 21 May, was held after French C-in-C Gamelin was finally sacked and replaced on 19 May, by General Maxime Weygand. This sprightly 74-year-old, who when tired of office work would jog a few hundred yards, had been Marshal Foch's Chief of Staff during the last war and had commanded the French troops in Lebanon and Syria until called back to France to replace Gamelin. His personal history is interesting as he was born 'of unknown parents' in Brussels and many speculations were made as to whom his parents actually were, since the Belgian royal family paid for his upbringing and later his studies at the French military academy.[18] Taking over from Gamelin, Weygand came to Ypres to organize a two-pronged attack against the German offensive, towards the sea. Flying over German-held territory in northern France, he

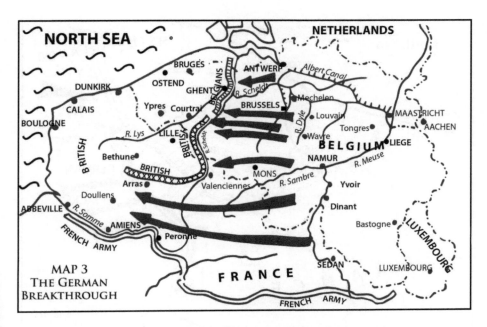

MAP 3
THE GERMAN
BREAKTHROUGH

heard from the Belgians that the Panzers had already reached Abbeville – he had not bargained for this, but maintained his plan: the northern group of armies, surrounded in Belgium, would attack towards the south while other French troops would attack from the south to meet them and thus cut the German advance off. Not much eventually came of it but it was also decided to withdraw the Belgian Army from the Scheldt River, where it had fought from 20 to 23 May, to the next river, the Lys and the canal linking Ghent to the sea. The Belgians now occupied a longer line, so as to free the British troops slated for the offensive southwards ordered by Weygand. As things eventually developed, this taking over of a longer part of the front by the Belgians covered, unknown to most of them at the time, the withdrawal of the BEF to Dunkirk.

On 23 May, the 1st Carabiniers and 2nd Guides resisted stoically at Zelzate, on the Dutch border south of the Scheldt estuary near Terneuzen, in spite of extremely heavy German artillery 'softening up'. This action won both Regiments battle honours.

As German air superiority was total, the withdrawal to the next line was made at night. There the Belgian soldiers again made their stand, after three exhausting night treks, on foot for most.

Lord Gort, who had missed the Ypres conference, disagreed with the planned southward offensive planned by Weygand. Since the evening of

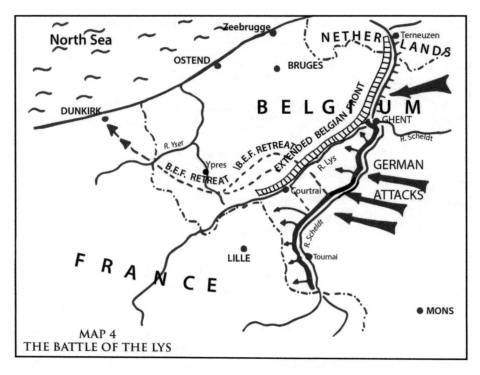

MAP 4
THE BATTLE OF THE LYS

18 May he had studied re-embarkation plans and had already received orders from London to retreat to France and the Channel ports, so he refused BEF co-operation with Weygand's offensive and started his retreat on 23 May. This British withdrawal left the Belgian Army fighting on its left, and the French contingent on its right, in the lurch. At the request of the British and to cover their retreat, Léopold III decided to fight for as long as possible starting on 23 May on the River Lys, taking over the part of the front that had been defended by the BEF so far. The Battle of the Lys became one of the bloodiest of the Eighteen Days Campaign, half the Belgians killed or wounded being lost there. Indeed of the 80,000 total casualties suffered by the Belgian Army during the campaign, 40,000 were inflicted between 25 and 27 May, the other half during the previous fifteen days. For almost five days, until the morning of 28 May, the Belgians fought on the Lys and a canal linking it to the sea, beating off repeated furious German attacks, while the British and French were re-embarking at Dunkirk. However, this depleted their remaining ammunition and fuel, preventing a further, contemplated withdrawal to the Yser River. There was fighting in the old battlefields of the First World War.

The Lanciers Regiment lost Passchendaele and Zonnebeke and on 26 May, British Engineers blew up the Menin Gate bridge. In some instances, such as Knesselaere on 27 May, another successful local counterattack by the 4th Carabiniers Cyclistes even yielded 120 German prisoners. German *Gründlichkeit* (thoroughness) is never found wanting – when the German commander found the Belgian captors were inefficiently fumbling the disarmament of his men he ordered the latter, with loud shouts of command, to stand in line so they could be more easily searched by the Belgians!

'Zivilisten haben geschossen!' (Civilians have fired shots!)

Most, in fact almost all of the British, French and Belgian troops behaved gallantly and in orderly fashion during the campaign and thoughout their retreat, but a few French and British soldiers looted abandoned homes, while others were seen throwing their weapons away to run faster. An action that was to say the least objectionable, was the execution of Félicien Vervaecke, a well-known Belgian bicycle champion, by Polish troops of the BEF because he refused to cooperate in turning his house and furniture into an anti-tank barrier. One of the worst acts of indiscipline was when Belgian 14e Linie and 20e Linie Regiments of the Ghent garrison surrendered practically without firing a shot, a fact about which some Flemish nationalists were later to boast to the Germans.

A number of other Belgian infantry units were notorious for their indiscipline even before the war, but at that time sanctions were frowned upon for internal political reasons and some officers considered too tough with recalcitrant called-up reservists were posted away. Some reserve officers or NCOs were also said to be mediocre.

Deliberate machine gunning by Stukas, of what the pilots could not fail to see were civilian refugees fleeing, was obviously a war crime, but few if any ever referred to it as such. Those who were at the receiving end and survived certainly have not forgotten it. Beautiful cities like Nivelles and Tournai were cruelly bombed, with heavy loss of life and destruction of buildings of high architectural value, as well as works of art. So were Brussels and Ostend, the latter repeatedly. The Luftwaffe was inflicting on Belgium and the Netherlands, where the bombing of Rotterdam caused at least 1,000 dead and 85,000 homeless, what the German cities were to suffer a few years later on a grander scale.

In 1940, the German command bore in mind the atrocities, especially the many summary executions of Belgian civilians, that the Kaiser's troops had committed in 1914, and the skilful use Allied propaganda had made of them to influence public opinion in their own and in neutral countries. Orders to behave had obviously been given to the German troops. Civilians were usually left alone, though in several instances Belgian POWs or civilians were pushed forward as a screen by their attacking German captors, an obvious breach of the laws of war. The low morale and poor showing of a Belgian regiment that surrendered (some soldiers even fired on their officers) at Meigem, together with a break-down of German discipline, was to trigger one of the worst massacres committed in Belgium in 1940, at Vinkt. On 27 May, the 1st Chasseurs Ardennais, again in the thick of it, as their status of elite unit justified, were told to stop the gap opened at Vinkt, the village next to Meigem. The by now battle hardened Chasseurs did just that – inflicting heavy casualties on their poorly trained opponents, who themselves were in combat for the first time, they threw back repeated German attacks. They lost 39 men and killed 170 Germans. Their commanding officer, Major Lecoq, had replaced Colonel Deschepper, killed at Namur. When they eventually withdrew under orders, their enemies, the 377th Infantry Regiment (IR 377), mainly recruited in Hamburg, entered Vinkt, started rounding up the local inhabitants and summarily executed eighty-six men, their ages ranging from 16 to 89. The direction from which you have been fired on is sometimes difficult to determine, especially in a built-up area, and the more so by raw recruits. At least one German motorcyclist was shot off his machine without a Belgian soldier being in sight and some of his colleagues may have genuinely thought civilians had fired at them, thus triggering the famous German psychosis about *'franc-tireurs'* (armed civilian irregulars) that dated back to the Franco-Prussian war of 1870, and which continued to claim many innocent civilian lives in both world wars. Anyway, mindful of the consequences and of the (far worse) incidents of the sort in 1914, the Belgian government never gave arms to civilians, warning them on the contrary against any hostile behaviour against the invaders. What made these events so much worse for the reputation of the German Army (this was not the SS), was that executions were not performed in a single burst of collective madness or temporary loss of control by the officers, but lasted several days, even after the ceasefire with the Belgian Army, and were preceded in two cases by the sitting of a kangaroo court, convicting two men as spies – one for having in his possession a private letter in French (Vinkt is in Flanders) and another for having picked up a spent cartridge. Many victims were forced to dig their own graves before being executed. Some of the German soldiers apparently refused to be part of the firing squads which, if true, is indicative that there were individuals who felt what was happening was not right. It seems the German high command was not happy with this shameful episode either, because all officers of IR 377 later had to answer questions in writing about their actions during these days. But the matter went no further.

Oberstleutnant (Lieutenant Colonel) Hodissen, the CO of IR 377 who ordered the executions, was later killed in Russia so could not be brought to trial in Belgium after the war, but two other responsible officers were alive and spent five years in jail. For the local population of Vinkt and Meigem, where tens of civilians were locked up by the Germans in the local church and died when a Belgian shell hit it, life changed forever after May 1940. The more so because they could not openly express their sorrow and grief for five long years. About 140 Belgian civilians died in the two small rural villages, including children. It is well known that the behaviour of the German armed forces was infinitely more brutal in Poland and Russia during the Second World War than in Western Europe, but that does not excuse the execution of innocent civilians, or of British prisoners at Le Paradis in France at about the same time, or the summary execution of hundreds of black soldiers serving in the French Army, on racist grounds.

The rope will break: surrender
On 24 May, the *Haltbefehl*, the famous order given by Hitler for the Panzers to stop advancing, was monitored by the Belgians. Various reasons were given for this strange order, which was met with disbelief by the Wehrmacht hierarchy who rightly pointed out that it was military nonsense because it gave the enemy more time, especially the British in full retreat.

The first and main reason might have been political, that Göring was jealous of the success of the old caste of army generals, most of them still loyal to the Kaiser,[19] and wanted his Nazi Luftwaffe to reduce the Dunkirk stronghold just by bombing it (which it proved unable to do). Another political reason could have been that an SS division was too far away at that point to intervene and so was given the necessary time to move up, so that Nazi propaganda could make use of their feats of arms. It might also have been that the Führer had grown concerned by the high degree of attrition the Panzers had suffered and wanted to spare them for the further onslaught on southern France. Both Hitler and his Chief of Staff Keitel had served in the First World War mud of Flanders, where the water table is just below the surface, and might have feared their tanks would bog down if sent north from the Amiens-Abbeville region where they now were. Finally, Hitler knew there were Nazi sympathizers among the population of Flanders and did not want to risk antagonizing too many of them by destroying the beautiful mediaeval cities of Bruges and Ghent (and reconstructed Ypres) by fighting in their streets. If this was it he miscalculated, because there was a lot of resistance to Nazi rule in Flanders during occupation, as we shall see.

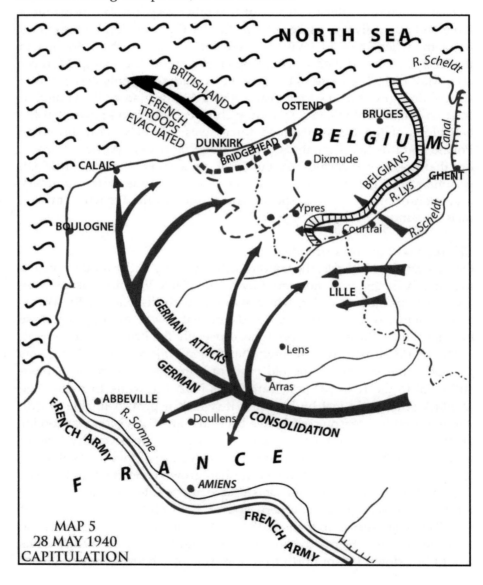

MAP 5
28 MAY 1940
CAPITULATION

Léopold III and his staff already knew by 15 May what the Sedan break-through meant, and by 23 May that the Franco-British coalition was fast disintegrating and the British were cutting their losses and running for the Channel ports. He realized the only hope of a later victory lay in the refurbishing and training of a new British Army. At Dunkirk, while the Belgian Army was fighting on, a maximum of British soldiers (215,000, together with 123,000 French, most of whom returned to southern France however) were in fact evacuated during the period of 24 May to 4 June, far more than had originally been hoped. About 400 Belgians and some Luxembourgers and Dutchmen were also taken away.

On 27 May, the Belgian forces could do no more. Short of ammunition, fuel and food, thousands of wounded, many of whom were untended, morale was at rock bottom. They had endured almost three weeks of un-interrupted fighting, followed by repeated withdrawals (because the French, not their own, front had been pierced), long night hikes and bomb-ings by Stukas, boxed in a very small territory together with 1.5 million refugees, on top of the 800,000 local residents and about 500,000 military, all lacking food, lodgings and medical attention – it was clear the end was near. A complete dispersal of the army cut into small groups was thought to be dishonourable. The hospitals and hotels in Ostend were overflowing with wounded, medicine was lacking, water mains at some places had been ruptured and cases of typhoid started to appear. The French and British guarantors had come to Belgium's aid but, beaten in France, had proved unable to defend the country and were withdrawing. It was felt that Belgium had fulfilled the moral obligation it had of helping to defend itself when asking Paris and London for help and could not be expected to do more when the Belgian Army was on its last gasp, civilians were being needlessly killed and wounded left to die. A further with-drawal to the Yser River, as had happened in 1914, was contemplated but rejected, for the reasons that unlike thirty years earlier a small territory could not be defended against modern artillery and air attacks, the ammu-nition dumps would have to be evacuated, fuel was by now too scarce, and it was not at all sure that the morale of the troops would not completely collapse. Furthermore, it was calculated that the tides would not have helpfully filled the low-lying ground in front of the Yser River with sea-water, as they had in October 1914.

An eminent jurist, Hayoit de Termicourt, Advocate General of Belgium's Supreme Court was consulted about the legal aspects of a military sur-render of the Belgian Army. The deputy chief of the general staff, Major General Derousseaux was sent under a flag of truce on the evening of

27 May to find out what the German conditions would be. The answer he was given at Von Reichenau's headquarters came from Hitler himself: 'Bedingungslose Waffenstreckung' – unconditional surrender.[20] It deeply disappointed Léopold III, who had hoped for more favourable terms, but in the circumstances there seemed to be no choice and it was accepted for the next morning at 0400hrs, when the ceasefire was sounded. In the meantime however and even much earlier, contrary to what was later said by some, ample warning had been given both to the British and French military missions, as has been attested by Lord Keyes, the personal British envoy to Léopold III. Keyes, who was the King's confidant and friend and who later loyally defended him in Britain, including against Churchill and the press, had had all latitude during the whole campaign to observe everything and report it, which he had diligently done. On 26 May for instance, the King's military adviser General Van Overstraeten, who played a very important role during these days, told him the Belgian Army was almost at the end of its tether and used the metaphor of a rope that is worn more and more until it breaks. Indeed, Churchill himself in his memoirs wrote that he was not surprised by the news. The 60th French Infantry Division, which had been placed under Belgian command, was transported back to the French lines at Dunkirk in Belgian lorries, so as not to be taken prisoner with the Belgian troops.

Since, as we shall see, this decision was used to make King Léopold and his army the scapegoats for the ultimate Allied defeat, it should be noted that France and Britain were each pledged not to make separate peace with Germany, but that no such engagement bound Belgium, who had asked her Locarno guarantors to help when her neutrality was violated. Military surrender also did not entail anything about the political future of Belgium, internally or externally.

The Air War
The Belgian Aéronautique militaire airfields received their alert orders around 0400hrs on 10 May 1940, and the planes started taking off immediately to fly to their allotted dispersal fields all over the country. But at Schaffen field near Louvain the Luftwaffe had time to destroy eighteen planes on the ground, including seven Fairey Foxes and, far worse, nine of the eleven operational MkI Hurricanes, the only Belgian planes that were a match for the Messerschmitt 109 E. Near Tienen (Tirlemont), three Gloster Gladiators successfully fought off the German planes, allowing the others to head off to their auxiliary fields. These were however quickly identified and received the Lufwaffe's attentions in the afternoon and for

the next few days. Already by the evening of 10 May, the Belgian Air Force had lost more than half of its 230 planes, including forty-seven modern ones, and the next day thirty-seven more were destroyed, some in the air, some on the ground. With their mostly obsolete aircraft, the Belgian pilots flew hundreds of missions and Luftwaffe General Galland later remarked that he felt sorry for them having such inferior planes. Again at Tienen, Lieutenant Dufossez's nine Fairey Fox biplanes, flying at a top speed of 340km/h took on eleven better-armed Me 109s flying at 570km/h. Four Belgian planes were shot down, with two pilots, including Dufossez killed and the rest parachuting down, like Sergeant Detal, who was badly burned and temporarily blinded. (After convalescing Detal made his way to Britain via Portugal and flew Typhoons in the RAF.) Still they managed to take one Me 109E down. Apart from the attacks on the bridges near Eben Emael the dwindling number of Fairey Battles flew tens of reconnaissance or light bombing missions, until these stopped because of total attrition of the planes. The nimble biplane Fiat CR 42s were more successful, although handicapped by the constant breakdown of the Italian machine guns mounted on them, usually in the middle of a dog-fight. Even so Premier Sergent Michotte managed to shoot down a Me 109 and so did Capitaine de Callataÿ on May 13. Their tactic was usually to keep turning on and on when pursued by a Messerschmitt and since the turning radius of the German plane, with a higher wing loading was larger than the biplane Fiat's, they would let loose a volley at the right moment so that the faster enemy fighter flew straight into the barrage in front of it. The same day Second Lieutenant Offenberg shot down his second German plane, a Me 109 again. Jean Offenberg and Alexis Jottard each brought down one Luftwaffe bomber. Offenberg, Jottard, and Leroy du Vivier were all to join the RAF later and fight in the Battle of Britain as well as London-born Captain Ortmans. As their resources dwindled, the Aéronautique militaire even sent pilots out in hopelessly obsolete Fairey Fireflies. Eventually the remaining Fiats CR 42 were withdrawn to France, where they helped defend French airspace and bases.

The slow, Belgian-built Renard 31 soldiered on to the last day, flying reconnaissance missions over enemy territory until the last ones were shot down or became unserviceable.

Apart from a few exceptions the RAF planes were conspicuously absent from Belgian skies in May 1940 and repeated Belgian requests for more air support met with as little success as the French requests, for the same well-known reasons. It was only on 27 and 28 May the RAF finally started to appear in force, to cover the retreat of the BEF – too late to help the hard-pressed Belgians.

Total German air superiority had the pernicious effect that Belgian troops on the ground mistrusted and systematically fired at their own planes, the black, yellow and red roundels notwithstanding. Several Belgian planes were brought down by 'friendly fire' and in some cases pilots had to prove their identity to suspicious army officers, even when speaking with a heavy Brussels accent, like Le Roy du Vivier. Another pilot was locked in a cellar and forgotten by Belgian soldiers, only to be 'freed' by the Germans!

Regimental colours hidden

Some regimental colours were burned but most, many of them with World War One battle honours, were called in by the GHQ and hidden in a false attic, which was then walled in at the Zevenkerken Benedictine Abbey outside Bruges, where they remained until September 1944, when the area was liberated by Canadian troops. Ironically the monks were turned out of their abbey in 1942 by the Todt Organization (a Third Reich civil and military engineering group in Germany named after its founder, Fritz Todt), which used the building as its headquarters during the building of part of the Atlantic Wall. However, the 37 regimental flags and some secret documents remained well hidden and those in the know held their tongue. The abbot and two monks were decorated after the war. Many of those regimental flags serve again or are now to be seen at the Royal Military Museum in Brussels.[21]

The Belgian Army in captivity in Germany

After the ceasefire Hitler publicly declared that on the whole the Belgian Army had fought bravely. The officers were to be allowed to keep their swords or side arms, but predictably all firearms were confiscated before they entered the POW camps. There was some confusion as to whether weapons and stocks were to be destroyed or delivered to the enemy intact. Official orders, now monitored by the Germans, gave instructions for the latter as doing otherwise would, it was said, jeopardize the ceasefire. In the event some artillery guns were rendered up but most, having fired almost continuously for so long a time, were no longer usable anyway. In other cases vital components like the breech or recoil cylinder were removed and disposed of, more in keeping with military traditions. Some of these guns would eventually find their way to the Atlantic Wall.

Demobilization of the troops was even more confused, as the surrender terms were unclear on that point. The different echelons of the German military hierarchy gave inconsistent and incoherent orders. More than a few servicemen just made off and simply went home, 'demobilizing themselves' in the confusion. Finally, Berlin gave clear instructions: most Flemish enlisted men were immediately to be sent home (due to the confusion, most weren't) but the French-speaking Walloon troops and all officers, including reserve (volunteer) officers went into captivity. This was clever wedge-driving by the Germans, who favoured the Flemish. In some cases Flemish nationalist politicians who had collaborated in the First World War and fled to Germany in 1918 to avoid facing the music were used to determine which troops were actually Flemings, and to be sent home. Later, many Flemish non-regular officers were also released and in some cases when it was difficult to determine someone's mother tongue the Germans allowed the Belgians to decide for themselves. So 'language examination juries' sat and in fact many Flemish officers helped their fellow Walloon officers go home by declaring their Dutch to be excellent when sometimes this was far from true. In some regiments like the Chasseurs Ardennais the Flemish officers decided to stay anyway.

Major Ordies was taken prisoner on 25 May, as he had been in the first war on 6 August 1914, then a *Sous Lieutenant*. In all he spent nine long years of captivity during the two world wars.

Like all POWs, the Belgians soon started to try to escape from Prenzlau, Eichstätt, Fischbeck, Neubrandenburg and other *Oflags* and *Stalags*. Some were sent to the famous Colditz fortress, where a large contingent of 'ordinary' Belgian officer prisoners was sent in the beginning, before it became a camp for recidivists from all nations late in 1940 when most of the Belgians there were removed to other camps. Like their British and other colleagues, the Belgians became experts at building small radios and compasses, tunnelling, faking papers and passes and transforming some of the camp theatre wardrobe into convincing German uniforms. Some escapees made it to freedom, many were caught. Once back in Belgium it was easy, since many Belgian POWs had been freed and the Germans were not especially looking for escapees. Others wanted to continue fighting and managed to reach Britain via Spain and Gibraltar and join the RAF or the Belgian Brigade in Britain, like two officers who, on their way sent their colleagues a colour postcard of a Portuguese beach ('The sea was so blue, blue, blue!' later remembered a recipient in dreary, wintry Pomerania).

Some others, including prestigious General Chardome, a hero of the First World War and cofounder of the Chasseurs Ardennais, were seduced by German propaganda and by Degrelle, now doing the Germans' bidding. Chardome bore a grudge towards the French and British, whom he felt had left Belgium in the lurch in 1940 and insulted the King. He agreed to be freed to fight communism in Russia and was allowed some days of home leave. His wife however, who was sympathetic to the resistance, made him realize the enormity of what he had done. He asked to be re-interned but to no avail. This was the first time a general had ever asked to be made a prisoner, a German officer ironically remarked. Though he never actually went to Russia, after the war he lost his rank and was condemned to fifteen years of hard labour, serving only a short part of it.

Enlisted men, almost exclusively Walloons, were taken to Stalags and/or put to work in farms or factories.

At the end of the war, most Belgian POWs had been freed; only about 67,000 were still being detained, mostly all the regular officers and French-speaking other ranks, since most Flemish conscripted soldiers had been liberated, while the Flemish regulars were kept. This was roughly 10 per cent of the Belgian Army of 1940. Most of them, held in camps far to the east of the Reich to discourage evasion, were liberated by the advancing Soviet Army in 1944 or 45, after five years of harsh captivity and privation. Religion, letters from home and Red Cross parcels had been their main sustainment but several hundred had died in Germany, had been shot while trying to escape, died from illness, or in the bombings or crossfire of the liberation combats. On the whole, they were held by their German captors in the same conditions as the other Western POWs, generally respecting the Geneva conventions, with a few exceptions, and far less harshly than Soviet Army prisoners.

A few of the soldiers or other young men hailing from Eupen and Malmédy, having become German citizens through the re-annexation, were drafted into the Wehrmacht, and in a few cases later ended up in prisoner-of-war camps in Siberia.

Conclusion
Hitler's personal Focke Wulf 200 transport plane landed in Brussels on 1 June 1940 and he had himself driven around the Belgian capital.

The Belgian Army had taken the first shock in the Western campaign: it was beaten in about three weeks by a far larger and better equipped army, the fighting spirit of its propaganda-fed soldiers bordering on fanaticism. That same army was going to beat the French in three more weeks, that same army everybody – including Churchill – thought was the world's finest and strongest. Belgium's Army lost about 6,800 killed and three times that number wounded in these eighteen days of fighting, the number of civilians killed or wounded being unknown. The total military losses (killed, wounded, missing or taken prisoner before the ceasefire) are estimated at about 80,000.

A quotation from William L. Shirer's *The Rise and Fall of the Third Reich* may serve as the last word on the May 1940 Eighteen Days Campaign of the Belgian Army:

> Whatever may be said of Leopold's behaviour, there should be no dispute – though there has been – about the magnificent way his Army fought. For a few days I followed Reichenau's Sixth Army through Belgium and saw for myself the tenacity with which the Belgians struggled against insuperable odds. Not once did they break under the unmerciful and unopposed bombing of the Lufwaffe or when the German armour tried to cut through them. This could not be said of certain other Allied troops in that campaign. The Belgians held out for eighteen days and would have held out much longer had not they, like the BEF and the French northern armies, been caught in a trap which was not of their making.

Chapter 3

All the King's Men

Political situation in Belgium
Belgium only became an independent and sovereign nation state in 1830, although the people that now live within its borders had long had common rulers. In fact almost all the countries that today form Benelux were united by conquest, inheritance or purchase during the Hundred Years' War by a family related to, but enemy of, the kings of France – the house of Burgundy. After a few generations the Lord of the Counties of Flanders and Holland, the Duchies of Brabant, Hainault and Luxembourg was the same person, among others Philip the Good and then his son Charles the Bold. Their wealth was larger than that of the English monarchy and certainly than that of their ruined and beaten cousin of France. Flemish painting started then and flourished. In the sixteenth century everything was inherited by the Habsburg kings of Spain and protestant reform took hold – more so in the north, which became the independent protestant Dutch Republic, than in the south which remained under Catholic, Spanish Habsburg control. In 1713, at the Treaty of Utrecht that also gave Gibraltar to Britain, the Southern, until then Spanish, Netherlands were transferred to the Austrian Habsburg Empire. Rule from faraway Madrid and then Vienna and a certain autocracy gave the Belgians a sense of belonging together and when the French revolutionaries invaded in 1792, burning down cathedrals and chateaus, they were welcomed by few, especially when they simply annexed the place to France and drafted young men for wars in Spain and Russia. After Napoleon's final defeat at Waterloo, outside Brussels which he was trying to reconquer, the Powers gathered at Vienna tried to glue Belgium and Holland back together as a buffer against France. The Kingdom of the Netherlands was thus created, to this day the official name of what is also known as Holland.[22]

This arrangement, however, did not last more than fifteen years and the Belgians revolted against Dutch rule in 1830, throwing their troops out of Brussels. The Powers were at first reluctant to see the Kingdom of the Netherlands collapse, the more so because the Belgians were soundly defeated by the returning Dutch Army. However, French diplomatic skill and Lord Palmerston's sense of realism worked out a compromise whereby Belgium became an independent country that had strict neutrality like that of Switzerland imposed by the Treaty of London in 1839. Moreover the German-born British Prince Léopold of Saxe-Coburg Gotha, widower of Charlotte, heiress to the British throne,[23] was sworn in on 21 July 1831 as first King of the Belgians (not of Belgium), the Constitution, rather progressive for the times, strictly limiting his powers. Two articles in that Constitution are important to the student of the Second World War in Belgium: one (Article 64) says no act signed by the King is valid unless countersigned by a minister responsible before Parliament; the other (Article 68), says the King commands the armies (of land and sea). Since Léopold I had done well as an army officer fighting Napoleon this was supposed to give the fledgling Belgian Army a competent leader, as was indeed proven a few years later, since the Dutch did not give up until 1839. These arrangements proved sound for exactly a century, as Belgian neutrality was respected by both sides during the Franco-Prussian war of 1870, but his son Léopold II[24] took great care to mobilize the Belgian Army and to deploy it along the border.

It can be seen that there is a contradiction between these two constitutional articles as regards the exact line between the head of state's attribution, which has to be sanctioned by a minister bearing political responsibility for running the Executive Power of the State, and that of the commander-in-chief, whose capacities are not strictly limited to moving divisions about. This already had created conflicts between Léopold II's successor, Albert 1, who effectively commanded the Belgian Army during the First World War, and his ministers who had taken refuge in France and wanted to have a say in the general conduct of operations. It never came to a serious clash because the army managed to cling to a small part of Belgian territory and the King always stayed with it and never effectively left Belgian territory. This was to haunt his son Léopold III, as we shall see.

By 1914 Europe was a very different place. Germany had united under the Kaiser in 1870 and was the rising power on the continent, while France mourned the loss of Alsace and part of Lorraine. The famous Schlieffen plan to invade France obviously rode roughshod over Belgian neutrality. When its amended version was put into practice in August, Berlin did not expect the small Belgian Army to resist and even offered financial compensation for possible damage if free passage was allowed. This was denied.

Léopold was only twelve when the First World War erupted. Having attended Eton with his younger brother Charles (who went on to join the

Royal Navy) he was later drafted, still a teenager, into the elite 12e de Ligne as a private and later into the Grenadier Regiment as a second lieutenant. In 1926 he married Princess Astrid, a niece of the King of Sweden. Three children were born of this marriage, two future Kings of the Belgians and one Grand Duchess of Luxembourg. Léopold became king in 1934, after his father's accidental death while mountain climbing. Next year disaster struck again in the form of a car crash in Switzerland and the extremely popular Queen Astrid was killed. Léopold was driving and broke an arm.

These were years of political instability, governments sometimes lasting only weeks or even less (one lasted just six days, another one was formed in the late morning and collapsed in the afternoon, each time failing through internal, trivial matters while the international climate grew ever more worrying), with the extreme right rising like everywhere else in Europe and the Flemish nationalists, some outright separatists, ever more vocal. Many have criticized Léopold as authoritarian, tactless and unable to listen. It should be noted that the Belgian constitution, drawn up in the early nineteenth century, gave large powers to the king, far more than is the case with English monarchs. And King Léopold publicly stressed more than once his country's instability, and the fact that power being increasingly held by the political parties, rather than the executive branch he headed, was unconstitutional. This did not endear him to these parties and was to have consequences in 1940.

The times were troubled both internally and internationally. Parliamentary democracy was by no means as generally accepted then as it is today. Indeed in the 1930s it had regressed in Europe and by 1940 only the (future) Benelux and Scandinavian countries, Czechoslovakia, Britain and France could be called democracies. All the others (Germany, Italy, Spain, Portugal, Rumania, Bulgaria, Poland, Greece and Yugoslavia, not to mention the USSR) had dictatorships of some sort, while in Britain Sir Oswald Mosley's Union of Fascists was by no means lacking in followers. In February 1934 heavy clashes had opposed French right-wing movements, partly monarchists, and the police, and many – who would rejoice in their own Republic's defeat in 1940 – wanted a strong regime.[25] In 1936, Léon Blum's Front Populaire government came to power. It included communists, hardly reassuring news for France's neighbours.

Belgium was at the time an overwhelmingly Catholic country and the political establishment was in large part recruited in the Parti catholique or its sympathizers. In May 1940, the Government was led by Prime

Minister Hubert Pierlot, in coalition with members of the Liberal and Socialist parties.

Born in the Ardennes, Pierlot was a practising Catholic, from a conservative background, perhaps lacking intellectual suppleness. For him, the Catholic party, religion and duty were foremost. He had studied at the famous Jesuit school, the Collège Saint Michel in Brussels, where a large part of the Belgian elite also went and which could be compared, with a few other such institutions across the country, to an English public school. After some years at the military academy he decided the army was not going to be his career. He took a trip overseas to Britain, Canada and the USA. Influenced, like de Gaulle, by the French political philosopher Maurras, he was and remained, even when at loggerheads with his king, a convinced monarchist. When the First World War broke out, Pierlot volunteered and served in the trenches as an officer. This experience made him think he knew a thing or two about military matters, but mobile warfare in 1940 was to be very different from the trenches of 1918.

A complete contrast was the Foreign Minister Paul Henri Spaak. Impressively quick and bright, with malice and humour, a good orator, Spaak came from a Brussels family that had long been prominent in the arts and in liberal politics. His mother was the first female member of the Belgian Parliament and his uncle several times a minister. To their shock, he chose the socialist party, where he rose swiftly and even briefly made it to prime minister. Together with the somewhat more sedate Pierlot and Finance Minister Gutt, who had Jewish origins, as well as the Flemish Liberal De Vleeschauwer, who had recently become Minister for the Colonies, they were to have a determining role in Belgium's destiny in the early 1940s, and in Spaak's own case in the foundation of the United Nations, NATO and the EU, being considered as one of the 'founding fathers' of the latter. The 'London Four' as they would become were, by coincidence, representative of the main political parties existing in Belgium, and De Vleeschauwer was Flemish.

The Parc de Bruxelles, also called De Warande in Dutch, in central Brussels may be one of the most symbolic parks in any capital city. From its centre you can see buildings associated with all three powers. In one direction the massive domed structure built by Léopold II in 'Babylonian' style, the Palais de Justice, represents the judiciary, somewhat set back, as befits the independence of that power. Neatly opposed on two sides of the park itself are the Palais de la Nation, where both Houses of Parliament are sited and where they exercise legislative power, and across from it, in clear sight, the Royal Palace, where the King holds executive powers which are delegated, as neatly defined by the Constitution, to the ministers he appoints and whose laws Parliament has to approve. The fourth incumbent of that palace, who had more power than most constitutional monarchs of his time and certainly of ours, surrounded himself, as had always been the case, with personal advisers he freely chose. They were the famous 'entourage' and have been much abused, even blamed for the crisis between Léopold III and his government. Baron, later Count, Robert Capelle was his secretary and Léon Frédéricq his *Chef de Cabinet*, that is, his chief of staff.

Two other men were playing an even more important role than these two just mentioned, and they were not spared criticism either. Général Major Raoul Van Overstraeten, had already been Albert I's military adviser and stayed on with his son. A brilliant mind, he made many enemies by displaying arrogance, especially towards his fellow generals and the political establishment, whom he almost openly despised. If the King himself always made it a point to scrupulously respect the Constitution and his oath to abide by it, Van Overstraeten certainly was no lover of parliamentary democracy and scarcely disguised the fact. He was to play a determining role in the events that unfolded and, for instance, was blamed for having inspired the King's unfortunate initiative to sound out the Allies after the Mechelen affair, or the King's 'political testament' (about which more later). When the Army capitulated, those who did not expect it also heaped blame on him, some sitting at an impromptu Council of Ministers held at the Belgian embassy in Paris even calling for his execution.

Another man much blamed was Henri De Man, former president of the Belgian Socialist Party, whom the King often consulted and who also stayed close to him during the Eighteen Days Campaign. He had been called up as reserve officer and officially put in charge of both the soldiers' welfare and the Queen Mother's security. De Man, who had developed a *Plan du Travail*, a plan to better the lot of the working classes, underwent a political evolution that took him away both from Marxism and from parliamentary democracy as well. At the beginning of the occupation, he published a manifesto that in essence welcomed the collapse of parliamentary institutions. That completely discredited him in the eyes of his fellow socialists, as they were bracing themselves to fight Nazism. Exiled in Switzerland as early as 1941, he met a bizarre end in 1953: he used to drive every day along the same route and cross a railway line at the same hour. The Swiss railways are famed for their regular timekeeping, but that day a train was late.

De Man is said to have influenced Léopold III to ask for terms on 27 May, when it was clear the Belgian Army was exhausted and something had to be done before it collapsed completely, while Van Overstraeten thought the troops could hold on for another day or two. However, De Man pointed out to the King that France and Britain had proved incapable of effectively guaranteeing Belgian neutrality and independence by military means as they had pledged themselves to do.

The falling out of 1940
Immediately after the beginning of the German invasion a great number of the civil servants, either local or in the ministries, remembering the summary executions of 1914, abandoned their posts and fled to France, making running the country almost impossible. The King, as head of state, wrote an angry letter to the ministers about it. During the campaign he saw the ministers but made little effort to thoroughly inform them of the military situation. In fact he barred them from attending the Ypres meeting with the new French Commander-in-Chief General Weygand, and the three main ministers – including Defence Minister General Denis – had to buttonhole the French general afterwards to find out what had been said.

On 25 May the Army had retreated into the small north-western part of the country around Bruges, where it was eventually to surrender. Foreign Minister Spaak did not know where King Léopold was and actually had to check the telephone number he had with the local telephone directory to find out the King's place of residence at the time. It was the chateau of Wijnendaele, a few kilometres south of Bruges and close to the last command post of the Belgian Army general headquarters. Pierlot, Spaak and Defence Minister General Denis drove there and asked to see the King. It was 5.00am and the monarch was resting (it had been a trying time for him since 10 May) but he rose to see them, obviously not in the best of moods. A momentous conversation began, whose consequences were eventually to lead to civil strife after the war and Léopold III's abdication a decade after the meeting took place. The ministers informed the King of their intention of leaving the country for France (as their predecessors had done in 1914), to continue the fight there. Léopold told them the Army was on its last gasp and surrender would have to take place soon. This surprised Spaak, who had just seen a camp of Chasseurs Ardennais looking to him disciplined and in good spirits, little realizing they were not representative. The King warned them that by going to France they would put themselves under French control (which they later found out was true enough) and informed them of his intention of staying in Belgium, with his troops. So far, everybody had been standing but Pierlot now asked if they could all sit down. They did and a more relaxed conversation took place. The King, no doubt influenced by the fact that the Germans had started throwing leaflets calling on the Belgian Army to surrender 'as your leaders will soon flee by plane', as well as the fact that Queen Wilhelmina's army had collapsed as soon as her departure for England had been known, refused steadfastly to follow them to France. Unlike the ministers who were banking on a repeat of 1914 and a new Battle of the Marne that would save France, he had realized long ago the French Army would also soon collapse.[26] The British were heading for the Channel ports, and at this stage the Soviet Union was an ally of the Reich, while even if willing and allowed by the American Congress, there was little President Roosevelt could do to help the democracies. So a damage limitation exercise was the least costly option under the circumstances. The ministers remonstrated with the King, saying that by calling on the British and the French, Belgium had accepted a moral obligation to fight on with all the resources at its disposal (such as, though they were not mentioned, the Belgian troops in training in France and the young future recruits, called the CRABs, the central bank gold, the merchant fleet, and, last but not least, the vast resources of the Belgian Congo). Léopold, however, considered the only moral obligation Belgium had to the Allies was to play its part in the defence of its territory. This the Belgian Army had done, to its utmost, and was about to be overwhelmed. Léopold recognized the ministers were sincere, but would not budge in face of their repeated exhortations that he should leave for France with them. In his memoirs, Spaak admits he was tempted to stay with his king, for whom he felt great affection, but was dissuaded by warning looks from Pierlot. More was said about a possible government the King might want to form and the situation this would create if the Pierlot government stayed on as well. This was important because, when in Paris a few days later, the ministers thought they had reason to believe Léopold would indeed want to fire them to form a government to negotiate peace with Germany, or at least economic arrangements.[27] Thus the protagonists of what has been called a Greek tragedy separated, each going his own, very separate way. Spaak, writing later, said he still shivered at the thought of what might have happened to him (after the war) if he had stayed...

At Wijnendaele, what Pierlot and Spaak already suspected soon became clear – there were two different concepts of Belgium's interest, in fact two different Belgian foreign policies. The King considered Belgium's interest to be paramount, and its only obligation towards the guarantors was for the Belgians to do their utmost to defend themselves, and the (neutral) Belgian territory which the French and British had been asked to help save from invasion. This having been done it was now his duty to seek the most favourable possible outcome for his country. This did not entail his leaving the country, with or without the remnants of its army, for an uncertain future in exile and at the mercy of France – certainly not to prolong a massacre that had become militarily senseless. The ministers, on the other hand, thought that by having called in France and Britain who – unlike the King – *they still thought could win*, Belgium had entered a de facto if not de jure alliance with them and should continue the fight with the Allies of the former war, if only for moral reasons and for the sake of the democratic institutions these two countries were fighting to uphold. There was a formal agreement between Britain and France not to sign a separate peace with Germany (which Reynaud as we have seen tried to get out of by going to London), but there was no such undertaking between the Allies and Belgium. No peace treaties were signed by anyone, just two ceasefire agreements, signed on 27 May by Belgium, and three weeks later on 18 June, by France. But between these two dates, whilst France was still fighting, the ministers thought Belgium should do the same. Only after the French collapse were they to see things differently.

There were also two different conceptions of what the role of the King in wartime should be – the government did not agree that acts passed by him as Commander-in-Chief of the armed forces should not require a minister's backing, when they had obvious political aspects. All this could and should have been cleared up before war broke out and while there was still time. Unfortunately this didn't happen, and the growing mistrust between the King and his prime minister in the months before the war was to blame.

When a plenipotentiary was sent to the German lines on 27 May, he also enquired about the fate of King Léopold and the German generals were quite surprised to hear he had not fled abroad, as they had expected. After the Germans dropped leaflets inviting the Belgians to surrender, adding that their leaders were about to flee by plane, the King made a proclamation to his soldiers: 'Whatever your fate, I will share it.' As mentioned earlier, King Albert I never formally left Belgian territory during the First World War (except for meetings in London or Paris), but it is not clear whether he would have gone into exile if the Belgian Army had been overwhelmed[28] and had lost the small part of Belgian territory behind the Yser River it clung to. In fact it is quite possible he would have surrendered with his army if he had believed all hope was lost, as his son did.

Unlike other monarchs, as has been mentioned, the Belgian kings are, con-stitutionally, commanders-in-chief of the armed forces. A commander is an officer and an officer does not abandon his soldiers, especially not in bad times. Neither King Albert nor his son Léopold III did so. Queen Wilhelmina of the Netherlands did not command the army in the field and in fact did not leave her country entirely of her own volition, as seen earlier, while King Haakon VII of Norway only left because the Germans wanted to force him to accept Quisling as prime minister. King Christian X of Denmark stayed in Copenhagen throughout the occupation and was never censured for it.

After the failed Wijnendaele meeting, Prime Minister Pierlot and Foreign Minister Spaak went to Paris, where they heard of the Belgian capitulation from French Prime Minister Reynaud who, knowing full well the French Army was being soundly defeated, found in King Léopold, against whom he bore a grudge for not having allowed his troops in when Belgium was still neutral, a very convenient scapegoat. He told the Belgian ministers he would have to announce the King's surrender in terms which meant he could not guarantee the safety of the million-plus Belgian refugees now on French soil – thus using the helplessness of those refugees to blackmail the ministers into joining him in blaming Léopold III for the impending disaster and collapse of the French Army.

Paul Reynaud's broadcast of 28 May stated that the Belgian King 'with-out a word of warning and without care for his allies, who had rushed to his help when he anxiously called upon them, has capitulated in the field.'[29]

Churchill, in a first statement to the Commons on 28 May, was more measured and said he would suspend judgement, while acknowledging the bravery of the Belgian Army. But a week later he made a far harsher statement, under pressure from Reynaud to align himself,[30] telling the House that Léopold had suddenly and without consultation, with the least possible notice, without the advice of his ministers and on his own initiative ... and so on. This he also wrote later in his memoirs.

As for Pierlot, his broadcast on Paris radio, which he was forced to modify to a harsher tone by French Minister Georges Mandel, who con-trolled the French wireless senders, may have seemed more moderate but was far more damning in spelling out the political consequences for the future:

> Casting aside the unanimous and formal advice of the Government, the King has opened separate negotiations and is dealing with the

enemy. Belgium will be stupefied, as the King has broken the bond that united him with his people. According to Article 82 of the Constitution, the King having put himself under the control of the enemy is unable to reign. [...] Officers and civil servants are no longer bound by their oath of allegiance to the King.

It has long been disputed (and still is) whether by surrendering the Army Léopold had broken his oath to respect the Belgian Constitution. Most find he had not, since surrendering was a purely military act, within his prerogative as Commander-in-Chief, though it obviously had political consequences. But even if he was not within his rights, the Belgian government also took some liberties with the Constitution. The relevant article on a monarch's inability to reign had obviously been intended for cases of dementia, serious illness or other medical incapacitation. It could indeed be applied (though it never had before) in the case of a king being the prisoner of a hostile state, but the Constitution only allowed the ministers to exercise the king's power for as long as it took for a regent to be appointed. In fact, the government took no steps to find one (his younger brother Prince Charles was appointed for about five years but only in 1944, when Léopold's return was disputed) and exercised the royal power themselves for the years the country was occupied. Another liberty they took with the law was to relieve the officers and civil servants of their allegiance to the King, which it certainly was not their business to do, as some officers and a few Belgian ambassadors in third countries pointed out. Reynaud went as far as asking Pierlot to adopt the French Constitution, an absurd idea if there ever was one, but Pierlot refused.

The French press and London tabloids went for Léopold with a will. Poltroon, coward, rat, traitor, felon king, fifth columnist were the usual epithets. Joining the fray were Lord Derby, who spoke of 'perfidy and treason' and former prime minister Lloyd George, whose pre-war visits to Hitler ('a man of peace') had raised more than one eyebrow and who now wrote in a British paper: 'You can rummage in vain through the black annals of the most reprobate kings of the earth to find a blacker and more squalid example of perfidy.' Maybe the elderly Welsh statesman was past his best by the 1940s.

Apart from the excessive language that discredits the speakers, all these statements rely on at best half truths, if not outright lies. But they were motivated by political expediency. For Reynaud, who had known very well for several days that his army was tottering on the edge of total collapse, and had until then blamed French generals, finding a convenient scapegoat, and one who could not defend himself, was the main motivation and no Frenchman tried to contradict him. By positioning himself alongside, in more temperate terms but to the same effect, Churchill was trying to bolster French spirits, as he still hoped he could. He was immediately contradicted by someone very well placed to know the truth about the much touted lack of warning to the British and French, Admiral of the Fleet Lord Keyes who had spent the Eighteen Days Campaign at King Léopold's side, often sleeping under the same roof. Keyes was supported by Colonel Davies, the liaison officer to the Belgian GHQ, and both men told the British Prime Minister that his statement was untrue, with some pluck in a mere colonel's case. 'I hear you don't like my statement, Colonel Davies !' was Churchill's opening salvo. They in turn were joined by no less than Randolph Churchill, who also wrote to his father to say these were unfair accusations. Churchill, both in 1940 and later, never budged however and wrote that he saw no reason to change his statements in Parliament. To his son he wrote back somewhat cynically that 'a lie has already gone around the world while Truth is still pulling its boots on.' Roger Keyes and Winston Churchill (who had been helped by Keyes ousting Chamberlain) were close friends, but when the former refused to give in, the matter erupted into a serious row between the two. Churchill reminded Davies and the much decorated Keyes that they were serving officers and even had Keyes's papers impounded at his home. For his part, Admiral Keyes sued the *Daily Mirror* for libel and in 1941 won his case.[31] Churchill later entrusted Keyes with organizing the Commandos[32] and starting raids on the Continent ('Set Europe ablaze!' Churchill told him) whilst the army was being reorganized after Dunkirk, maybe to give him something else to think about. Admiral Keyes died shortly after the war but his second son, also named Roger, wrote a book in the 1980s vindicating Léopold.[33]

If King Léopold and his staff had failed to inform the British and the French before surrendering, it would certainly have been very serious and the opprobrium well deserved. A study of the facts shows this was not the case. Indeed, on 25 May Keyes had informed Churchill personally that without help the Belgian Army would have to surrender within a day or two (it actually held on for three more). On 26 May, Van Overstraeten told the French that the situation of the Belgian Army was grave and the *limits of resistance had been reached.*

Indeed if anyone failed to inform others of important facts it was the British, who did not tell the Belgians of their decision, taken as early as 20 May, to evacuate the BEF. Only on 27 May, the very day the King sent a plenipotentiary to the Germans, did Churchill wire Keyes that 'it is now time to tell the Belgians [of the withdrawal] and 'We are asking them [the Belgians] to sacrifice themselves for us.' Indeed Keyes reported (and this is quoted in Churchill's memoirs) that when he told the Prime Minister King Léopold was asking for a ceasefire, Churchill was not surprised because of the warnings he had received. 'Do the Belgians think us awful dirty dogs?' Gort asked Keyes who had come to visit him on 21 May, hardly a statement from someone who suspects he might be deceived, but rather the other way round. From the military point of view the accusation does not stand scrutiny either. The idea still held by some, that the Belgian Army's sudden surrender left the flank of the BEF exposed and the road to the sea open, is wrong because in fact Gort withdrew three of his divisions on 22 May (right after his conversation with Keyes) to form a reserve to the west, while the Belgian Army took up the task of flanking and rearguard action to cover the BEF from the east. On 25 May, he decided to abandon the Weygand plan altogether and leave for the sea and the French General Blanchard gave orders to form a bridgehead around Dunkirk. By the time (27 May) the Belgians decided to ask for terms, the BEF was already in full retreat/flight to the coast, under orders 'to evacuate the maximum of [your] force possible' as set out by Secretary of War Anthony Eden. Eden had ordered preparations to be made as early as 19 May, while the Admiralty launched 'Dynamo', the evacuation from Dunkirk, on 26 May, the same day the War Office gave Gort leave to proceed to the coast. The Belgian front had been severely breached in the Menin–Courtrai area[34] and the deep thrust the Germans had made there isolated the British from the Belgians anyway, so the latter were no longer covering the BEF's back. Among several others, both the British military historian Sir Basil Liddell Hart and General Von Falkenhausen, the German military commander in Belgium during the occupation, have stated in writing that it was thanks to Belgian Army resistance between 20 and 28 May that most of the BEF managed to escape through to Dunkirk. And, it follows, that Britain was able with the cadre of the BEF, to rebuild the army that would eventually land in Normandy.

As for the French, it is possible (though far from certain) that Reynaud and Weygand were not aware the Belgian surrender was imminent, but that was due to the total breakdown of communications and confusion in the French Army and hierarchy (it was from the Belgians, not from his own sources that Generalissimo Weygand heard on 21 May that the Germans had reached Abbeville at the Somme estuary, thereby cutting his forces in two!), and the fact that the kindest comment that can be made of

General Blanchard when, in succession to the deceased Billotte, he held command of the French 1st Army Group, was that he lacked leadership. The fact that the important Lille telephone exchange was blown up by retreating British troops may also have played a role.

At the same time, the Belgian ministers, who laid down a wreath at the Paris monument to King Albert I, a very telling message indeed, sincerely believed the French were going to continue fighting and that the King had thus taken the wrong decision.

King Léopold had written letters to King George VI ('My dear Bertie'), to the Pope and to President Roosevelt, justifying his decision to ask for terms. To the British monarch he also added he would do everything in his power to prevent Belgian territory being used against Britain. The answer was an appeal to come over to London that didn't reach Léopold in time. The letter to Roosevelt was not published in Washington at the time, in the (vain) hope that withholding it would help the French will to resist, possibly under French or British pressure. Later, in January 1941, when things had become clearer and Léopold had been cleared by all of accusations of treason, the *Chicago Tribune* editorial ran: 'The only purpose the censorship of this letter served was to throw (in the eyes of the American public) upon the Belgians the full responsibility for the defeat for which they certainly were not more responsible than the British or the French.'

Although not the case everywhere, for many of the 1.5 million Belgian refugees in France Reynaud's speech had extremely unpleasant consequences. Until then French propaganda had concealed the catastrophic turn of events for the French forces, but the events of the previous two weeks and the announcement out of the blue of the Belgian 'defection', had the effect of suddenly making the French public, most of whom had not seen any fighting close at hand, realize the war might well be lost now, seemingly because of 'Belgian treason'. Having done nothing wrong, the unfortunate Belgian civilians in France now often, especially in the cities, found themselves ostracized, turned out of temporary lodgings, denied food or water, or overcharged for these. In some places they heard themselves being called '*Boches du Nord*'.

Most of the Belgian government, their bureaucracies and a large part of the parliament had moved to France during the campaign, including a mobile radio broadcasting facility. Now under French control, the Belgians had to submit their broadcast texts to French censorship and were assigned residences in towns and villages further and further to the south, including in one village where they ended up in a street called *rue*

Blanc Dutrouilh, this to the great joy of their detractors because it can be loosely translated as 'white with funk'. After the French capitulation they moved to Vichy and stayed, more appropriately, at the Hôtel Roi Albert.

This was a period of harsh recrimination between the King and the political establishment, culminating at Limoges in central France, where part of the Belgian parliament voted on a resolution using very strong language indeed – implying high treason if stopping short of the actual words. They also, though some proposed it, stopped short of calling for the abolition of the monarchy, which Reynaud had urged them to do. A politically confused (and bitter, because Léopold III could not and would not forget these insults) period followed, with contradictory instructions being issued to the Belgian embassies abroad from the King via the embassy in Bern, and from the government, communication between King and government taking place via emissaries, and the publication in Belgium of a pastoral letter from Cardinal Van Roey, approving the King's laying down of arms and pleading for reconciliation. On the whole Belgian public opinion, at this stage certainly, fully approved of the King's decision to end their ordeal and strongly condemned the ministers, who were held responsible for their defeat and misery. 'On vous vomit en Belgique!' ('You inspire total revulsion!') Spaak was made to hear when he enquired about a possible return to Brussels. The German occupying force, perhaps making a political mistake by not allowing the return of a government they could have controlled, also let it be known they would not permit the government to come back to Brussels and ignored them completely, on Hitler's specific orders. All of this, especially when France, on which they had staked so much, eventually also asked the Germans for terms on 18 June, caused the demoralized Pierlot and Spaak to despair, as the latter admits in his memoirs. Leaving for London was considered and discussed but eventually rejected, only the young Minister for Health Marcel-Henri Jaspar, something of a loose cannon, making the move. He was immediately stripped of his position by Pierlot for having abandoned his post (in France).

The CRABs

Again inspired by lessons learned in the previous conflict, when many hundreds of young men braved the electrified barbed wire separating the neutral Netherlands from occupied Belgium to join the Belgian Army, the government, immediately the invasion began, called upon all male citizens between 16 and 35, who for whatever reason were not already under arms, to make their way to camps in southern France, where it was anticipated they would receive military training. The young men who joined these *Camps de Recrutement de l'Armée Belge* were known as CRABs. Mostly by train or bicycle, about 200,000 of them started their journey south. In some cities they could find lodgings or places to sleep in French army barracks, but this was the exception rather than the rule. In fact, there was not much preparation at the camps themselves and the few Belgian officers detailed to look after them were left without orders or money. Since they had no military status as yet, discipline had to be by consent rather than imposed, and the few hundred staff were left to their own devices as to how to feed, lodge and keep the recruits busy and, where possible, useful. Many started working in farms or vineyards. Some later said it was the best vacation they had ever had. Drunkenness was not unknown and several said later they lost their sexual innocence during that long, hot summer. Nothing ever came of training them and most eventually trickled back home or were repatriated by the Red Cross. So too were many of the million and a half Belgian refugees in rural France, who had mostly been well treated, in contrast to those in the cities, where the reception was often far less friendly because of the Reynaud speech on 28 May.

Raymond V. and his brothers, together with some cousins and friends, started the long journey south by bicycle. Cousin Michel J. had a superb racing bike, but gave up after only a few days. Raymond ended up in a vineyard in southern France, where he made a little money spraying sulphate on the vines, whilst waiting for developments.

Back in Flanders, at the very 'Flemish feeling' S. household there were mixed feelings. There was gratitude to the King who had put an end to the useless slaughter, and also rejoicing that Belgium, to which no loyalty was felt, had been defeated. There was also hope that the Germans would restore full rights to the Flemings, as they had started doing during the previous occupation.

Arrest of real or imagined suspects
During the night of 14/15 May, about 6,000 persons were arrested by the Belgian police, acting on a law of 1918 and with prepared lists. This was justified by fears of fifth column actions (like those of Quisling's men in Norway), but whoever prepared these was overzealous to say the least and those who oversaw them incredibly negligent or incompetent. Among those detained were the leaders and key members of the extreme right parties, Degrelle for the Rex party and Van Severen of Verdinaso (in spite of the fact that the latter had made an appeal to his adherents to do their

duty as Belgian soldiers and stand behind the King), Flemish nationalists (Staf De Clercq), communist leaders and/or members of parliament like Grippa and Lahaut (not completely without reason, as the communists were at the time considered in many countries to be allies of the Nazis because of the Molotov-Ribbentrop Pact, and Stalin expelled the Belgian ambassador to Moscow on 10 May), and German and Austrian nationals. Bizarre, even outrageous was the inclusion of others who had done no worse than be too-vocal advocates of the (official) neutrality policy, or in the case of German citizens, the inclusion of anti-Nazi individuals and Jewish refugees in the lot! Apart from lacking common sense, no account was taken of the Belgian Constitution or parliamentary immunity. A look-alike of Flemish nationalist and arch collaborator August Borms was also arrested, while a Belgian unfortunately called Tirpitz, later turned over to the British, was to spend four years in the internment camp on the Isle of Man. First detained in jails across the country, sometimes beaten by Belgian gendarmes and called 'dirty Jews' (this must have rankled with the anti-Semite Degrelle), the detainees were put on buses when the military situation worsened and most were eventually taken to France and delivered to the French *Sûreté*.

These arbitrary arrests caused uproar with some Belgian politicians who managed to get a few, like Flemish nationalist De Clercq, freed while they were still in Belgium. Degrelle was later freed in southern France,[35] but not all were so lucky. One of the buses, holding seventy-seven detainees, including Verdinaso Party Leider Van Severen was driven to Abbeville in France. When the Germans were advancing on this city the local French military, not knowing what to do with their captives, summarily executed twenty-one of them, including Van Severen, two of his followers and a communist.[36] Most German (and Austrian) nationals ended up in camps in southern France and for the anti-Nazis and Jews among them all this was to have tragic consequences: at the armistice with France the pro-Nazi Germans were promptly freed, but the others immediately sent to concentration camps, from which few returned.

Chapter 4

The innocents abroad: London and Africa

Belgians in the Battle of Britain

In the summer of 1940, the RAF was short of trained pilots and those belonging to the continental countries that had been overrun were a very welcome addition. It is a little known fact that after the Commonwealth and Polish contingents the largest number of foreign pilots in the RAF during the Battle of Britain were Belgian, no fewer than twenty-nine of them, and in the summer of 1940 they made up about half of 609 Squadron, which was in the thick of the fighting. Some of them, as described earlier, had already faced the Luftwaffe in Belgium, in inferior biplanes. Seven were killed in the Battle of Britain, among them Paul Baillon whose Spitfire was shot down over the Isle of Wight by a Me 109E and who managed to parachute into the sea but did not survive. His lifeless body was washed ashore in France after a few days. The famous 609 Squadron itself would later be commanded by Belgian officers.

Later on, in 1942, two complete Belgian Squadrons were formed, Nos 349 and 350, the former at RAF Northolt and with the colours of the 2e Régiment d'Aéronautique militaire, smuggled out of Belgium. The latter took part in the Dieppe raid and the Battle of the Bulge. Some of these pilots merit special mention like Flight Lieutenant Jean Offenberg DFC, already a veteran of the Eighteen Days Campaign, who refused to abide by the ceasefire and together with Alexis Jottard escaped to French North Africa. From there, with a few other Belgians, they took ship to Gibraltar, arrived in England in time for the Battle of Britain and flew Hurricanes in 145 Squadron from Tangmere. Offenberg shot down two confirmed Me 109Es and one probable, but his close friend Jottard went missing, a great shock to him. On 5 May 1941 Offenberg, now flying a Spitfire Mk I, shot up two Heinkel 60s over the North Sea but was bounced by two Me 109s. After hectic manoeuvering he shot one down and saw white smoke coming out of the other's engine. Low on fuel he flew home. In June he joined 609 Squadron at Biggin Hill and in July, already with a DFC, he flew with the Squadron to Albert in occupied

France. On the way back they were attacked by several Me 109Fs and Offenberg went into a steep dive, which he knew a Spitfire could pull out of but not the Messerschmitt that was tailing him – which crashed, killing its pilot without his having fired a single bullet. Some have said Offenberg's victim was Condor Legion veteran and *Geschwaderkommodore* (Squadron Commodore) Wilhelm Balthasar of the famous JG 2, the Richthofen Geschwader, adorned with the highest German military decoration and with forty aerial victories, who died in similar circumstances in the same area at about the same date, but the slight discrepancy between dates in German and British records casts doubt on this. If Offenberg actually was responsible for *Hauptmann* (Captain) Balthasar's demise, he avenged the three Belgian Gloster Gladiators his opponent had shot down in May 1940. On 22 June 1942, while he was training younger pilots in combat tactics, a Spitfire from another squadron collided with his in a mock attack, damaging his tail. *Peike* ('little guy' in Brussels slang) Offenberg did not survive the ensuing crash, nor did the other pilot involved.

On 13 June 1942, Flight Sergeant Maurice Raes of 350 (BE) Squadron was returning from a flight over the Channel to protect British coastal shipping, when his Spitfire Vb hit the cable of a barrage balloon over Norwich. Rather than bailing out he steered his stricken plane away from the houses and forfeited his life. There now is a Maurice Raes Close in Norwich.

Later to be Wing Commander Mike Donnet DFC, stole a light plane and flew it to England. The title of his post-war memoirs was appropriately, *J'ai volé la liberté,* the pun being that the word for 'to fly' in French is the same as for 'to steal' (*voler*). In March 1944, he led an air-raid attack against a Gestapo headquarters in Copenhagen.

Wing Commander Le Roy du Vivier was the first non-Commonwealth officer to command an RAF unit in the Mediterranean. Quite a change from being locked up by his own compatriots during the Eighteen Days Campaign – having been shot down he had parachuted to safety but when picked up was suspected of being a German!

Rodolphe de Hemricourt de Grunne, scion of an aristocratic family, had flown Fiat CR 32s on the Nationalist side during the Spanish civil war and downed two Republican planes. He then joined the Belgian Aéronautique militaire and flew Hurricanes. It was in a Hurricane again that he shot down two Me 109Es during the Battle of Britain. Then in May 1941 he had to bail out over the Channel and was never seen again.

Pilot Officer Henri Picard of 350 (BE) Squadron, had an even more tragic fate. He was credited with shooting down two FW 190s in his Spitfire Mk Vb, but was himself shot down in 1942, and taken to Stalag Luft III. He was one of the officers who made the famous 'Great Escape' and was also one of those who were summarily executed on Hitler's orders after recapture.

If some Belgians excelled with the Supermarine Spitfire in all its versions, including the photo reconnaissance high altitude ones, others mastered another famous fighter plane produced by the British aeronautics industry, the Hawker Typhoon/Tempest, a new and difficult beast to tame. Belgian pilots flew Typhoons Mk 1b with 609 Squadron (half of 609's pilots were Belgian for most of the war) and with other squadrons. Someone who definitively preferred the Typhoon to the Spitfire, though not for its flying qualities, was Billy the goat, 609 Squadron's mascot. When allowed to stray out of sight, Billy was usually to be found licking the glycol coolant that seeped from the Typhoon's big Napier Sabre engine cooling circuit. The Typhoon outclassed all but the last versions of the slower Focke Wulf 190, and Pilot Officer Raymond Lallemant DFC, nicknamed 'Cheval' because of his love of horses (and his large healthy teeth), Van Lierde and de Sélys, all of 609 Squadron, accounted for fourteen FW 190s between them during the winter of 1942–43.

Flying Officer Jean-Michel de Sélys Longchamps DFC, who like several other Belgians in the RAF came from an ancient aristocratic family, had fought in the Eighteen Days Campaign, then managed to make his way to Britain, doctoring his papers because he was officially too old to be a fighter pilot. On the morning of 20 January 1943 his unit was tasked to attack rolling stock in occupied Belgium. After completing this mission, he flew his Typhoon 1b on to Brussels on his own. There he buzzed his parents' home, dropped Belgian flags, and strafed the building on Avenue Louise in Brussels, where the German *Sicherheitspolizei* (Security Police) had their offices, killing several including the deputy head, an SS Lieutenant Colonel, and causing havoc. His timing had been carefully planned so that the German interrogators were already in their offices, preparing for the day's 'work', while the *Résistants* were still locked away in the basement cells and escaped unharmed. This unauthorized action, of which the news quickly spread, boosted morale in the occupied capital and won him both a medal and a demotion. In February he shot down a Focke Wulf 190 in a frontal pass. In May 1943 he received a DFC, but on 16 August his Typhoon was hit by flak and he had to nurse it back to base. The damaged plane broke up during the final approach to land and he was killed. A monument to his memory now adorns the little grass square in front of the building he shot up in Brussels and which still stands.

'Cheval' Lallemant and the other Belgian and British pilots of 609 Squadron were also involved in the Amiens prison break, but apparently badly briefed and scrambled too late they could not prevent losses that might otherwise have been avoided, like that of Wing Commander Pickard, in command of Operation Jericho. In his memoirs Lallemant dwelled at length on it, although he was not to blame. He was later shot down and badly burned over Arnhem during Operation Market Garden. By then he was a squadron leader and another Belgian, 'Manu' Geerts took over command of 609 Squadron.

The first Belgian to command an RAF squadron was Léon Prévot, who in November 1942 took charge of the Typhoon-equipped Squadron 197.

Belgians who were shot down and killed included Squadron Leader Henry Gonay of 263 Squadron, lost in the Channel Islands, and 'Balbo' Roelandt over Normandy, whilst new blood arrived in the form of Pilot Officer Cooreman, whose grandfather had been prime minister of Belgium at the end of the First World War. Georges Nossin, who had flown Renard 31s in the Eighteen Days Campaign, travelled from Belgium to Portugal and on to the Congo, South Africa and Uruguay before joining 609 Squadron in September 1944. Serge Castermans, also coming from the Belgian Congo, Jean-Noël Van Daele, who was to be killed over Rotterdam, and many others also joined. Charles Demoulin, the third Belgian to command 609 Squadron, and Henri Goblet were shot down and taken prisoner, whilst Louis Bastin crashed his Typhoon in a wood after its engine stopped during take-off in the Netherlands. The heavy plane completely disintegrated under the impact but lucky Bastin was found, without a scratch, still sitting in his seat in the middle of the debris.

After D-Day the Belgian-manned Typhoons wrought havoc among the German tanks and other vehicles in Normandy with the four 20mm guns and the new 3in rockets slung under the wings, though later surveys after the battle showed that the psychological effect on German ground troops of the Allied fighter bomber attacks had been greater than the actual damage caused. Brussels slang and profanity could sometimes be heard over the RAF airwaves when some pilots were detached to accompany the ground troops and control strafings.

Flight Lieutenant (later Squadron Leader) Van Lierde from 150 Squadron later shot down no fewer than forty-four V-1s with his Tempest Mk V.

Two friends from Liège, Charles Delcour and Christian Deffontaine, the latter the son of a general, flew in the Aéronautique militaire in May 1940 and after the ceasefire fled together, via North Africa and Dakar. In England they joined Coastal Command, trained on Beaufighters and were sent to Egypt with Delcour in charge of the flight. Deffontaine disappeared over the Mediterranean but Delcour fought in the desert for two years, over El Alamein, Benghazi, and later from Malta.

Based in their home country after its liberation, some Belgian-manned RAF squadrons suffered heavily along with the rest of the Allied airpower during Operation Bodenplatte, on New Year's Day 1945, when the Luftwaffe launched a very strong attack on airfields all over Belgium and the south of the Netherlands, but on 10 January 1944, Flying Officer Jaspis shot down a Junkers 88 near Brussels. This was the 100th victory of a Belgian pilot in the RAF. Like their Czech, Polish and Dutch counterparts the Belgians flew planes that were painted and marked according to standard RAF regulations, but many added a little Belgian roundel or flag close to the cockpit, or the emblem of their former unit in the Belgian Aéronautique militaire.

On 27 April 1945, ten days before VE Day, Spitfires of 350 (Belgian) Squadron met with Soviet Yak fighters over Berlin.

Many other Belgian airmen flew with Bomber and Coastal Command, the USAAF or the South African Air Force. In all about 1,200 Belgians flew with the RAF alone during the conflict and 128 were killed in action.

Out of that core the post-war Belgian Air Force (now called Air Component) was built. Its units are still called 'Wings' and 'Squadrons', its uniforms clearly inspired by the RAF ones. In the 1950s and 1960s most of its generals, like Donnet and Delcour, were RAF veterans of the Second World War and in 1974 General Armand Crekillie, who had flown ninety-eight missions in Typhoons with 609 Squadron RAF in his early twenties, became Chief of the General Staff, the senior officer in the armed forces.

To this day two of the Belgian Air Force Squadrons, now equipped with F16s, proudly carry the names, crests and traditions of 349 (BE) and 350 (BE) Squadrons. The Belgian Air Force base near Florennes is called Base Jean Offenberg. It houses a museum that includes a Spitfire Mk XIV as flown by Colonel Aviateur Raymond Lallement DFC and Bar after the war.[37]

The London government in exile

Eventually Prime Minister Pierlot and Foreign Minister Spaak made their way from Vichy to London, via Spain and Portugal. This move was made after much hesitation and soul searching, and no doubt prompted by the impossibility of returning to Belgium, their first intention after the French collapse, but was decided on after a meeting with their colleague De Vlee-schauwer, who came to the Spanish–French border to see them. Having seen a complete collaborationist government installed in Vichy on the one hand, and the last appeasers having left the Churchill Cabinet on the other, and furthermore seeing that the Germans had no interest in dis-cussing any arrangements either with them or with the King (who would have been unwilling to do so anyway), they decided their best course was to leave for London. Most of the other government members progres-sively made their way back to Belgium and faded from political life.

In July 1940, De Vleeschauwer, who was in charge of the Belgian col-onies in Africa, obtained from the Portuguese consul general in Bordeaux, Aristides de Sousa Mendes,[38] visas for his family and himself to go to Portugal, where they were accommodated at Sousa Mendes' home. He left his family in safety in Portugal and travelled on his own to London, where he saw Ambassador de Cartier de Marchienne and had several meetings with the British government. In August he came back to meet Pierlot and Spaak at the French Spanish border, insisting they should come to London. Avoiding attempts to prevent them from doing so by the Vichy government, who even tried to convince them London would soon ask for terms,[39] the Prime Minister and Foreign Minister did cross into Spain but were put under house arrest by Franco's police. Spaak has described in his memoirs how, prevented from leaving Barcelona by the Franco government, they waited a few weeks until their police minders relaxed and left them on their own, going off to watch an important football match for which the two captives had cunningly bought them tickets. With the help of the local Belgian Consul they hid in a concealed compartment behind the driver's seat of a lorry that drove them all the way to the Portuguese border. There must have been few occasions when a head of government travelled in a less dignified way. The Portuguese government headed by Salazar, though neutral, was more pro-Ally than its Iberian neighbour,[40] and from Lisbon there were commercial flights to Britain.[41]

The Belgian Ambassador to the Court of Saint James at the time was Baron Emile de Cartier de Marchienne, who had been given the London Embassy at the close of his career. In fact he had reached retirement age but it had been decided earlier to keep him on, a wise decision indeed. He was popular in London with the political establishment and was known among his colleagues for his bushy moustache and the fine Luxembourg wines and gourmet meals served at his smart Residence in Belgrave Square.[42] Spaak has described how, both before and after their arrival, Cartier de Marchienne took a role far beyond that of an ordinary diplomat, rising to the occasion by convincing them that Britain would fight on and consistently encouraging them to come over to London. Spaak turned him out of his office at the embassy's chancery on Eaton Square, which became the temporary foreign ministry, the rest of the Belgian government in exile setting up shop in different buildings around Eaton and Belgrave Squares.[43] An Anglo-Belgian Club, still existing today, was opened on Knightsbridge.

Colonies Minister De Vleeschauwer was already in London and Finance Minister Gutt, who had gone to the United States on government business, eventually showed up too. Those four made up the core of the London Belgian government in exile. A Belgian 'Parliamentary Office' also existed on Hobart Place, regrouping the dozen or so members who also had made it to Britain, including First Socialist International veteran and former Burgomaster of Antwerp Camille Huysmans, who chaired it.

Relations with Churchill and Halifax became more cordial after the initial strong mutual mistrust. Especially so with Churchill, and Spaak has described how they sometimes would meet for an informal and friendly chat, though Pierlot's poor knowledge of English and lack of tact didn't help.

When Japan attacked Pearl Harbor and the British and Dutch possessions in the Far East, the Belgian government declared war on the Empire as stated in a telegram from Spaak to all Belgian embassies abroad, sent on 19 December 1941. The declaration of war on Italy was formalized at the same occasion.

Ambassadors were exchanged with several other continental countries who had governments in exile in London, in some cases a convenient way of getting rid of some politicians, and a few new Belgian ambassadors were sent abroad. The embassies in Spain, Portugal, Switzerland and Sweden became more important as travel and communication by mail between London and occupied Belgium was made through them and the embassy in Spain was also having to help all the Belgian refugees who crossed the Pyrenees, most of whom usually ended up for a while at the large internment camp at Miranda del Ebro in northern Spain. From Miranda most were eventually processed to Gibraltar or Lisbon to join the Belgian forces in Britain, if fit to serve. Elderly people, women or children were usually sent to the Belgian Congo if they had nowhere else to go or lacked means to look after themselves. Liberation of Miranda detainees usually kept pace with deliveries made in exchange of goods like cotton, coffee, jute, etc. from the Belgian Congo to dirt-poor, civil war ravaged Spain.

Raymond V. and his group were liberated from Miranda after a shipload of Congolese cotton arrived at a Spanish port. Washed and close-shaved, including their hair, they were taken to Madrid by train accompanied by an elderly Guardia Civil. *There, the Belgian embassy first paid for new suits purchased at the Corte Inglés. After that they went to have some pastries in a tea house on the Gran Via. Seeing a group of shaven-headed young men accompanied by an armed policeman, the female customers there thought they were seeing a group of criminals being escorted and held firmly on to their handbags. Next they went by train to Gibraltar where they had to wait for a convoy bound for Britain. On the sea trip north two ships of the convoy were torpedoed by German submarines. At the Liverpool railway station they beheld a large well-known poster asking 'Is your journey really necessary?' Recalling other posters, German ones in Belgium announcing recent executions, they decided it had been.*

They were then taken to something called 'Patriotic School' where they were interrogated to establish if they really were who they said they were, in other words to weed out possible spies infiltrated into Britain via Spain. They were asked pointed questions about their families and neighbours in Belgium, what they had been doing before they left, which shops they would shop at, etc. the answers to which could easily be verified. Since Raymond V. already had several cousins and friends who had preceded him to Britain, he was released after only a few days, but some of his group who had come all the way from Miranda disappeared and he was to see them no more.[44] *Upon his release Raymond V. was allowed to go to the Belgian Embassy on Eaton Square and volunteer for the Belgian Brigade.*

The Grand Duchy of Luxembourg, whose government was also exiled in Britain, was helped by the Belgian government in many ways and it was in London also that the first foundations of what was to become the Benelux group of nations were laid. Rubbing shoulders with colleagues from the Netherlands and Luxembourg led to discussions about the future of their countries after the war, indeed to negotiations. In October 1943 a monetary agreement was signed between the three and in September 1944 a Customs Convention. This was to lead to the Benelux Treaty of 1958 which introduced many innovations later adopted by the Common Market. Benelux is now acknowledged to have been the embryonic form, also the incubator, for what is now the European Union, and was brought into being in London during the occupation of its members.[45]

The Belgian government in exile also had 'internal' matters to look after. There were about 23,000 Belgian refugees in Britain. They had to be organized and administered, those who were already in uniform reorganized, those who were not drafted and/or unfit to serve put to useful work wherever possible. The government organized the Belgian units within the British Armed Forces and Merchant Navy, supported and controlled the internal Resistance back in Belgium, organized trade from the Belgian Congo and ran the embassies abroad, all of whom gradually accepted its authority.[46]

BBC V-signs
The BBC started broadcasting to occupied Belgium and the Belgian Congo. Jan Moedwil (a pseudonym for Fernand Geersens, a radio announcer since 1936 in Belgium), took over reading the Dutch language announcements on Radio België, *moed* and *wil* meaning 'courage' and willpower'. His catchphrase that rhymed *boffen* (to be lucky) and *moffen* (the Boches) was remembered in Flanders for many years after the war. Theo Fleischman and Victor de Laveleye read the news for the French language Radio Belgique. Fleischman was a pioneer of news broadcasting and radio-theatre shows before the war in Belgium, and would pursue his career after 1945. De Laveleye, for whom Pierlot had little time, was a Liberal Party member of the Belgian parliamentary office in London. As a young boy scout he must have realized that the first letter of his Christian name, V, when signalled in Morse code corresponded with the first bars of Beethoven's Fifth (Vth) Symphony, although a British announcer also claimed the idea. The letter V also begins *victoire* ('victory' in French) and *vrijheid* ('freedom' in Dutch). So the V-sign was launched with a little jingle (*V! V! V!*, lyrics by de Laveleye, music by Beethoven) on the Belgian broadcasts of the BBC on 27 June and immediately, as recommended, Vs were scratched, painted, pencilled, engraved or otherwise affixed onto Belgian walls, windows, trams and trains, public conveniences and even in some cases, daringly, on German military vehicles. Seeing its success had spread to northern France, de Gaulle took it over and it was consecrated by no less than Churchill himself, on July 20. The Germans first tried to repress the 'V-mania' but then thought of a clever countermeasure – German vehicles, buildings and other public sites suddenly were adorned with beautifully stylized Vs, signifying of course the Victory of German arms. Victor de Laveleye was to die shortly after the war, still young, having been briefly minister for education and a member of the

delegation which drafted the United Nations Charter. His place in the history of the Second World War however, is as the initiator of the V-sign.

The saga of the Belgian gold

In 1939, before Belgium was involved in the war, the Pierlot government anticipated the German invasion and took measures to prepare for a new occupation; again inspired by 1914 precedents and experience, they decided to send the gold reserves of the central bank abroad. This amounted to about 600 tons and the Banque Nationale de Belgique was tasked to divide this into three lots of 200 tons, to be send respectively to the United States, Britain and France, the last consignment would be minus 2 tons to cover the expenses of the Belgian Government in exile – again based on the 1914 precedent, they were to take refuge in France, if and when the Belgian territory or most of it had been overrun. Transports to the US, where the gold was deposited in the New York branch of the Federal Reserve, and to London went smoothly. The third lot, of 198 tons, entrusted to France had a very different war story. With French territory about to be completely overrun in June 1940, the Belgian government already in exile in southern France asked the Banque de France to have it removed. It was duly taken by railroad to a French port, loaded onto the cruiser *Victor Schoelcher* and taken to Dakar, the capital of what is now Senegal and was then French West Africa.

When France asked for an armistice the gold was still in Dakar but a joint British and Free French attack was feared (and later materialized) against this city, motivated in part by the presence of Belgian, French, Polish and Luxembourg (4 tons) gold in that port.[47] The French authorities decided to move the Belgian gold further out of reach and it was taken to Kayès, 600km inland, in the desert. During the negotiations instituted as a follow-up to the French Armistice, the Germans demanded the surrender of the Belgian gold under French control. The directors of the Banque de France at first adamantly refused, saying it would be a shameful breach of trust, but their hand was forced by Pétain's prime minister, Pierre Laval. Arch-collaborator Laval, who would face a firing squad after the war, thought (wrongly) he could obtain concessions like the freeing of French POWs by giving away what was not his to give. The legitimate qualms of the governor of the Banque de France were stilled with a law signed by Pétain, and the Vichy authorities started bringing back the gold from Kayès, across the Sahara to the French North African coast, where it was flown over to Marseilles in Air France LeO 242 flying boats, and from

The main 120mm cupola of Fort Eben Emael. Even partially patched up with cement, the damage caused by a German 50kg hollow charge can clearly be seen. The hollow charge was a new weapon and the Germans wanted to keep it secret, as well as their use of gliders which landed on top of the Fort. (*Author's collection*)

A 75mm gun cupola at Eben Emael. The hole made by a hollow charge can be seen on top, with the imprint of the camouflage netting that has been burned into the steel. The round cupolas were fixed to counterweights and would be raised to fire. They were normally flush with the base, not left in the raised position as here. (*Author's collection*)

A fixed triple 75mm gun bunker at Eben Emael. Unlike the cupola guns, which could fire all round, these fixed emplacements were oriented to specific objectives – the bridges at nearby Maastricht and Visé – and were named after them. (*Author's collection*)

Inside a 75mm emplacement. Considering their age and the fact the fort remained derelict for decades, this gun is in a remarkable state of conservation, as is the whole fort. (*Author's collection*)

The main entrance gate at Eben Emael. Apart from an escape tunnel, it was the only access. On 11 May 1940 at about noon, a white flag was flown. Almost all the fort's guns had been rendered unusable by then, the observation cupolas were destroyed and smoke had entered the underground galleries. (*Author's collection*)

Outside the main gate, one of several tin, dummy cupolas. The Germans did waste effort on these as their intelligence was not perfect, contrary to what was said later. The (reconstructed) peacetime barracks in the background were destroyed by the fort CO to give the main gate guns a clear field of fire, unfortunately using men who could have been manning the anti-aircraft guns to shoot at the incoming gliders. (*Author's collection*)

The strategically important Vroenhoven Bridge. There were bridges over the Albert Canal on each of the three roads leading out of Maastricht into Belgium. They were attacked by airborne troops at the same time as Fort Eben Emael. The bridge is in Belgium, but the Dutch border is a few hundred metres to the right and Maastricht a few kilometres behind.
(*Author's collection*)

Early this century a completely new bridge was built at Vroenhoven but the Belgian army pillbox that had defended it in 1940 was preserved. After the Germans took it, Belgian, French and British planes tried heroically to destroy the bridge, most of the pilots losing their lives.
(*Author's collection*)

A sergeant and a squad of Chasseurs Ardennais pre-war, wearing their characteristic large green beret with boar's head cap insignia. These elite troops gave a spirited account of themselves in May 1940. They are armed with the 1936 Belgian version of the Mauser rifle. (*Copyright Memo 5/1981*)

(*Left*) Chasseur Ardennais Dequand was, in civilian life, a cycling champion. Bicycles were a cheap and reliable transport on small tracks in the Ardennes woods. One battalion was equipped with motorbikes, acting as mobile reserve for the whole army – they suffered heavy losses. (*With kind permission of Cdt R. Georges Ch. A.*)

(*Right*) T13 and T15 light tanks were built in Belgium and equipped Chasseurs Ardennais and Cyclistes frontier troops. On this T15, a Belgian (black, yellow, red) roundel can be made out painted on the turret, as well as *LIII* (Leopold III). (*Copyright Royal Army and Military Museum, Brussels*)

Having abandoned the post-First World War alliance with France to revert to neutrality, Belgium had to build up a credible defence. In 1940 it fielded a remarkable 600,000 men, the strongest army Belgium ever had. We see King Leopold III (centre right) inspecting a 47mm anti-tank gun crew during pre-war manoeuvres. Left of him is General Denis, the Defence Minister. These guns proved very effective against the German tanks, which at this early stage of the war were relatively lightly armoured. (*Copyright Royal Army and Military History Museum, Brussels*)

The Renard R 31 armed reconnaissance plane was built in Belgium. These slow planes were in service until the last days of fighting in May 1940.
(*Daniel Brackx Collection*)

A few of the Fiat CR 42 Italian-built fighters acquired by Belgium on the eve of war. Most of the modern Hurricanes Mk 1 having been destroyed on the ground, Belgian pilots managed to shoot down several Messerschmitt 109s with these slower biplanes. (*Daniel Brackx Collection*)

Belgian Fairey Battles. Nine were sent to destroy the Albert Canal bridges on 10 May 1940. Only three came back and five airmen perished in the fruitless attempt. (*Daniel Brackx Collection*)

The impact of German armour-piercing shots can be seen on this steel turret at Fort Battice. (*Author's collection*)

This is all you could normally see of a retracted 75mm cupola. (*Author's collection*)

Breech of a 75mm gun inside a turret of Fort Battice. After the war, the forts around Liège were allowed to slowly decay, but by the turn of the century most were in the hands of private groups (sometimes including veterans), restored and open to visitors. (*Author's collection*)

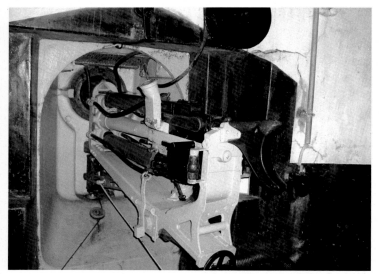

One of the thousands of Maxim machine guns received from Germany as reparations after the First World War, mounted inside a turret at Fort Battice. (*Author's collection*)

One of the smaller generators still at Fort Battice (some were removed by the Germans). Like the bigger ones at Fort Eben Emael, they have been restored to working order. (*Author's collection*)

Part of Fort Tancrémont, outside Verviers. Much smaller and less important than Eben Emael, it resisted far longer, in fact until 29 May, after the bulk of the Belgian Army had surrendered. (*Author's collection*)

One element of a Cointet barrier. When solidly attached to similar elements on each side and kept under fire it could stop light tanks and resisted artillery fire. Also called 'Belgian Gates', some were later used by the Germans on the Atlantic Wall. (*Author's collection*)

In the worst outrage by the Wehrmacht in Belgium, 86 civilians, aged 16 to 89, were executed at Vinkt on 27/28 May. Here a group are having their hands bound, moments before being shot. (*Copyright Royal Army and Military History Museum, Brussels*)

A group of Belgian RAF pilots congratulating their colleague Raymond 'Cheval' Lallemant on receiving the DFC. The 29 Belgians were one of the largest non-Commonwealth contingents in the RAF during the Battle of Britain. Lallemant later added a bar to his DFC and ended the war a squadron leader, hospitalized with severe burns. Both he and Manu Geerts, who is shaking his hand, commanded 609 Squadron, RAF. (*Copyright Royal Army and Military History Museum, Brussels*)

The former Belgian embassy on 103 Eaton Square. The building became the seat of the Belgian Foreign Ministry during the war. (*Author's collection*)

The plaque on 103 Eaton Square, commemorating the Belgians who volunteered here to serve in the Belgian armed forces in Britain. It was inaugurated by HM Queen Elizabeth, the widow of King George the VIth and Prince Albert of Belgium, son of King Leopold. (*Author's collection*)

The 'London Four', the Belgian government in exile. Left to right: Colonies Minister De Vleeschauwer who put the Belgian Congo's vast resources at the disposal of the Allied war effort, Prime Minister Pierlot, Finance Minister Gutt and Foreign Minister Spaak. Since they were the senior members of the constitutional, elected government at the outbreak of war their legitimacy was greater than that of most other exiles in London. (*Copyright Royal Army and Military History Museum, Brussels*)

Belgian Congolese troops entraining. Led by Belgian officers and in coordination with British troops coming from Kenya and Somalia, they helped conquer Italian-occupied Abyssinia (Ethiopia) in 1941. (*Copyright Royal Army and Military History Museum, Brussels*)

The Belgian ambassador to London in 1940, Baron Emile de Cartier de Marchienne played an important role in convincing important members of the Belgian government, demoralized after France's defeat, to come to London and stay in the war. (*Author's collection*)

The German military governor for Belgium and northern France, General von Falkenhausen, was a Prussian aristocrat with little time for the Nazis. How far he was involved in the Stauffenberg conspiracy is unclear, but he was in detention in Buchenwald. He stood trial in Belgium, and did not receive a death sentence. (*Copyright Royal Army and Military History Museum, Brussels*)

Leopold III, King of the Belgians during the Second World War, was a handsome man. In May 1940 he followed closely what his father, King Albert I did in 1914–18 or would have done if beaten, but lost his throne after the war because of action taken during the occupation, rather than for surrendering a fight that had become hopeless. (*Author's collection*)

Lilian Baels was without doubt a pretty woman. Many were shocked when Leopold III, widower of a popular queen, married her in December 1941 while so many of the soldiers he had pledged to stay with were suffering in POW camps. (*Private Collection*)

The entrance to the sinister Fort Breendonk. Used as GHQ Belgian forces in 1940 it was turned into a detention camp by the Germans, for about 3,500 persons. (*Author's collection*)

The torture chamber at Fort Breendonk. Prisoners were suspended from the hook by the wrists, tied behind their backs. (*Author's collection*)

The execution posts at Breendonk. (*Author's collection*)

The gallows at Breendonk.
(Author's collection)

They chose the wrong side: Flemish SS parading through the streets of Antwerp behind a Wehrmacht officer. Many lost their lives in Russia.
(Copyright Royal Army and Military History Museum, Brussels)

Another who chose to collaborate: SS Lieutenant Colonel Léon Degrelle of the SS Sturmbrigade Wallonien, third from left, has just received his Iron Cross First Class from the Führer. Degrelle's superior, SS General Gille, commanding the SS Viking Division, is furthest left. Like the Flemish SS, the French speaking Belgians of Légion Wallonie fought bravely for a wrong cause. *(Copyright Royal Army and Military History Museum, Brussels)*

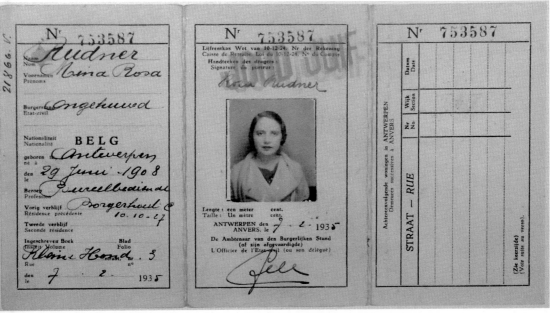

The identity card of a Belgian Jewish woman, issued in 1935 and on which, during the occupation a Star of David and the word 'Jew' was stamped in both the languages spoken in Belgium.
(*Copyright Kazerne Dossin Mechelen*)

Hergé, creator of Tintin, went through an anti-Semitic phase. Here Isaac, who has been asked by Salomon about the possible end of the world, answers in a heavy foreign accent: 'Ha! That would be good news. I owe my suppliers 50,000 francs, so I would not have to pay them!'
(Le Soir, *11 November 1941*)

The 'Hidden Children'. This moving drawing of a young Jew protected by a Belgian is by Israeli Belgian-born cartoonist Kishka, for the cover of a book written by another Israeli of Belgian origin, Sylvain Brachfeld. The title is *Thank you for saving us!* Brachfeld himself was hidden in a Catholic institution. (*With kind permission of Michel Kishka*)

One of the most surprising exhibits at the Dossin Barracks – the Iron Cross awarded to German Jew Max Cohen for valour while serving in the German Army during the First World War. It was taken from him before he was sent to Auschwitz. (*Copyright Kazerne Dossin*)

(*Left*) *Manneken Pis*, the famous statue in Brussels, 4 September 1944. He was later presented with an Irish Guards uniform, which he wears on the anniversaries of his liberation. (*Author's collection*)

(*Below*) Two on the right side: *Maréchal des Logis* (Sergeant) Salman and *Cavalier* (Private) Desy of the Armoured Squadron, First Belgian Brigade, observe the enemy in Normandy from their Daimler Mark I. On 4 September they were given a rapturous welcome in the streets of Brussels. (*Copyright Royal Army and Military History Museum, Brussels*)

there sent by train to Berlin. About 5,000 boxes of gold took this complicated trip, the Germans supplying the necessary fuel for the flying boats. The Reichsbank of course was not slow to renege on its promise to the French to put the gold in a special account 'for safekeeping for the Belgians until after the war'. Göring had the precious metal quickly melted down and recast in Reichsbank ingots, bearing false dates ('1937' and '1938'). However, a zealous German bank clerk wrote in pencil the Belgian serial numbers corresponding to the list of the new German ones being cast. This allowed for them to be traced after the war, some to the salt mines, where the US Army found about a fifth of it, others to the Swiss or Swedish vaults where it went as payment by Germany for arms or other supplies during the war. The weight of gold thus found added up almost exactly to the amount that had been entrusted to France before the war.

In the meantime, the Belgian government in London, having learnt of the transfer to Germany, had its representative in the USA, former Prime Minister Theunis, start a lawsuit in New York where the French had deposited their own gold, to claim part of that gold as compensation for the loss Belgium had incurred through the Vichy French breach of trust. The court proceedings dragged on and were stopped altogether in November 1942, when the Allies invaded North Africa and the Germans occupied the rest of France, as the French representatives in New York and their lawyers claimed they were now cut off from receiving instructions from Vichy. Discussions between the Belgian government in London and the Free French were held about this matter even before D-Day and not surprisingly the Gaullists took a very different attitude. As soon as the French territory was liberated the new authorities in Paris showed complete willingness to cooperate, and after some problems were ironed out France made, out of its own gold reserves, a series of phased compensatory payments that went on until 1953.

Belgian loan to the British Exchequer

One of the first matters to be discussed by the Belgian government in London was that of the Belgian gold. The tribulations of the part that had been sent to France before the war are covered in the previous paragraph, but cash-strapped Britain looked with envy on the part that had been sent into British care. In the winter of 1940–41 Britain's financial situation was as bad as its military reverses and its political isolation. In fact the gold reserves of the Bank of England had been so reduced as to affect the fiduciary cover of sterling. Negotiations were started with the London

Belgian government, which was quite willing to lend its gold to Britain for the duration: 'We are in together for better or for worse. What is ours to-day should be yours to-day, what is yours tomorrow should be ours to-morrow,' wrote a somewhat carried-away Finance Minister Gutt to the chancellor of the exchequer on 16 October 1940. All the same, the London Belgians wanted political guarantees for Belgium's independence, as well as guarantees of its colonial possessions in exchange (with good reason in the Belgian Congo's case, as we have seen), plus economic cooperation and customs-free access for its goods in Britain and its dominions during and after the war (British protectionism had hit Belgium hard during the great 1929 crisis). Halifax replied that Britain was 'deeply appreciative of the generous spirit in which Mr Gutt's letter was written [...] and, indeed, sensible to the contribution Belgium has made to the Allied cause.' As Antony Eden, Halifax's successor, wrote to Churchill in a secret memorandum of 10 February 1941, now in the British National Archives: 'It should be noted that even if, legally, we are in a position to vest the Belgian gold in the Custodian of Enemy Property or buy it from him in sterling (which is doubtful), it would be undesirable in view of the not unreasonable attitude the Belgians have adopted, to proceed to such a drastic step.'[48]

The political guarantees were granted or in fact reiterated, as they had already been given earlier by Churchill in the House of Commons in June 1940, including an association in any peace negotiations with Germany and pledges of economic, financial and transport assistance at the liberation of Belgian territory. But for customs-free access it proved more difficult, especially when it came to the Belgian Congo's goods, which had for the duration of the war been given the same access to Britain as those from the Dominions and Empire, to continue to do so after the war. However, negotiations with Ministers Gutt and Spaak and Ambassador de Cartier were satisfactorily concluded by an exchange of memoranda. It has been written that this saved Britain from bankruptcy in 1941. It certainly gave the Belgian government in exile prestige and standing in London.

The Congo's war effort
Even more than the gold deposits, the new Belgian government in exile's greatest asset was the Belgian Congo's vast resources, which were put at the disposal of the Allied war effort. In the Anglo-Saxon world Belgium's colonization of central Africa is usually thought of as one of the bloodiest and most predatory. During the last decades of the nineteenth century,

the second King of the Belgians, Léopold II, *privately* acquired a large domain in Central Africa, the Congo Free State, later to become the Belgian Congo. It is indisputable that very severe abuses were committed against the local population at the time, as was established by both Belgian and international experts commissioned by a worried Belgian government, and as also was the case in other parts of Africa (as well as Asia and America) colonized by other European countries. There is no documented evidence however, that millions lost their lives, as has been claimed by some. In 1908, the Congo became a Belgian colony, in part because public opinion in Belgium and abroad became increasingly concerned by the situation in what was King Léopold II's private realm, and most abuses stopped. Serious historians agree that on the whole the Belgian Congo was run neither better nor worse than the neighbouring colonies in British, French, German or Portuguese Africa, as was also reported by visiting American journalists like Paul Gunther in his book *Inside Africa* (12).[49]

The negotiations on the Congo between the British and Belgian authorities in London did not go as smoothly as those about the gold loan to the British exchequer. Research in the archives of the British Foreign Office has revealed London had decided to militarily occupy the Belgian colony with its vast resources if an agreement was not reached, and its attitude towards the Belgian government in exile sometimes bordered on the arrogant, while their private recriminations against the 'insufferable' Belgian Colonies Minister De Vleeschauwer were uncharitable to say the least. In fact the Colonies Minister was playing 'bad cop' while Gutt and Spaak were 'good cops'. The Belgians sometimes fielded with the Americans, who did not always see eye-to-eye with London on these and other matters, against the British. During the negotiations the British demanded and obtained a 30 per cent devaluation of the Congolese currency, which meant in fact they were getting its products at a bargain price, cheaper than similar products coming from their own colonies. Eventually an agreement was reached and any danger of seeing the British simply taking over the rich Belgian colony disappeared. The Congo's value for the Pierlot London government in its relations with the British became even more important after early 1942, when the Dutch East Indies (today called Indonesia), the British Asian colonies of Malaya and Burma, as well as the Philippines, all exporters of similar commodities produced in tropical climates, especially rubber, fell prey to the Japanese. Colonies Minister De Vleeschauwer and the Belgian Governor General in Léopoldville (now called Kinshasa) Pierre Ryckmans were instrumental in diversifying and driving up production of copper, gold, zinc, cobalt, industrial diamonds, cadmium, tantalum, and manganese, as well as rubber, cotton, palm oil, coffee, gum and jute, evidently all extremely valuable for wartime production of armaments, ammunition, clothing, means of transport, food, payments in gold to neutrals etc. These commodities, whose production increases were impressive, were transported to Britain, the US, Canada or South Africa for processing, sometimes in Belgian merchant vessels. It is worthy of note that delivery of some of these goods to hesitant neutrals, especially Spain, were an important factor in keeping them neutral and out of the Reich's total economic dependence.

Driving up the production of Congolese goods by so much was an extremely important contribution to the Allied war effort, now largely forgotten, but it did not take place without a heavy price. The high production rates demanded caused discontent, and sometimes accidents and loss of life. This was especially true for rubber, the British appetite for this commodity being such that its production rose tenfold, and the methods used to achieve it, forcing the Congolese population to harvest more latex both in hevea plantations and also in the forests, being sometimes identical to those that had been so criticized by British philanthropists at the time of Léopold II. The disruption this caused in the rural population was denounced by the local Catholic Church. Strikes by both Belgian and Congolese workers erupted in the mines, factories, railways and docks. In December 1941, some strikers were shot at by the *Force Publique*, the local army/police force, leaving hundreds dead. Until then only Belgians had manned the skilled supervisory jobs, but with increased production their numbers were insufficient. Local manpower was trained but paid less than whites with the same qualifications and responsibilities, which naturally caused resentment. Logically enough, these newly formed African cadres would later support the pro-independence parties of the 1950s. Discontent was also rife among the 15,000 Belgians living in the colony, because the high production rates meant a far heavier workload – this while many able men were away with the armed forces – and also because wages had not followed price increases and the devaluation of the currency had made imported goods dearer. Contrary to expectations not even the colonial companies profited much from the production boom because of heavy war taxes, sometimes up to 40 per cent. On the positive side the vast territory hugely improved its infrastructures in transport and production facilities, assets that would serve it well after peace had come.

Uranium
Uranium-235 was also produced in the Belgian Congo and merits a special mention. Union Minière du Haut Katanga (UMHK) was by far the largest mining group in the Belgian Congo, especially active in the copper-rich province of Katanga, bordering Northern Rhodesia (now Zambia). UMHK also extracted uranium at the Congolese mine of Shinkolobwe. Until the late 1930s it was shipped to Belgium to make radium, used in the medical industry, or for colouring ceramic tiles. The discoveries of Otto Hahn in Germany and the Joliot-Curie couple in France indicated that by enriching uranium and bombarding its core with neutrons enormous energy could be liberated and Einstein wrote his famous letter to Roosevelt, warning him of a possible German atomic bomb and indicating the main source of the mineral as the Belgian Congo. The Roosevelt administration contacted UMHK in the person of its chairman Edouard Sengier, who promptly shipped 1,140 tons of the stuff to be unloaded on Staten Island, in the port of New York. When General Groves was put in charge of the Manhattan Project to build the bomb and sought to acquire uranium he called Sengier, who happened to be in New York and who told him about the stock already in the US. Sengier had a pretty good idea of what it was needed for and was later decorated by the Americans.[50]

Thus the cores of the Trinity test bomb first detonated in the New Mexico desert and of the Hiroshima U-235 bomb and the Nagasaki plutonium bomb were made with Congolese uranium ore. Since the presence of uranium in other parts of the world was not yet known, the US government sought to acquire a monopoly on the Congolese uranium and, under great secrecy, negotiated an agreement to that effect with the London Belgian government, which was promised preferential treatment in nuclear research in exchange. The Shinkolobwe mine was closed before the Congo became independent in 1960 and subsequently flooded, but North Korean agents were reported to have been seen there in the 1990s.[51]

The Abyssinian campaign and the Battle of Saio
In the early days of the war, just after the Belgian Army's surrender and before the Belgian Brigade could be organized, the only armed force under Belgian colours was the 15,000-strong police/army force in the Belgian Congo, the Force Publique, with local troops and Belgian officers. Well-equipped and disciplined, spread out over the colony, it had occasionally been used to suppress disturbances, just like the corresponding forces in the neighbouring French and British territories. Manned exclusively by

volunteers it had even developed a specific language, so overcoming the problems of communication between soldiers speaking the different local languages of the hundreds of different ethnic groups in this vast land. In the First World War it had played an important role in the conquest of Deutsch Ost Afrika, now Tanzania, then a German colony, skilfully defended by General Von Lettow-Vorbeck. The Belgian colonial troops conquered a large part of German East Africa, including one of its largest cities, Tabora. Two districts, Ruanda-Urundi (now Rwanda and Burundi), had been given in trust to Belgium by the League of Nations, because of this contribution. After the collapse of the Belgian Army and the occupation of the homeland in 1940, the officers manning the Force Publique, as well as many Belgians living in the Congo among whom were numerous reserve officers, were all itching to do something about it. Seeing – or perceiving – the government to be doing next to nothing, or rather preferring business to warfare, disturbances, not to say an outright mutiny, broke out in Stanleyville, the third largest city (now called Kisangani). Governor General Ryckmans, to whom an ultimatum had been sent, had to send a senior member of his staff to calm them down, by explaining that their economic contribution to the war effort was at least as important as a military intervention, the organization of which would be fraught with problems. These were firstly the enormous distances involved: the closest Axis territory to the Belgian Congo was Abyssinia (Ethiopia) recently conquered by Italy and thousands of kilometres away from the garrison cities of the Congo. It was ruled by the Italian viceroy, the Duke of Aosta, a cousin of the King of Italy. A legal problem existed also, because technically Belgium and Italy were not at war, but the Belgian government, at first reluctant because of the dynastic links (which had their uses as we have seen), finally declared war on Italy on 23 November 1940, having taken into consideration that Mussolini had sent air force units to occupied Belgium from where they attacked Britain, and also the fact that an Italian submarine had sunk a Belgian cargo vessel.

Plans were coordinated with the British who were in overall command, General Cunningham simultaneously attacking from Kenya in the south of the Italian colony and General Platt from Somalia in the north, the offensive from the Congo in the east completing the encirclement. After protracted preparations about 8,000 men, including many porters, set out in February 1941 under the command of General Gilliaert and reached Juba, on the White Nile, after having trekked some 1,000km. They then marched on into Italian-held Ethiopia through mountainous terrain and took the Italian garrison town of Asosa by surprise on 10 March 1941. An Italian counter-offensive was repulsed by a charge with bayonets, followed by a stalemate along the banks of the Bordaï River, where another Italian attack was foiled by a machine-gun platoon led by Sergeant Bobozo, who was later to command the Congolese armed forces after independence. Logistics had been mismanaged and the soldiers were poorly fed on dried fish and had too little water. Hundreds of African soldiers and porters died of exhaustion and illness, mainly dysentery, as well as some of the Belgians. Intensive heat of up to 50° C alternated with diluvian rains in this most inhospitable region.

After a pause, combat was rejoined with better artillery that had arrived in the meantime, together with the support of the South African Air Force, including a Belgian-manned squadron. The important Italian garrison town of Gambela was taken on the first day of July 1941. The Italians made a stand on a riverbank, with a second line on a hill at Saio a few days later. The British liaison officer present transmitted an order to attack and on 3 July the Belgian/Congolese force made a two-pronged attack, one battalion in a frontal advance against the Italian line, the second making a large flanking movement around the Italian left, while a third was held in reserve to watch the other flank. Two artillery batteries gave covering fire. At 1500hrs three Italian officers were observed carrying a white flag. Ceasefire was ordered and rather generous terms were agreed on and signed, the Italian officers retaining their sidearms, servants and baggage. The Belgian/Congolese force captured 6,500 men including General Pietro Gazzera and nine other generals, who willingly surrendered to the Belgians rather than to the Ethiopians whom they had harshly treated, fearing reprisals like emasculation. Among the generals was one called Van den Heuvel, untypically for an Italian, who was of Belgian origin. Twenty cannon, 200 automatic weapons and 250 lorries, as well as 500 mules, were also taken. In all the Force Publique expeditionary troop had marched for 6,500km over rugged terrain. It lost 527 men, including four Belgians. This marked the first success for Belgian arms after May 1940, a welcome morale booster. It also contributed significantly to Britain's campaign, coordinating with their aim of conquering Italian-occupied Abyssinia/Ethiopia and restoring the deposed Emperor Haile Selassie.

Another contingent of Belgian colonial troops was taken to Nigeria in 1942, where for several months they trained and prepared to help conquer the Vichy-held French colony of Dahomey (now called Bénin), but before fighting started the local authorities in all of the French colonies in black Africa decided to side with the Free French after the Allied landings in

Morocco and Algeria. The highly motivated but disappointed Belgian/Congolese force was then taken on to Egypt and Palestine, a part of the troops being trucked 6,000km across the Sahara, but in the Middle East again, to their despair, they were confined to training or guard duties. A medical unit also served in Madagascar and even in far-away Burma. To this day a few hundred elderly Congolese, veterans of these campaigns, draw pensions from the Belgian State.

The Belgian Brigade
Several hundred Belgian military, mainly officers, made their way to Britain over the summer of 1940. The government decided to form an armed unit with them, under command of the senior Belgian officer present and First World War veteran General van Strijdonck de Burckel. There were plenty of officers, but apart from a few troops who had been evacuated through Dunkirk, other ranks were proportionately lacking. However, keen young men soon started trickling in from the Congo, from occupied Belgium, usually via a long detour through Spain and either Portugal or Gibraltar, or were drafted willingly or not from the Allied or neutral countries, some as far away as Brazil and Argentina. A few coming from faraway lands, sons or grandsons of emigrants, did not speak either French or Dutch. Luxembourgers also joined and were to form an artillery battery, while the future Grand Duke Jean joined and fought with the Irish Guards, of whom he later became Colonel-in-Chief.

If morale was always excellent among Belgian airmen and sailors, whose busy schedules and exhausting duties probably kept them from dwelling on things anyway, this was not the case with the Belgian land troops. In the beginning discipline was lax, rumours abounded and opponents to King Léopold clashed with loyalists. But intensive training, first at Tenby in Wales and Leamington Spa, took care of that and in July 1943 the 1st Belgian Infantry Brigade, part of the Belgian Forces in Great Britain, was formed under operational command of Colonel Piron. A year later it became the First Belgian Independent Brigade, colloquially known as the Brigade Piron and was declared operational, complete with three motorized infantry companies, three troops of field artillery, including the Luxembourg troop, a field engineer company and administrative and training units. Issued with British kits and uniforms they used Belgian rank insignia with a 'Belgium' shoulder patch or Belgian flag. An armoured squadron was equipped with Humber and later Daimler scout cars and drilled for reconnaissance duties.

Raymond V. arrived at the Belgian camp of Leamington Spa on a sunny day. Colonel Piron, the CO of the Belgian Brigade, happened to be there and asked him if he was related to Major V. with whom he had served in the First World War. When Raymond answered that that was his late father Piron told him to choose the unit he wanted to serve with. Raymond chose the armoured squadron and started training at Malvern in the platoon of Lieutenant Dewandre. The Belgian NCOs were stern and unforgiving. The men in training slept in tents and the sergeant major would throw all their belongings out into the mud if everything was not perfectly aligned and spic and span, rainy days being preferred for this treatment. One day they were told to assemble and were taken to another military camp in the vicinity where Polish soldiers were stationed. A drinking bout had got out of hand and turned into a riot and they had to help the British and Polish MPs and officers to re-establish discipline.

One evening, several months after Raymond had left, the telephone rang at the V. home back in Belgium. His mother picked it up and heard a voice say, 'The parcel you have sent abroad has arrived at its destination.' The anonymous caller immediately hung up. It took Berthe V. a few seconds to realize the import of the message, but she was immensely relieved to know her son was safe.

In May 1942, other Belgian volunteers formed the Belgian Independent Parachute Company under Captain Blondeel and joined the British SAS Brigade, later to become its 5th SAS Regiment. A Belgian Troop was also formed in the 10th (Inter Allied) Commando with Norwegians and Poles. They fought in Algeria, at Anzio, at the Garigliano River in Italy and in Yugoslavia before D-Day.

Belgians in the Royal Navy
A Belgian section in the Royal Navy was created in April 1943 and two Flower-class Corvettes, HMS *Godetia* and HMS *Buttercup*, a fisheries protection vessel, HMS *Zinnia*, as well as patrol ships, minesweepers etc. were all manned by Belgian crews. These ships flew both the White Ensign and the Belgian flag. The crews trained at HMS *Royal Arthur*, Skegness. The corvettes took part in the Battle of the Atlantic in the extremely harsh conditions of that vital part of the conflict and HMS *Zinnia* accounted for a U Boat. Several Belgian naval officers and ratings were assigned to larger Royal Navy vessels and played a part in the Normandy landings. The minesweepers worked in the Harwich area. In 1944 they cleared the port of Ostend of mines and helped clear the Scheldt estuary up to Antwerp. It would take the fledgling Belgian Navy three more years to clear the entire Belgian coast of mines and to this day the odd one is still sometimes found

amid the shifting sandbanks, allowing its sailors to announce a 101 per cent success rate at the end of a de-mining exercise, when a real one is fished up alongside the practice ones.

A number of Belgian sailors were also detailed to serve in military roles aboard merchant vessels, Belgian or others, like manning deck guns and communication gear.

One of Raymond V.'s first cousins, Christian J., served in the Belgian section of the Royal Navy, having come to Britain via Portugal.

One naval officer, Lieutenant de Vaisseau Billet, was particularly active in recruiting Belgians, mainly Flemish fishermen, into the RNSB (Royal Navy Section Belge). Assigned to other duties he went missing in action during the Dieppe landing, where he was in command of a tank landing vessel.

After the war, in 1946, the new Belgian Navy called Force Navale/ Zeemacht was created out of the Belgian Section of the Royal Navy and maintained the tradition of calling some of its ships after the Belgian-manned RN vessels. To this day, there is a Belgian Navy Ship *Godetia*.

In all three branches of the armed forces where Belgians fought, but especially in the RAF, Belgian officers reached senior rank and were given command over British or other nations' units. This was partly thanks to fairness in recognizing leadership or ability without regard to nationality, but also in some cases simply lack of skilled cadres. By 1943, Belgians commanded several British fighter and flying training squadrons, while others held important positions in naval, aerial and land staff planning and executing the Normandy landings and other Allied operations.

The Merchant Navy
Under government instructions, most vessels of the Belgian merchant navy, both passenger liners and cargo ships, as well as fishing boats, made their way to British ports in May and June 1940, some after helping in the Dunkirk evacuation. The pilot boats were requisitioned by the British. The 280 fishing trawlers and their crews, about 3,500 men, were immediately put to good use and their catches made a welcome addition to British rations.

The nine mail boats of the regular (now defunct) Ostend–Dover line, an organization whose charter dated back to the Battle of Waterloo, were sailed to British ports between 16 and 18 May 1940, some after having helped in the evacuation of military personnel from Dunkirk and other

French ports. Among them were the *Prince Albert*, the *Prince Baudouin* and the *Prince Philippe*, all 25-knot fast car ferries. With three more Belgian mail boats they helped evacuate British troops from Saint Malo in June 1940. *Prince Baudouin* made several trips to Cape Town before being converted to a Landing Ship Infantry and used in the Normandy landings. *Prince Philippe* was lost after having been rammed in thick fog by the British ship *Empire Wave*. *Prince Leopold* was torpedoed off the Isle of Wight by U 621 and sank under tow. *Prince Albert*, which was to sail all the way to Burma and Singapore, won for itself the nickname 'Lucky Albert' for having successfully dodged several torpedoes fired at it.

Not all Belgian ships were so lucky. Like the other 'Ville Boats', mixed cargo/passenger ships, the ill-fated SS *Léopoldville* had plied her trade before the war between Antwerp and the Belgian Congo. On 24 December 1944, she was transporting most of the US 66th Infantry Division to reinforce the troops already landed on the Continent, when she was torpedoed by U 486 outside Cherbourg. The lights of that French port were in sight, but because help was slow in coming 736 American soldiers lost their life, though a number of others were saved by a British destroyer escorting her. This only became known long after the war, the families in the US being told at the time simply that their sons or husbands had been killed, with no further details. The Belgian crew were accused of saving themselves first in the lifeboats, but it is fair to say that American safety arrangements both before and during the trip were far from adequate.

Most Belgian cargo vessels were quickly chartered by the British, pooled into the Allied convoy system and used across the Atlantic, in the Mediterranean and in the North African, Italy and Normandy landings. About two thirds of their tonnage was lost during the conflict, with heavy loss of life among their mostly Belgian crews. Armement Deppe, the main Belgian cargo carrier, suffered crippling losses. Out of the twenty-eight ships it owned at the outbreak of war, only seven survived the hostilities, a loss of 90 per cent of the tonnage. Also 183 Belgian sailors lost their lives, as well as many lascars from various countries including the Congo.

SS *Antverpia* was lost to Luftwaffe bombs near Boulogne on 21 May 1940, whilst evacuating Allied troops and SS *Luxembourg* was torpedoed off the French coast on 21 June. SS *Bruges*, sailing from South America to Europe was sunk by the gunfire of a German auxiliary cruiser. The crew was taken on board the German vessel sailing under the pretence of a Yugoslav flag, which exchanged fire with the British auxiliary cruiser *Alcantara* on 27 July. After several weeks the Belgians were transferred to another German ship, the *Rio Grande*, which took them to Bordeaux and five years of captivity in Germany.

On 31 October 1941, SS *Anvers*, laden with scrap metal, approached the Clyde but was ordered to sail around the top of Scotland and down the coast to London. Four days later a German plane attacked her. Return fire was opened with the lone Hotchkiss light gun on board, which soon jammed. The plane raked the bridge with its machine guns and dropped six bombs, two of which hit home. A fire started and Captain De Jonghe was trapped on the bridge. His son, on board as a sailor, tried in vain to save him. As the ship started to settle the only remaining lifeboat was freed and they tried to make way. The ship then suddenly sank and the wash capsized the lifeboat, throwing all its occupants into the sea, though some of them managed to struggle back to the now upside-down lifeboat. The next day two Norwegian vessels saw the distress signals and rescued the few survivors. Father and son De Jonghe were among the twenty-one dead.

SS *Roumanie*'s loss was even more tragic. The ship had sailed in the Mediterranean and around Africa and sustained heavy Luftwaffe attacks at Liverpool. In July 1942, it left the Western Approaches for its fourth trip to the United States. On reaching Baltimore its captain received a commendation from the US Navy for the exemplary way he had discharged his duties as Convoy Commodore on part of the voyage. Ten days later *Roumanie* left Halifax in a convoy of forty-seven ships bound for England. Four ships were sunk during their first week of passage. After suffering serious damage in a heavy squall, Captain Marbée decided to leave the convoy and head for Iceland for repairs. On 24 September the *Roumanie* was torpedoed by U 162 and immediately capsized. The lifeboats had been carried away or damaged by the tempest. Only one life-raft could be put to sea and Chief Engineer Suykerbuyk managed to take his place in it with four other sailors. The German U boat then surfaced and took Suykerbuyk on board to interrogate him, realizing he was an officer because of his stripes. The German captain refused to take the other survivors aboard, in spite of Suykerbuyk's insistence. The chief engineer was taken to Germany in captivity and was to be the only survivor of a crew of forty-two. Nothing was ever heard again of the other occupants of the raft, left drifting without water or food and away from the convoys' usual routes.

SS *Portugal* remained several months immobilized in neutral Lisbon, the object of several attempts at sabotage by German agents, who also tried to entice her crew to desert, the dynamic young captain somehow managing to keep his flock together. Finally, after a few trips to Setubal and Gibraltar, SS *Portugal* sailed for Britain but was lost on the way with all twenty-three hands.

SS *Brabant*, SS *Hainaut*, SS *Gand* and SS *Leopold* were all lost to enemy torpedoes, *Brabant* in the Caribbean and with heavy loss of life, while the SS *Escaut* braved Stuka bombs off Tobruk and was the first Allied ship to enter Benghazi after its fall to the Eighth Army, only to be sunk later at the entrance of the Suez Canal. MV *Limbourg* was torpedoed at night on 29 March 1941, broke in two and quickly sank into the Atlantic, only two sailors out of a crew of twenty-four surviving to tell the tale.

SS *Belgique* was sunk as a block-ship/breakwater in Normandy.

Chapter 5

Occupation

During the occupation the attitude of the population in all occupied countries of Western Europe – Belgium, the Netherlands, Luxembourg, Denmark, Norway and France – was very much the same: the majority waited things out and first and foremost tried to survive and keep themselves fed. This was by far the main preoccupation, as we shall see later. Only minorities, not more than 5 per cent of the population in each case, engaged actively in either resistance or collaboration. However, the proportion of those resisting tended, not unnaturally, to increase progressively as time went on and an Allied victory was perceived to become more likely, while that of active collaborators, just as logically, dwindled.

In Belgium, schools reopened as soon as the fighting stopped in May 1940. Some located in less affected regions did so even while the fighting was still raging elsewhere. Universities also reopened.

In Leuven (Louvain) Raymond V., a student at the Law faculty, attended a meeting held by VNV leader Staf De Clercq, with a dozen of his friends. They sat in the back of the room, near the door. At a given signal during the speech they started heckling: booing, whistling and loud shouts of 'Verrader!' (traitor) and 'Pas op, Stafke!' (Be careful, little Gustaf!). When the black-shirted 'Ordedienst' drew menacingly near they decided it was wiser to make themselves scarce.

Newspapers started to reappear after the Germans had set up the necessary censorship arrangements, and radio broadcasts in both languages also restarted. The papers linked with political parties like VNV and Rex were swiftly given every facility, but their circulation was never very large. The main papers, the French language *Le Soir* (soon nicknamed *'Le Soir volé'*), and the Dutch language *Het Laatste Nieuws* also found their way back to the newsstands. Their circulation was, at the end of 1941, respectively 260,000 and 201,000. There was also a German language *Brüsseler Zeitung* with a print run of about 25,000 copies. Swiss newspapers could sometimes be found but the main source of news was of course listening (clandestinely) to the BBC. A simple device, a spool wound around a cardboard cylinder, could diminish the German jamming and how to make one was the subject of a Resistance pamphlet.

People went to the cinema more than before the war, to German films which had been dubbed and French films. Theatre (obviously censored) and music both classical and modern (Swing was tolerated but Jazz, considered decadent 'nigger' music by the Nazis, was not, at least not on the controlled airwaves) were also much sought after means of distraction.

In normal times there was no curfew but at night one had to brave the blackout to get home. If light could be seen from the street, a shouted warning in German, 'Licht aus!' ([Put that] Light out!) from a passing patrol, might be followed, in the absence of a quick reaction, by a rifle shot through the offending window.

Immediately after the beginning of the invasion, even before the campaign was over, the cities of Eupen, Malmédy and their environs, as well as some territory that had never been part of Germany, were re-annexed to the Reich, with all the legal consequences. German became the only official language and no less important, young males, even those who had served in the Belgian Army, were drafted into the Wehrmacht.

German plans to also annex Arlon, a city at the extreme south-east of the country, did not go ahead though. The argument in favour was that the local dialect was close to German but the legal grounds were shaky as, unlike Eupen and Malmédy, Arlon had never belonged to Germany. It is possible King Léopold's intervention with the Germans to prevent it also had an effect.

The different boroughs of the larger cities which, by ancient tradition dating back to the Middle Ages have always enjoyed a large degree of autonomy, were now administratively merged. There now was a *Gross Brüssel*, instead of nineteen *Communes*.

Along the Belgian coast a *Sperrgebiet*, a zone of controlled access, was set up, and the northernmost *départements* of France, including the cities of Lille, Calais and Dunkirk were bundled together with Belgium under a joint military administration called Militärverwaltung Belgien und Nord Frankreich, placed under the control of General von Falkenhausen. He was to remain in command until June 1944, when the SS replaced him by a far harsher 'civilian' administration, in fact the SS. Apart from deliberate sabotage, hosting clandestine British citizens (i.e. pilots) became punishable by death at the end of 1940 and listening to the BBC could get you up to twelve years of hard labour. Strikes were illegal, though some broke out as soon as September 1940 among the hardworking and undernourished coal miners of Liège and Charleroi, and again in May 1941, the Germans forcing the bosses to raise wages, which had not kept pace with the huge increases in food prices.

At the onset of occupation, the Führer's instructions to the German military administration in Belgium were to keep all options open: nothing was to be decided about the future of the Belgian State, the Flemings were to be given preferential treatment as much as possible and the Walloons were to be accorded no favours. In fact Berlin saw Belgium mainly as a resource to be exploited for the benefit of its war effort and little thought was given to what should be done about it after the war.

The newly installed Military Governor Von Falkenhausen belonged to a family of Prussian nobility, where military careers were a tradition, and his uncle, also a general, had served in the same capacity in occupied Belgium at the end of the First World War. He spoke several foreign languages and considered the Nazis to be boorish, ignorant parvenus. He had served in the Boxer Rebellion and in Tokyo as military attaché. In the First World War he fought with the Turks in Palestine and Mustafa Kemal later sent him to the Baghdad front to fight against the British. After the war he went to China as adviser to Chiang Kai Shek. In Belgium he was flanked by the SS General Eggert Reeder, who was much closer to the Nazis and Hitler. It should be noted that compared to the Netherlands, where the Austrian Nazi Seyss Inquart led a civilian administration all along, Belgian conditions were milder, thanks to the fact the German Army was in charge for the greater part of the occupation. The SS, Geheime Staatspolizei (Gestapo), Geheime Feld Polizei (GFP), Sicherheitspolizei/Sicherheitsdienst (SIPO/SD) and their like were ever present and did their worst. An incredibly complicated German administration was put in place with different offices reporting to different ministries, headquarters, institutions or police forces in Berlin, rarely collaborating and more often doing what they could to thwart each other, such as supporting rival collaborationist movements.

Governor Von Falkenhausen in some cases commuted death sentences passed on Belgians, had some Belgian Jews freed (though most were caught again later), tried to insist that detentions at Fort Breendonk concentration camp respect certain norms (without much success), and so on. Immediately upon arrival he even told Henri De Man that the Jews would be left in peace and that he wanted the Jewish diamond-dealing community in Antwerp to resume their trade as soon as possible because of its importance to the economy! He may have been sincere, but we shall see what actually befell the Jews in Belgium. After the war a Belgian court tried and condemned Von Falkenhausen and the Dutch did the same with

Seyss Inquart, but the former escaped execution, the latter did not. Von Falkenhausen, whom Berlin found to be too weak, was replaced in July 1944 by SS *Gruppenführer* (Brigadier General) Jungclaus, who during the last months of occupation made full use of the powers of life and death he had been given.

The Todt Organization, named after one of Hitler's followers, now started building fortifications along the Belgian coast, parts of which can still be seen today,[52] planting long stakes in open fields to prevent Allied planes from landing. They were later dubbed 'Rommel's asparagus' by the locals. Local labour was hired and Russians and other POWs also used.

Most of the monuments and cemeteries of the Great War which dotted the Belgian and especially the West Flanders countryside were left in place and respected and a German NCO who had urinated at the Menin Gate in Ypres after a drunken binge, was punished. There were a few exceptions, as when the inscriptions about 'furious German barbarity' in Leuven (Louvain) and Dinant were rendered indecipherable. The monument where they were accused of having made first use of poison gas, in Langemark-Poelcapelle north of Ypres, was blown up – the Germans always considered they had not been the first to use chemical weapons. The Edith Cavell Street in Brussels kept its name, even though the monument to the same person in Paris was destroyed. A guard was posted at the Gabrielle Petit monument in Brussels to prevent passers-by from laying flowers there.

Most of the Luftwaffe units engaged in the Battle of Britain were stationed in Northern France but Mussolini sent a *Corpo Aereo Italiano* which was stationed on the Belgian bases of Maldegem (Fiat G 50 bis fighters), Chièvres, Ursel (Fiat CR 42) and Evere outside Brussels (Fiat BR 20 bombers, Fiat CR 42 and Fiat G 50 fighters, as well as Cant 2007 bis reconnaissance planes). They raided Ramsgate, Great Yarmouth, Ipswich and Harwich as well as merchant shipping and were withdrawn in January 1941. Contrary to wartime Allied propaganda the Italian pilots were just as brave as their British or German counterparts, but inadequate combat training and obsolete planes, the fighters having open cockpits and lacking radios, caused their mission in north-west Europe to be less than successful.

The King, POW
The King was now a prisoner of war. His expressed wish to be taken to Germany along with the army was not accepted and he was assigned

residence, under armed guard and with a called-up diplomat and First World War veteran, Major Kivietz as 'minder', at his Laeken Palace, the royal residence outside Brussels. The royal children,[53] who had been sent to safety in France, along with the King's private papers, were now brought back.[54] The King was allowed to keep his advisers and his mother, Queen Elisabeth, shared his lodgings. It was not generally known at the time that he was allowed relative freedom of movement – that is, he was not confined to the palace but was allowed to take some trips around and even outside Belgium, though of course never without his German 'tails'. The trenches the East Surrey Regiment had dug in the garden before withdrawing in May, to the great indignation of the head gardener (who got a very short two-word English answer to his recriminations) were filled in and a small farm started. King Léopold's Legion of Honour, taken away by Reynaud, was restored to him. His Knighthood of the Garter was never withdrawn, nor was his honorary colonelship of the 5th Inniskilling Dragoon Guards, which had also been held by his father.

The King's prestige with the Belgian population was in fact at its zenith at the time, because it was felt he had put an end to the senseless bloodshed the campaign had become during its last days. That of the government was at its nadir, as we have seen, and when the dust settled down and especially when the ministers realized the King was not going to form a new government as they had feared he would, they sent out peace feelers. Léopold however, no doubt because of the very strong language indeed they had used against him, kept them at arm's length. One curt answer written by his chief of staff to a long letter wherein the ministers proposed to organize the return of the million-plus Belgian refugees still in France, consisted of just two sentences: 'The King does not see politicians. The Red Cross looks after the refugees.'

All through the occupation, the government in exile, especially after it had reached London, tried to mend fences with the King, sending emissary after emissary (one of whom, Pierlot's brother-in-law, lost his life in the process, though in unrelated circumstances[55]) but to no avail. In June 1941, the British press reported the outcome of the Keyes case against the *Daily Mirror* and wrote more balanced accounts of King Léopold's behaviour during May 1940, indeed now vindicating him. With the findings of the case Belgian embassies abroad, especially in neutral countries, were instructed by their government in London to give the local press a new version of the May 1940 events that completely exonerated the King's attitude. The government now referred to the 'glorious prisoner of Laeken, an inspiration to all'. Camille Gutt, finance minister and acting foreign minister in October 1940, had as early as that penned a strongly worded reply in the *Daily Dispatch* after author H. G. Wells had called for the Belgian king's execution.

In a Brussels museum[56] a curious letter from Hitler to Seyss Inquart can be seen. The Führer confides in the ruler of the Netherlands that 'after the war we can do what we want in Holland, because we are rid of the Queen, but in Belgium, we still have this damned King [*Dieser verdammte König*].' This comment, which the Führer seems to have repeated a few times, can be interpreted as confirmation that the King's presence in Belgium inspired some respect in the Germans, and had a moderating influence on their behaviour and indeed on their plans for after the war, especially since they knew he was very popular with the Belgian public, at least in the first years of occupation.

Since the Belgian government and Parliament, in application of the relevant article of the Constitution, had declared him to be incapacitated from reigning and, more relevantly as he himself saw it, since he was indeed a prisoner of the enemy, Léopold refrained from purely internal political acts. However, he considered that should not prevent him from using his prestige and whatever chivalrous respect the Germans showed him. Indeed, at that stage they had made statements to the effect that he had led a brave army into inevitable defeat and that by defending his country he had behaved honourably. It is always easy and sometimes profitable for victors to be magnanimous. These assets the King now thought he should put to use to try to better the Belgian people's lot under the occupation, since nobody knew how long it would last or who would win the war in the end. That it would be Germany was in no way unthinkable in the summer and autumn of 1940.

During her visit to Hitler in October 1940, Princess Marie-José, Léopold's sister and wife of the Crown Prince of Italy, asked the Führer, apart from freeing the Belgian POWs, also if he would see her brother. This meeting with Adolf Hitler did not help Léopold's cause when it was revealed to the public during the controversy about his future as head of state after the war, especially at that time when the full horror of the Nazi regime was being revealed and with a strong communist party in Belgium. But it should be placed in the context of the time just described. Dates for the visit were discussed with German officers in Belgium and it was at first decided the Führer's train would make a stop at Yvoir, on the way back from interviews with Franco and Pétain. Meeting in Belgium might have been slightly less controversial than the King going to Berchtesgaden, as eventually happened on 19 November 1940, the Yvoir plan being cancelled when Hitler had to hurry off to Florence. (He was trying – unsuccessfully – to stop Mussolini, who had, partly as tit-for-tat for not having been informed of the Führer's plans on earlier occasions, decided to invade Greece without telling him.[57])

Though there are slight discrepancies about the subjects discussed, we have a reasonably clear picture of what Léopold and Hitler said at that meeting, both through Belgian accounts and the account of Hitler's interpreter.[58] The main reasons the King wanted to see Hitler were to alleviate the heavy financial burden of occupation, to improve the food supply situation and to plead for more prisoners of war to be released. He also wanted to seek reassurances about Belgium's future after the war, but as regards that he did not get much out of Hitler who would not commit himself. Leopold had decided that he would not reign over Belgium under German rule, but since he had also decided not to be the one to raise this first and Hitler didn't (and wasn't at all considering it anyway), it was not discussed. No less important were the two other subjects that were discussed at length: the food supply in Belgium (see below) and the liberation of Belgian military prisoners of war. On both subjects Hitler made vague promises for the future but no more and the visit, which was later to cost the King a high political price, did not bring any important result. He did obtain a stay of execution for three young Belgians condemned in Liège for sabotage.

The trip to Berchtesgaden did not become known about until after the war. In the years 1945–50, to be known to have asked to see Hitler and to have shaken his hand, was not at all the sort of thing you wanted your enemies to know, if they were plotting to ease you from the throne. But since it was certain to be made public anyway (though the Germans hadn't done so) Léopold's supporters thought it wiser to announce it themselves, with the explanations about content and context explained here.

The Berchtesgaden visit, although rumoured, only became known for certain after the German capitulation, but on 7 December 1941 (Pearl Harbor day) Léopold III's wedding was announced by the Belgian Catholic Primate Cardinal Van Roey. That this stunned the Belgian population and had a devastatingly negative effect on his popularity might seem surprising, since marrying is normally an honourable and popular thing to do. However, the general reaction was hostile and here again the context should be taken into account. Firstly the Belgian Constitution expressly forbids a religious marriage to precede a civil one, and this was overlooked. But what had a far more serious impact was that the King married whilst a 'prisoner', when many POWs, especially Walloons (since the Germans had released most Flemish soldiers) were in camps in Germany, far from their families. 'Our wives are cuckolding us with Germans back in Belgium while we are stuck here, and he gets married!' one soldier was heard to grumble, while in London one Belgian scornfully joked, 'He called for us to get back to work; if that is what he meant, I am all for it!' In at least one Oflag, the King's portraits were thrown out of the window by young officers, to the great scandal of the more senior ones. Then there was the matter of his chosen bride. There certainly was nothing wrong with Miss Lilian Baels per se, or probably would not be today. But there was more than one 'but'. First, the Belgians still worshipped the memory of Queen Astrid, a Swedish princess whom the King had married in 1926, who had borne him three children and was tragically killed in a road accident in Switzerland in 1935. By remarrying he destroyed the rather popular image of the inconsolable widower left to raise three young children. Second, there was the family background of Miss Baels. Her father, who was in the fisheries industry and had spent the First World War in Britain, where Lilian was born in 1916, had flirted with Flemish nationalism, become a government minister and in 1940 was Governor of West Flanders, the province around Bruges.[59] In May 1940, though he later disputed this, he was dismissed for having abandoned his post and fled to France, his future son-in-law signing the order revoking his appointment on the proposal of the relevant minister.[60] Third, in a country where this still was important, Lilian's family did not belong to either Belgian or foreign nobility. Her brother had a somewhat dubious reputation. Many books and articles have been written about this woman who became Princess of Réthy (Prince of Réthy being a pseudonym her husband used when travelling abroad incognito) and about her family, ranging from the positive to the outright nasty, if not outrageous. She once complained of being the most detested woman in Belgium. That she was ambitious and influenced some of her husband's decisions seems certain. Intelligent and extremely pretty, she bore Léopold two daughters and a son, who were excluded from the royal order of succession by an act of their father. Lilian made her husband very happy for the rest of his life. But the marriage itself and especially its faulty timing were used extensively against Léopold during the controversy about his future after the war. Receiving congratulations and flowers from the Führer, thanking him for them, going to Austria on honeymoon and staying part of the time in a château belonging to a Nazi party member there, was all bound to raise controversy. One of Princess Lilian's sisters would later marry Spaak's former chief of staff, Edouard Le Ghait, which is ironic because Spaak, though he had befriended King Léopold, was one of the most prominent of his opponents after the war.

If Léopold's marriage in these circumstances caused a serious dent in his popularity, that was nothing compared with the uproar his 'Political Testament' caused when it became known immediately after the war. In the spring of 1944, just before he was abducted to Germany, the King put on paper a few ideas about the political situation. He seems to have written this paper, which became known as the Political Testament, bearing in mind he might not survive the conflict. It comprised several points about the economy and education problems, and about how to deal with those who had betrayed the country by collaborating, calling for only the really high-placed traitors to be punished. It also declared all international agreements signed by the government in exile in London to be null and void, because they had not been signed by the monarch. But the paragraph that caused the loudest uproar was when Léopold asked for those who had insulted him and the Belgian Army in May 1940 in Paris and in Limoges, in essence Pierlot and Spaak, either to make full amends and apologies or to be excluded from politics. If its contents were controversial, what was lacking in the Political Testament was even more so: no mention was made of the Allies who in the summer of 1944 were about to liberate the country, no mention either of the Résistance. Nothing positive was said about the London government which had upheld Belgian sovereignty, maintained democratic institutions and had contributed to the Allied war effort. Pierlot and Spaak had made mistakes in May and June 1940, but when the Testament became known many thought it would have been wiser for Léopold to let bygones be bygones and to make reconciliation the priority above reparations for insults which, though grave enough, it would have been more expedient to forget if not to forgive. Through high-ranking magistrates, the King made arrangements for copies in sealed envelopes to be handed to Pierlot ,when he returned to Brussels in September 1944, and through British ambassador Knatchbull-Hugessen to Churchill. The British Prime Minister, after reading it, declared it 'stank' and Anthony Eden compared the King to the Bourbons of the Restoration after Napoleon, who were famously said to have learned nothing and forgotten nothing. Churchill (and the Americans) also had reasons to dislike the paragraph about agreements entered into by the London government because it included the accord on uranium shipments, at a time when it was thought the Belgian Congo might well be the only source for that mineral. There was already not much love lost between Churchill and King Léopold, and this didn't help. Pierlot and Spaak, bent on reconciliation with the King and with his partisans, who were mainly to be found in Pierlot's own Catholic Party, at first tried to ignore and keep the paper secret, but its contents gradually leaked out. The Socialists and Communists were not slow in using it against Léopold, and despite the efforts of the new, socialist prime minister, Van Acker to find a solution, calls for the King's abdication grew ever louder as other facts became known, like the Berchtesgaden visit, or contacts his close advisers had had during the occupation with well-known collaborators now on trial for treason. In the months and years right after the Liberation, Léopold's controversial remarriage was also used in articles and pamphlets against his return.

On the whole it could be said that if the King's popularity had been at its highest in the summer of 1940, and that of the government at its lowest, there was a gradual inversion while the occupation went on. Léopold's image remained high in the first months and years, when the populace were still thankful to him for having put an end to the senseless killing the conflict had become at the end of May 1940, when he was a prisoner of war and was seen to intervene on behalf of the population's welfare and even to have condemned *résistants* reprieved, in favour of Jews or organizing welfare institutions for children etc. But as the war progressed and it was gradually seen that the Allies had the upper hand, Belgium's London government became more popular.

Late in 1942, Léopold wrote a letter to Hitler protesting among other things about deportations of young people to work in Germany, to which the Führer responded by threatening to have him detained under harsher conditions. This exchange of letters was not known at the time, but afterwards the King became less active and his popularity diminished for the various reasons or factors cited above, while that of Belgium's London government which was increasingly expected to come back with the Anglo-American troops, went up.

It is undisputed that King Léopold had a deep sense of duty, which had been fostered by his upbringing and education. That this last, through circumstances (the Great War) had been more focused on military matters than on handling politics (and politicians) is something he himself complained about. His initiatives and decisions during the war, especially during the occupation, were not uncontroversial. That they were inspired by what he knew at the time and what he saw, rightly or wrongly, as his country's interest should be recognized, with the notable exception of his marriage during the occupation and the circumstances surrounding it – factors such as the Austrian honeymoon – which was a serious psychological blunder.

Allied air raids

Allied bombings of military objectives sometimes caused grievous damage and loss of life to the civilian population in Brussels and Antwerp. In Mortsel, outside Antwerp, the bombing of the ERLA aero-engine factory caused 396 deaths, including 209 children, in April 1943. (In 2009, the US embassy in Belgium recognized its country's responsibility for this.) German propaganda was quick to use these statistics, for example in posters showing a big four-engined bomber spewing out its load of bombs, with the comment: *'Liberation is nearing; prepare your testament!'* And when in Brussels in September 1943 another particularly clumsy bombing raid caused about 120 civilian deaths and destroyed more than a thousand homes, all the German top brass came to the collective church funeral of the victims to 'show their solidarity' and be seen and photographed. In another of these bombings one prominent member of the Comet Line, the escape route many Allied airmen used to get back to Britain, was unfortunately killed, being at the time detained in a Brussels barracks by the Germans. The Rex party of course also made political capital out of it, especially after the bombings intensified in 1944. The overwhelming majority of Belgian public opinion, however, blamed all these things on the occupying Germans. The long lines of bombers on their way from East Anglia to the German cities, often flew over Belgium and the locals, well informed by the BBC, knew their ominous significance for the Nazis.

Economic life

The Belgian government, who had sent most of the gold reserves abroad, arranged in May 1940 for the major banks to pay the salaries of the civil servants, since the fiduciary guarantee of the Belgian central bank could not be expected to support such payments for long. Before leaving, Camille Gutt, the finance minister, signed a government collateral guarantee note to that effect.

Severe rationing of foodstuffs, fuel and cloth was instituted and a huge black market was not slow to develop despite being the object of severe repression by both the Belgian and German police. Large numbers of German soldiers, sometimes whole units, also engaged in it.

The Germans instituted an exchange rate between the Reichsmark and the Belgian franc that was artificially biased in their favour and made Belgian goods very cheap for them to purchase. All major enterprises had to make significant regular cash contributions to the vast impositions the Germans made on the country, as a 'contribution for fighting Judeo-plutocracy' and later defending Europe against communism, according to the occupiers, or as a price the country had to pay for and on top of being occupied, as the people more accurately felt.

Belgium is a built-up country, with relatively little arable land. Even then it produced only about 50 per cent of its food needs. Feeding the population with imported agricultural products has always been a necessity, these imports being paid for by the export of manufactured goods or with services. Feeding the Belgian populace during the four years of occupation in the First World War had been a serious problem. An agreement had been reached, thanks to the American minister in Belgium, Brand Whitlock, for grain shipments in vessels especially chartered for the purpose to be made from the United States via ports in the neutral Netherlands. Future President Herbert Hoover became the chairman of the Commission for the Relief of Belgium, and the Germans, though they were themselves under severe blockade by the Royal Navy, had respected their agreement not to seize relief shipments which were clearly marked as such.[61] A similar arrangement was sought in 1940 but Britain refused. So the problem of feeding about 8 million people was the most urgent to be addressed, especially since the Germans were carting away huge parts of the country's wealth, including produce and coals, and would carry on doing so to an ever greater extent. Inflation set in and since salaries were frozen it hit many households very hard. The problem became more serious over time, as the German administration itself became acutely aware. Some help came from charitable groups linked to the Catholic Church or of whom King Léopold was the patron, and the 'winter help' organization, which also existed in Germany and was politically tainted because of this, distributed food or set up mobile soup kitchens. After a while it became possible for Belgians in London to pay a firm in Portugal to send food parcels to their families and friends in Belgium. Tins of sardines, olive oil, sugar, coffee, tea and so on, as well as soap and other requisites, were a welcome arrival in households that had not seen them for many months and were, for some, dangerously close to starvation. This was of course, but a drop in the ocean.

Undernourished children were a serious concern during the whole occupation in many families, though the Germans allowed groups of them to go to Switzerland under the auspices of the Red Cross for a couple of weeks at a time. Medical supplies and drugs also became very scarce or could only be purchased at prohibitive prices. Firewood also fetched high prices and though the country had several coalmines, many homes had to make do with 'war coals' or *schlamm* (German for mud) to keep warm. The newspapers were full of tricks to keep heat in, reuse old newspapers for fuel or worn fabric for clothing, and recipes to cook wild plants or vegetables, like nettle, rutabaga (swede) or Jerusalem artichoke, which were easy to find or grow. Something resembling coffee could be brewed with suitably prepared acorns and all sorts of plants were used to replace tea, which was drunk without sugar. People stopped eating bread with their meals. Many started raising chicken and rabbits in their backyards and those with farmers among their family or friends were of course at an advantage. Those who had a garden also grew vegetables and most city parks had their grass or flowers removed for the same purpose, plots sometimes being rented out. Night wardens had to be appointed to keep off marauders.

The *Secrétaires généraux*
In the Belgian administrative system a *Secrétaire Général* (or *Secretaris generaal* in Dutch) is the senior civil servant of a ministry, reporting only to the relevant member of the government. He controls the running of the ministry and all the civil servants who are junior to him. The position can be compared to a British permanent under-secretary.

Inspired by the experience of the previous occupation in 1914–18, the Pierlot government had taken steps to organize economic life under a possible new occupation, and to keep control of all essential public services like health, police and other home affairs, administration of justice, allocation of (rationed) food and fuel etc. In anticipation that the ministers themselves would take refuge abroad, as they had in France in 1914, legislation was passed entrusting each ministry and all civil servants to the *Secrétaires-généraux* (secretaries general) who were tasked with keeping the country going and especially keeping the population fed, treading a fine line beyond which economic activity would become collaboration with the occupiers, and reporting on progress by keeping tabs on who was doing what. This law allowed them to enter, by necessity, into regular contact with German occupation authorities, especially Eggert Reeder, with whom they frequently clashed and who had a few of them sacked and replaced by more pliable men, usually from the Rexist or Flemish nationalist parties. They also started meeting regularly themselves, forming a kind of government in miniature. A common cause to try to preserve the best state of affairs in the Belgian interest existed between the secretaries general and the top magistrates, who had to determine the extent of their powers under the law passed before the war.

In April 1941, the secretary general at the ministry for home affairs, obviously a very important post for the Germans to have a man they could trust, was replaced by Gerard Romsée, who came from the Flemish nationalist party VNV, along with a few of his colleagues.

As mentioned above, in May 1940, just before taking refuge in France, at the same time as the Pierlot government entrusted the *Secrétaires-généraux* with their powers, Foreign Minister Spaak and Finance Minister Gutt asked the heads of Belgium's three main banks to pay the civil servants for the duration of the occupation while keeping as much cohesion as possible in the country. One of these men was Alexandre Galopin, head of the vast Société Générale, who during the occupation developed the *Galopin doctrine* guidelines as to what should be done to keep the population in as much comfort as possible, and what would be classed as helping the enemy, outright economic collaboration. This was a fine line to toe indeed. Galopin kept records on many institutions and persons. In February 1944, at Himmler's prompting, he was assassinated at his home by members of DeVlag and of the Algemene SS Vlaanderen.

Apart from 'paying for being occupied' and enduring cold and hunger, the Belgians also suffered when hundreds of the nation's works of art were carted away. Paintings by Flemish masters, wall tapestries for which the country had been famous since the sixteenth century, sculptures such as the only known marble work by Michelangelo outside Italy, the metre-high *Madonna with Child* of Onze Lieve Vrouw (Our Lady) Church of Bruges were all shipped off from churches, galleries or private collections, the ones belonging to Jews being the first but not the last to go. The idea behind this shameful plunder was to centralize them in the great museum Hitler planned for Linz, the Austrian city where he grew up, but not much justification was even offered and nothing ever came of the museum. Göring was also a keen 'private collector' and much went his way, though Bormann, Hitler's secretary, who hated the head of the Luftwaffe and vied with him for influence, made him give some back – to the curators of the putative Hitler museum, that is. Most of the purloined works of art were rediscovered by the Americans in Germany at the end of the war, as we shall see. Prominent among them was Flemish fifteenth-century painter Jan Van Eyck's famous masterpiece, the incredibly detailed, multi-panelled retable *Lam Gods* ('The Lamb of God'), formerly (and today again) to be found in Ghent Sint Bavo Cathedral. It was incomplete until 1919, but the missing panels had been given to Belgium by the estate of the Kings of Prussia (in essence the Kaiser's) under the terms of the Versailles reparations. In May 1940 it was driven in haste to a chateau near Pau in southern France, after being hidden for a few days at a farm when the lorry driver transporting it saw his path blocked by Panzers on their way to Abbeville. When the Germans found out its whereabouts they promptly went to fetch it (the whole lot, not just the panels that had been rendered up under the reparations) despite the protests of the local French authorities, who were overruled by the Vichy government then in charge of non-occupied France.[62] The occupiers also took away many archives, both public and private, including those of the political parties.

As they had done in the First World War, from 1944 on the Germans started collecting non-ferrous metals for their war manufacturing, as these were in increasingly short supply. Down from the steeples came the church bells, an exception being made for those ancient bells which could be proved to have been cast before a certain date. Of course fake documents to that effect flourished. The railway *résistants* managed to spirit some away – in one case, in Ath, they derailed a train and buried the bells deep into the railway ballast.

What shocked most Belgians even more was the introduction of a compulsory requirement for unemployed persons of both sexes between 18 and 50 to go and work in Germany. This too was a repeat of what had happened in the First World War and was introduced in 1942, though most departures did not take place until 1944. Although the German military administration in Belgium warned against it, Sauckel, responsible to Hitler for the working force, gradually introduced this diktat in most occupied countries. About 190,000 young Belgians, in fact mostly male and under 35, took trains to Germany willing or not, approximately 80,000 others refused. Most of the latter went underground, feeding them being a serious problem since their food coupons were no longer delivered, and this at a time when scarcity of food was becoming ever more acute. In fact it brought about a huge influx into the ranks of the Resistance. Their lot in Germany varied wildly, depending on the time and place they were sent to. At first most were decently treated, but conditions deteriorated rapidly as Germany's fortunes declined. Not a few were killed in Allied bombing attacks. Léopold III protested against these deportations and wrote, as mentioned earlier, a letter to Hitler in which he alluded to the dangers that girls especially would be exposed to. That brought a scathing reply from Hitler, who would not accept that Germans could misbehave and who threatened the King with a considerably less comfortable position than he currently enjoyed as a POW detained in his royal palace, if he failed to understand that the war had become a life or death struggle against communism, in which all of Europe should be taking part, and of which Germany was bearing the brunt ...

Chapter 6

Resistance

11 November 1940

As in all the other capitals of the Western countries that had fought against Germany, an unknown soldier was buried with great solemnity in downtown Brussels following the end of the First World War. The *Soldat inconnu/Onbekende soldaat* tomb, with an eternal flame, was placed at the foot of a column commemorating the National Congress that had adopted the Belgian Constitution, in Rue Royale, a main thoroughfare of the capital. Each year on Armistice Day, a parade and wreath-laying ceremony was (and still is) held. On ordinary days men passing the monument would usually take their hat off when walking by. Defying a ban by the Germans, a few hundred young men gathered there on the first Armistice Day after the beginning of the occupation, having been called upon to do so by a leaflet campaign. This was later considered to be the first act of open defiance against the occupiers and more than a few who were present would not survive the war, having gone on to engage in varying forms of resistance.

Brussels Free University closes

The presence of several students of Université Libre de Bruxelles (whom they were however unable to clearly identify) at this demonstration of defiance was used, among other pretexts, by the Germans when they made clear to the directors of the Brussels alma mater that great changes were to be imposed on it, because of its evident anti-German and Masonic characteristics, as their first letter to the Rector, Franz van der Dungen stated. The university was told to fire its Jewish professors and to accept others sent from Germany, among them Flemish activists who had fled the country under a death sentence for treason after the First World War. This was deemed unacceptable by the ruling council of the university who decided, on 25 November 1941, to suspend teaching – in essence to close down, though the academic year had only just begun. Told to report to the Gestapo headquarters, Rector van der Dungen thought that this inevitably meant deportation and took a small suitcase of essential belongings with him. He was however allowed to go home.

Belgian politics in the nineteenth century was dominated by the opposition between the Liberal Party, whose principles were derived mainly from the ideas of the French Revolution on humanism, freedom of expression and creed etc., as opposed to the more conservative Catholic Party, closely linked to the Church of Rome. The oldest university in the land, at Louvain (Leuven) had been run by the Catholic Church since its beginnings in the Middle Ages. Since, apart from the universities of Liège and Ghent, which were state run, there was no other independent institution of higher learning in Belgium apart from Louvain, which they considered as wholly in the grip of Catholic obscurantism, the Liberal Party, itself strongly influenced by the Free Masons, decided in 1834 to open the Université Libre de Bruxelles (ULB) whose motto is *Scientia vincere tenebras* (It is for science to defeat darkness), a clearly anti-Catholic statement. Young persons of Catholic background went to Louvain, those from liberal families to the ULB, and doing otherwise was almost unheard of. This political and religious (or anticlerical) context made what followed the closure of the ULB all the more remarkable.

In a gesture of national solidarity transcending ideological and political rivalries, all other Belgian universities opened their doors to the ULB students, the Flemish Ghent University being no exception, but most prominently and remarkably considering the past history, about 600 (mainly medical) students from ULB were welcomed in and allowed to continue their studies at the Catholic University of Louvain by the rector, Monsignor Van Waeyenbergh. They were told no attempt would be made to impose any aspect of Christian creed on them and they were exempted from the otherwise compulsory religion classes. Other ULB professors and students organized clandestine classes in private homes or other dwellings in Brussels, some even in the Institute of the Holy Heart of Jesus. Mgr Van Waeyenbergh, in full accord with his superiors in the Belgian Church hierarchy also repeatedly intervened to save the ULB's library and to have some of its incarcerated professors freed. After the liberation of Belgium the reopened ULB officially thanked both him and his university. Tensions between the two institutions, though they have not disappeared, are now far less acerbic in large part because of this episode.

After the war, both Winston Churchill and Charles de Gaulle were made Doctors *honoris causa* of Brussels University.

The Press
As in many other circumstances, a repeat of what had happened during the previous occupation occurred. Most of the prewar press started to

reappear, but obviously under German censorship. *Le Soir*, quickly re-acquired its nickname, '*Le Soir volé*', while *La Libre Belgique* again became '*La Belgique*', since the country was no longer free. During the first occupation a paper entitled *Libre Belgique* had been regularly published, one copy always finding its way to the desk of the German Military Governor, and the legally responsible publisher being stated as: Peter Pan, Oberfeld-kommandantur, 1 Place du Trône, Bruxelles.

About 700 other clandestine papers were printed during the occupation and proved a great morale booster. Whether consisting of a single Roneo-typed sheet, or four or five pages, they never kept going for long – that was not the idea anyway. The average lifespan of a typical clandestine publication seems to have been about six months. They were more an opinion press than designed to inform. There was not much emphasis on international news (the public had other sources for that, mainly the BBC which was widely listened to), but one could read in them politically inspired editorials, denunciations of local conditions and/or collaborators and so on. Those producing them had to solve numerous problems of paper supply, finding safe places to print, distribution etc. Most were linked with a political party, prominently the Communist Party or particular sectors such as the miners, the streetcar or railway workers, the trade unionists, factory workers or farmers. They included *L'Usine*, *Le Tram*, *Le Métallo* (the Metalworker), *L'Intersyndical*, *La Mine*, *De Mijnwerker* (The Miner, in Dutch), *De Hamer*, *De Boer* (The Farmer), *Het Vrije Woord* (The Free Word), or the more generally politically oriented *L'Anti Boche*, *La Voix des Belges*, *Front*, *Vaincre* (To Win), *De Vrije Belg* (The Free Belgian), *Eenheid en Strijd* (Unity and Struggle) and many more. Some clandestine papers or pamphlets were also written in German and destined to demoralize members of the Wehrmacht, giving hints on ways to report sick with a self-induced fever and tricks of that sort.

On 9 November 1943, a unique event in occupied Europe occurred: the *Faux Soir* printed a run of about 40,000 copies. Five thousand of these were directly distributed to newspaper outlets all over Brussels at the precise time the real, German-controlled edition of *Le Soir* was due out. Printed clandestinely by five Resistance fighters, one of whom was linked to the communist-controlled *Front de l'Indépendance*, it poked fun at Hitler, the Wehrmacht, and Degrelle, whom it decorated with the Knight's Cross First Class of the *Stoeffer* ('braggart' in Brussels slang) with dandelion (*pissenlit*) rather than oak leaves. Witty and full of cryptic humour and allusion, it won plaudits all over Europe, wherever the rest of the copies were sent. In Brussels streetcars some surprised readers could not suppress their giggles and read out loud the funniest extracts. Unfortunately the authors were caught by the Germans, including one accomplice who worked at the real *Le Soir* and had lent the font for the title. All were sent to concentration camps in Germany and some did not return.

Other fake issues of existing papers or magazines were also put out by the Belgian Resistance, including *Signal*, the German armed forces publication, and William Ugeux, an important member of the Resistance and head of the Zéro spy ring, published a clandestine *Libre Belgique* for a while. Mathieu De Jongh, who took over from him was gassed at Mauthausen camp in July 1944. His was the 'free' version of *La Belgique*. And since the 'Boches had ruined Belgium' it was free of charge, as was written on the front page.

Although one risked a heavy penalty by doing so, as noted earlier, practically everybody (even arch-collaborator Degrelle, as he was later to write in his book) listened to the BBC for general news on the war and some followed the progress of faraway campaigns by updating maps with coloured pencils. It was wise not to leave your set tuned to the BBC wavelength after listening, in case the German police paid you a visit. The Germans tried to jam the broadcasts from London all through the war, but never with total success. Apart from the BBC, surprisingly, some Swiss newspapers could also be bought freely and their news was less contaminated by German propaganda.

Berthe V., Raymond's mother, had little reason to befriend the Germans. Her husband, a regular officer who had fought for four years in the trenches of the First World War without any possibility of coming home on leave, had died in 1926, of wounds sustained in the final offensive in October 1918 when he had been machine-gunned in the legs. Her eldest son Raymond was in hiding and trying to make his way to Britain because the German police were looking for him, while her other son, Jean V., had already been arrested by them. So when a German officer presented himself at their home and produced papers to the effect that he was going to be billeted there her reaction was less than sympathetic. When after introducing himself he tried to shake hands she kept her hands where they were. During his stay he did not make further overtures, he had his own key and in the evening would let himself in and go straight to his room. When they happened to pass each other on the stairs they pretended not to see one another. One afternoon, after about six months, he called the housemaid to his room. She saw he was packing his belongings in a suitcase. On the table was a big bunch of flowers and he told the girl they were for Madame V., that he was leaving, that

*someone else was going to come and stay in the room and that since he didn't
know who this other fellow was, she should be more careful and lower the volume
of her radio when listening to the BBC 'because one could hear it in this room'.*

Espionage
The gathering of information by civilians in wartime has been called the
second oldest profession. Like the first it never completely shook off
the opprobrium surrounding it. The Belgians had, in 1940 the (dubious)
advantage over the other occupied countries of having already endured
that experience once before. During that earlier time, intelligence gathering by Belgians for the benefit of the Allies had been very active. In the
interwar years it was praised as patriotic and the victims of the inevitably
harsh German repression were unanimously described as heroes in
articles in the press and in numerous books exalting the deeds and courage
of those who had been executed or had died in captivity. Hence those who
had not accepted seeing their neutral country invaded and plundered once
again were more inclined to engage in spying when the second German
occupation came. Moreover some leaders of intelligence networks that
had worked for the Allies in the First World War recreated them. Prominent among them was Walthère Dewé, leader of the Dame Blanche network that had closely monitored railway movements in occupied Belgium
for the British Intelligence Service, who could thus accurately predict
build-ups of troops and supplies and so coming offensives in Flanders.

Apart from Dewé's Clarence, many other networks like Zéro, Luc-Marc,
Les Amis de Charles, Zig, Tégal, Mill, Beaver, Portemine, Tulipe, Fidelio,
Bayard and the Moscow-led Orchestre Rouge (aka the Red Orchestra, or in
German, Rote Kapelle), to name only the most prominent, spied on the
Germans and on general conditions in occupied Belgium. With the excep-
tion of the communist Red Orchestra they all eventually reported to
London,[63] that is to the Belgian Sûreté which had been recreated in the
British capital, and to MI6, the two having agreed in August 1941 on procedures: all information gathered would go to the Sûreté, who would pass
it on to British Intelligence, who in turn could ask specific questions,
mainly of a military order, and would arrange for training and dropping
of agents as well as supplies of radios and so on.

Churchill, in the fourth volume of his memoirs of the Second World
War, *The Hinge of Destiny*, wrote that the Belgian agents should be specially
mentioned among the providers of information on the Continent, as by
1942 they were supplying 80 per cent of all intelligence. This included a
map stolen by two of them from a Luftwaffe officer, which gave the RAF a

clear view of German radar coverage and air defence over Europe. Prime Minister in exile Pierlot said he saw everything he needed to know about the Germans in Belgium as if it were a glasshouse, thanks to the Resistance.

With the exception of Clarence, which relied on its previous experience and for whom Dewé had already made arrangements during the phoney war with the British and recruited several former members of Dame Blanche, the Belgian intelligence gathering groups struggled at first. Not many volunteers came forward at a time when practically everybody saw a German victory as inevitable. Then there was the problem of communicating data to London, which was only gradually solved – very few radio sets had been left behind by the retreating British in May and June 1940 for that purpose. There were unsuccessful drops in late 1940 of a few agents who were almost immediately caught and shot like former Chasseur Ardennais Emile Tromme.

Also in late 1940, Prime Minister Pierlot left France for London and his chief of staff Pierre d'Ydewalle, who had several small children, in agreement with his former boss went back to Belgium and began sending him regular reports on the general political and economic conditions in the occupied country. Gradually, with some of his relatives (*including Raymond V.*) he also gathered more military-oriented information in the coastal region, where his cover as member of a charity allowed him to circulate freely.

Since Dewé worked for the Belgian telephone and telegraph system RTT, where he was a senior engineer, he recruited agents who could intercept telecommunications. Beagle specialized in collecting and transmitting meteorological data which were of course very important to prepare RAF and later USAAF raids. The Mill network was especially active among the railway workers, whilst in several cities postal workers often intercepted letters addressed to the German authorities denouncing real (or supposed) *résistants*. In Liège they were warned in time of the fact that the Germans, suspecting this, had started sending themselves letters so as to track where they became 'lost'. Thousands of such letters were sent during the occupation; many in fact were trumped-up accusations by jealous husbands, unpaid creditors or the like, but some were genuine and did indeed lead to the arrest of *résistants* or Jews. Even some Germans expressed shock at the number of denunciations they received (all over occupied Europe) by mail or other means. Several members of the Ixelles police belonged to an espionage ring and some warned individuals in advance when they were going to be arrested.

Luc, to which many Brussels judges and lawyers belonged, was named after the son of one of its leaders who had been killed in the Eighteen Days Campaign, while the Zéro network chose its name because one of its founders had cynically said all their effort would come to nothing. Some of the networks expanded into the Netherlands and Luxembourg. Zéro-France numbered several hundred agents of both nationalities and was mainly active in northern France, opposite the Kent coast, obviously an area of particular interest for the British. An elderly lady was recruited into one of the networks when it was learned that officers of the Corpo Aereo Italiano in Belgio, including one of Mussolini's sons, were billeted in her château and were expected to be talkative (they were).

From May 1942 on, networks became better organized, learned lessons from their mistakes, which had often had catastrophic consequences, and communications with London were improved. Because Belgium is very built up and flat terrain is rare in the less inhabited Ardennes, very few Lysander flights were used, parachute drops being preferred. About 250 Belgians were dropped between May 1942 and May 1943, mainly radio operators, sometimes with more than one radio set, some destined for different networks, as well as money, spare parts, etc. Photographers, draughtsmen and even typists were also sent. Sometimes they also brought goodies like chocolate, or rare medicines, or rubber bicycle tyres, which had disappeared in occupied Europe – such things were morale boosters, as were medals, sometimes also dropped. It has been estimated that at that time about 21,000 persons were engaged in or supporting intelligence-gathering activities in Belgium, in seven main networks and several smaller ones. With a few exceptions for coordination, all networks of course had to work in complete isolation from one another, and within each group only a cell of three to five persons would know each other. Typically it was three: the person you reported to and the one (or two) who reported to you, in a pyramidal structure. A total of 1,000 members was considered the maximum controllable number for a network. Messages gathered were compiled and collated, usually in a central clandestine office and the resulting abstract either written on light paper, to be smuggled through France and Spain to agents there, or radioed through. Pigeons were also used, as they had been in 1914–18, Belgium being a country where keeping courier pigeons is a national pastime. The BBC sometimes (but not always) gave a coded answer to a question asked by a network, or acknowledged the arrival of an agent or an important message.

The meaning of the personal messages sent by the BBC were sometimes obvious and destined for a certain agent or group, whose codenames were used, like 'From Maurice to Joseph: there is a fire at the travel agency', warning those wanting to contact some escape line that it had been infiltrated, or 'Six friends will come tonight' for a network to expect a parachute drop of six agents. Others were more cryptic and had been agreed on in advance, like 'One can't see the forest for the trees' and 'King Salomon is shod with heavy clogs' sent respectively on 1 and 7 June 1944 to prepare and to execute prearranged sabotages of railroads, bridges, electricity power boxes and other targets, on D-Day.

Taking written messages to Spain and beyond meant running the gauntlet of the well-guarded Pyrenees crossings and agents sometimes themselves compromised, usually working with networks like the Comet Line or others. One group discovered that a disused sawmill on the French side of the border had a cable contraption with which they formerly carried logs all the way to the Spanish side – they soon put it to use for their own purposes. Of course the Belgian embassies or consulates in Madrid, Barcelona, Lisbon and Stockholm had large contingents of undercover agents in charge of receiving and dispatching agents and messages. In Bern they acted independently from the embassy. At Gibraltar people would debrief, interrogate and send on released internees arriving there from the big Spanish camp at Miranda del Ebro.

Trust between London and the networks in Belgium was essential, but relations were not always smooth and sometimes were complicated by mutual recriminations. Questions raised by 'the people who were risking their lives' were not always satisfactorily answered by the 'lazy bureaucrats who live in comfort in London'. Desperately needed radios or funds were not sent, or even more infuriating, when an agent trying to recruit a hesitant candidate asked London to transmit an agreed message as proof that he was actually working for the resistance, his credibility was of course lost when that message was not broadcast for some reason, London not always realizing the urgency. When someone in London misguidedly sent an extensive list of the chemicals needed to develop photographs, including some which were obviously not obtainable in Belgium, the agents in Brussels ironically answered they had been to the local department store but had been told all the stuff was sold out. Indeed rivalries in London between SIS (Secret Intelligence Service) and SOE (Special Operations Executive) also sometimes complicated things. Calls for money merit a special mention. One might think the agents should have been working without pay, out of sheer patriotism and this was indeed almost always the case, but expenses for travelling, or for sustaining the families of arrested or executed agents had to be covered, as well as buying food for persons in hiding, like Jews or compromised agents, since they of course had no access to ration stamps. After the Germans introduced compulsory work in Germany for (in theory) all unemployed men aged between 18 and 50 this brought in a huge number of '*réfract-aires*', many of whom joined different forms of resistance, but the problem of food supplies was also hugely magnified.

The main motivations of the agents were of course patriotism, a desire to avenge the country that had been twice invaded or the loss of a loved one, love of adventure and thrills, the influence of charismatic leaders like Walthère Dewé, or political and philosophical convictions. It should be noted though that apart from the communists, extremist political parties were under-represented in the intelligence gathering networks, their members coming mainly (but not exclusively) from French-speaking, well-to-do, politically moderate backgrounds, who were in favour of parliamentary democracy. Being an anglophile was also mentioned in a post-war enquiry, since Britain was seen as both the country that had come to Belgium's aid in 1914, where many had taken refuge with their families during the first occupation, and (at least until the end of 1941) in whom some saw the only hope of seeing their own country liberated from Nazi oppression. Since many books in the interwar years had exalted (and sometimes exaggerated) its role in the First World War, the British Intelligence Service benefited from high prestige and many took pride in working for it.

Apart from those who had, through their jobs, access to information – for example by listening in at the telephone exchanges where they worked – there were other ways of gathering useful information. Matters of a political and economic nature, like how public opinion saw the King and the London government, the collaborators, the state of the economy in general, inflation, black market, hopes for after the war and so on, were readily obtainable just by asking the right people, like former politicians, church leaders, lawyers and magistrates, those civil servants working in the ministries linked with economic affairs or at the Central Bank, etc. These were the types of information that especially interested the Pierlot government in exile, and some of the material gathered was used for reforms taken directly after liberation, like the change in currency notes. Indeed Pierlot said he knew everything he needed to know about what was happening in Belgium and his former chief of staff Pierre d'Ydewalle, who provided him with a lot of that information, later wrote that the government in exile in London knew more about the real situation in Belgium than the King, locked in his palace outside Brussels and isolated by his courtiers and German guards.

Some networks made lists of the works of art, of other precious objects or church bells the Germans plundered, and these records proved very useful after the war when they were able to be recovered.

The Belgian military intelligence Deuxième Bureau in London and the various branches of British military intelligence, later also the American OSS (Office of Strategic Services), were of course far more interested in the German armed forces in Belgium. Agents of Clarence, later Les Amis de Charles, Zig, Luc-Marc and the others, had to learn how to distinguish different German uniforms and insignias of rank, and especially the unit badges painted on the Wehrmacht vehicles to determine which ones were stationed where. Another way of finding this out was to recruit someone working with an optometrist, where German soldiers in need of new spectacles would go and would fill in a form mentioning their unit. Bakers could deduce quite accurately how many men were stationed at a barracks just from the number of loaves ordered.

Apart from the very important information on Luftwaffe radars and air defences, the Belgian Resistance managed to regularly inform London about the results of Allied air bombings, helping to determine if 'second tries' were necessary and thus lessening the need for dangerous reconnaissance missions by air. They reported on all important road or railway movements of troops, the state of rolling stock, and the plans of the new German planes – Junkers 188, Focke Wulf 190 and Messerschmitt 410. Clarence sent the plans of the jet engines powering the Messerschmitt 262 several months before they were used operationally and Luc-Marc was asked for a complete survey of all bridges in Belgium in preparation for the liberation campaign, with a classification as to how much weight they could withstand. Agent Roger Morsa copied about a thousand plans of defensive works built in the Atlantic Wall by the Todt Organisation. Clarence also traced accurately the strength and itinerary of the 1st SS Panzerdivision Leibstandarte Adolf Hitler which was recalled from Russia, reorganized, re-equipped and retrained at the former Belgian army camp of Leopoldsburg before being sent to France in July 1944, and it was duly harassed and slowed down by Allied air attacks on its train journey south. In all, the Belgian intelligence rings managed to keep track of fifty-one of the fifty-nine German Army Divisions that were in Belgium at any time during the war.

It was a Luxembourg member of Clarence working at the Peenemünde proving establishment on the Baltic who first reported, in January 1943, the existence of what was later to be called the V-1 flying bomb. Later reports also came in and were sent on to London about the V-2, the Messerschmitt 262 jet fighter, the HS 293 radio-guided flying bomb and many more. When the V-1 campaign against London began there was an urgent request to pinpoint the launching sites along the French coast so that they could be bombed and Clarence managed to locate 370 such sites.

In all about 65 per cent of the information gathered by the Belgian net-works was of a military nature, mainly linked to the war in the air.

Risks and arrests
The Germans obviously spared no effort to catch the Belgian spies they knew were all around them, with the multiple aim of stopping the damage, punishing the culprits and dissuading others by letting it be known what terrible treatment would be meted out to them. At least until the summer of 1944, when it was absorbed in the Reichssicherheitshauptamt (RSHA, the Reich's security head administration, in fact the SS) the institution mainly responsible for the repression of espionage and sabotage was the Abwehr, which was under the control of the Wehrmacht. We now know that its leaders, mainly Admiral Canaris, actually plotted against Hitler, but that was obviously not known at the time and did not stop his men from doing what they were there to do.[64] They were helped by the 500 men of the Geheime Feldpolizei (GFP) which usually carried out arrests and house searches and the Feldgendarmerie, in fact the military police in charge of menial jobs like manning checkpoints, searching passers-by and checking their papers, catching German deserters, or persons engaged in the black market and so on. Since they carried a metal gorget plate around their necks the Belgians nicknamed them *Cognacs*. In addition the Sicherheitspolizei-Sicherheitsdienst (SIPO-SD) was a branch of the Gestapo and took over particularly serious cases of espionage or sabotage.

The methods used were on the whole much the same as in the rest of occupied Europe. Infiltration, agents provocateurs, calls for denuncia-tions, torture, 'turning' of captured agents, blackmail, executions (which were much publicized so as to discourage others), deportations to the camps or jails in Germany and sometimes trial and execution there, threats against the families (and sometimes their deportation or at least taking them as hostages, sometimes to be shot later in reprisals for an attack on Germans) etc. In all the Germans executed 240 hostages in the years 1942 to 1944 alone.

Agents of most networks were told to try to hold out for 48 hours under torture (in some cases only 24), so as to give time for others they knew to be warned and to go underground. Hiding places had to be prepared or asked for in advance when possible. Some never spoke and eventually died under torture, were executed without having spoken, or committed suicide, but many, understandably, eventually did. Many chose not to tell their families about the activities they were engaged in, others did. A radio operator caught red-handed was pretty sure to end up being executed and only the bravest refused, after a reasonable delay, to speak and collaborate, thus escaping certain death. Of course there were codes arranged with London for a radio operator to let it be known he was transmitting under German control, but equally, the Germans also knew this. For example the insertion of deliberate or obvious errors in a message could be noted and if so it could mean a quick end for the operator.

The most (in)famous infiltrator was Prosper Dezitter, who was paid handsomely by the Germans. Helped by his mistress Florentine Giralt he wrought havoc in some networks. Apart from pretending to be a Canadian pilot he sometimes used the names and identities of captured agents. Both Dezitter and Giralt were executed after the war.

Collecting information can be difficult and risky but transmitting it is sometimes even more so. Couriers were extremely important and sometimes women or younger men would be used. Some would memorize the (shorter) messages, others hid vital papers between several layers of wrapping paper on a parcel, or in a suitcase, carrying unthreatening items such as small quantities of black market goods – a little butter or part of a sausage. If these were discovered at a checkpoint the culprit could then pay the fine, but nobody would think of having a closer look at the wrapping.

Since, at least after 1942, many if not most of the messages were sent by radio to England, the Germans developed the *Funkabwehr*, or radio defence. Lorries were equipped with radio (goniometric) direction finding devices, two or three of which could establish from which direction a radio signal was coming, down to a circle of about 100 metres. Of course the longer a transmission was, the more time the Germans had to pinpoint its origin, so messages had to be kept short and never sent at regular hours. One thing that soured relations with London was that the operators listening there at first did not work at weekends, to the understandable fury of the agents in Belgium. If they were unable to accurately determine the site of transmission the Germans would sometimes shut down the electricity supply from the public grid to small areas of a town, or even a street, in succession. If the signal stopped they then knew from which block or street it had come and each house would be thoroughly searched. Or they would let the power through but would ring at the doorbells of each house in succession in a given street where they knew someone was sending a message, since hearing the bell ring would immediately make an operator stop transmitting. Sending signals from a crowded city centre rather than from an isolated farm in the countryside had both advantages and disadvantages. But in this game of cat and mouse things did not always go the cat's way. Some networks would post lookouts outside the garages where the lorries of the Funkabwehr were normally stationed, to send a warning by telephone when they had seen them drive away, so that the radio transmission could be stopped in time. Or, when a *réseau* (network) had more than one radio transmitter and a long message to send, this would be split between two or more radio operators and the separate parts sent to London from different locations on the same frequency, thus defeating the Funkabwehr triangulation efforts.

Unlike in the Netherlands, where large-scale infiltration and the turning of numerous radio operators only became known in London after the Germans had practically dismantled and almost destroyed the Dutch networks, in Belgium intelligence gathering activities in favour of the Allies never stopped throughout the occupation.

It took nerve to be an agent in occupied Belgium and those individuals lived in constant fear for their own lives and those of their families. Someone not showing up at a rendezvous might mean he or she had been arrested and that 'they' would come for you next. Or it could just be that a train was late. A constant dilemma was to find a balance between the efficiency needed to fulfill their mission and the necessary precautions, mainly secrecy, to be taken in order not to be caught.

One might feel surprise that the Germans through either ignorance or incompetence failed to arrest Walthère Dewé right at the start of the occupation since his real name, along with those of most of the other agents who had worked with him during the First World War, had appeared in a book published in the 1920s. In 1940 he composed a network, Clarence, partly made up of people who had already worked for him in the first war – like Thérèse de Radiguès, who was in her seventies – and partly new recruits, many of them businessmen, some regularly travelling to Germany. The Germans, of course, soon suspected him and his house was searched three times in 1941. His wife died in January 1943, in part due to the stress the whole family was enduring. In early 1944, he was warned by his agents working at the telephone exchange that the Germans were actively looking for him and had the names of many in the network. Two of his daughters were arrested. Dewé went at once to the home of Thérèse de Radiguès, who lived near the corner of Avenue de la Couronne and Rue de la Brasserie in Brussels in order to warn her. However the Gestapo had arrived there first and lay in wait to catch whoever might show up (an old police technique called *la souricière*, 'the mousetrap' in French). They arrested Dewé without knowing who he was, but he managed to escape as he was being taken to a waiting police vehicle. He tried to flee by jumping on a passing tramway but it stopped at a red traffic light. Dewé got off again and started running down Rue de la Brasserie, which slopes downwards, with two armed Germans in hot pursuit. A Luftwaffe officer who happened to be there and was walking up in the opposite direction saw what was happening, took out his service pistol and shot Dewé dead, to the great dismay of the Gestapo who obviously would have preferred to take him alive and told the Luftwaffe officer so in no uncertain terms. Dewé was carrying forged papers and the Germans in fact never realized who he really was, the head of one of the largest and most successful intelligence networks in Belgium and perhaps in occupied Europe. A plaque on the wall of 2 Rue de la Brasserie commemorates his death on that spot, on 14 January 1944.

Those agents who had been working in the Clarence group who had escaped arrest went to another network, called Les Amis de Charles, the friends of Charles Woeste, who belonged to a Belgian family long active in politics and including two former prime ministers. This group was mainly active in collecting data on the Kriegsmarine and Organisation Todt arrangements along the Belgian coast and after the war Sir Colin Gubbins, head of SOE expressed his high appreciation of their work.

One of these agents was young Raymond V., who was contacted by one of his cousins in their home town of Bruges. Since this was close to the Sperrgebiet, the strip of land along the Belgian coast, he was asked to act as courier and to bring messages to Brussels, there to be forwarded to London. Going regularly by train from Bruges to Louvain, he frequently passed through Brussels where he had to change trains. The Bruges cell of Clarence was headed by Gerda Van de Kerchove, who had a small bed-and-breakfast where several Kriegsmarine and Organisation Todt officers stayed while working on the coastal defences. Rather naively they thought she could not understand German and spoke freely in front of her. She would also look at their papers and wastepaper baskets whenever they were out for the day. Some years ago a message from Clarence reporting on the damage after a bombing on the Belgian coast could be seen exhibited at the Imperial War Museum in London. It is quite possible it was brought to Brussels by Raymond V.

One morning Raymond's mother Berthe and his younger brother were having breakfast at the family home when Gerda Van de Kerchove's sister suddenly arrived, announcing Gerda had just been arrested. Raymond immediately fled the house for a couple of weeks and took refuge at the Château d'Acoz belonging to the d'Udekem family.[65] *After some time, thinking the coast was clear Raymond came back and spent the night at home. But next morning at dawn, the maid entered his room in great excitement saying, 'Sir, the Germans are here!' They had indeed come for him, but while his younger brother Philippe led them into the garden, where he said Raymond might be feeding the rabbits and chickens, Raymond had time to hide in a small room whose access door was concealed inside a closet. When one of the Germans opened the closet and began to look through the hanging coats and suits, Raymond's heart beat very fast indeed. But the German didn't see the internal door. The Feldpolizei took his other brother instead, mixing them up because Jean's name had been found written in a book at the home of Gerda, to whom he had lent it. He was led to a waiting Kübelwagen, the military version of the Volkswagen and taken to the local jail. After they had gone, Raymond came out of hiding, bundled some clothing together and scaled the back wall of the garden to get away. It would have been unwise to use the front door in case it was being watched.*

Escape routes

In a memorandum he wrote for Churchill at the close of the war, Anthony Eden listed the different contributions Belgium had made to the Allied war effort and he especially emphasized the help given to downed airmen in attempting to get back to Britain.

Though there were other escape routes, like that run by Belgian army doctor Guérisse (aka Pat O'Leary), Andrée De Jongh's *Réseau Comète* or Comet Line, is by far the best known, especially in Anglo-Saxon countries, because about 400 Allied flyers used it to get back to Britain after having parachuted into occupied Europe. The total number of airmen helped by Belgian escape lines is said to be about 1,500. They inevitably had to contact locals to survive and if they were lucky they were taken to members of the Comet Line. Usually after a waiting period in a safe house, small groups were then briefed ('Don't sleep on the train because you might betray yourself by speaking English when dreaming,' that sort of advice), given civilian clothes and false papers with identification pictures they had been told to bring with them, before taking off in Britain, and passed from one agent to the other, each only knowing the 'deliverer' and the 'receiver'. The usual itinerary was Brussels, Valenciennes at the French–Belgian border, Paris, the demarcation line between occupied and not occupied France and the small French city of Pau, at the foot of the Pyrenees. There another Belgian woman, who incredibly was never caught during the war, lived in the chateau of the family she had married into, and she organized Basque guides to take small groups across the Pyrenees and into neutral Spain. Once there the British, Commonwealth, and American aircrews were usually taken charge of by the local consulates and military attachés and quickly sent back to Britain.

The Comet Line was also used by French, Belgian, Dutch and others who had been in the Resistance and were sought by the Germans, and/or wanted to volunteer and join the embryo armed forces of their countries in Britain like the Free French or the Belgian Brigade, and by Jewish fugitives or those who had other reasons to leave occupied Europe but could not get the necessary papers and visas. Some Belgian soldiers who had escaped from POW camps in Germany and wanted to continue the fight against Germany, and a few Italian deserters also used the line young 'Dédée' De Jong had set up with her parents and a few dozen friends and relatives.

All this was obviously very dangerous, because the Germans quickly got wind of what was going on and infiltrated fake Allied flyers who spoke perfect English and who either were tasked to help dismantle the line or were sent to Britain as spies or both, the traitor Prosper Dezitter, already mentioned, among them. Dezitter worked for money and was paid an extra bonus by the Luftwaffe for each Allied airman he helped capture. Fluent in English, he sometimes pretended to be a 'Captain Jackson, RCAF', who had been shot down. The fact that he had lost part of one finger soon became known and other men who had the same handicap were turned away, being mistaken for him. More than once several members of the Comet network were arrested and sent to concentration camps, including Andrée De Jongh herself. In all, 23 members of the Comet Line were killed, including her father who was executed, and 130 members never returned from the camps in Germany. After the war Dédée received the George Medal and became a nurse in the Belgian Congo. Other members of the group also received the George Medal, the Distinguished Service Order, MBE, OBE and Belgian medals.

Crossing the Pyrenees by narrow mountain tracks was sometimes done at night to evade the German patrols and during winter, with strong winds and heavy snow, appalling conditions had to be endured.

Arriving in neutral Spain by no means offered quick deliverance, as those without valid papers were interned in the huge Miranda del Ebro camp. It should be said Franco's Spain never extradited non-Germans but the combination of conditions in the camp, and not knowing for how long you were stranded there, was demoralizing.

After crossing France by train via the Comet escape line, Raymond V. arrived at Pau at the foot of the Pyrenees. After a small group had gathered there a guide took them through mountain tracks. In the group there were French and Belgian young men wanting to go to Britain to join their respective armed forces, a few Italian deserters and a Jewish family with children and an aged relative. These last had to be carried uphill in turn by the younger men. At one point the guide urgently told them to hush and they hastily took refuge in a mountain hut. Lower down an armed German patrol could be seen, looking precisely for groups like theirs. When they arrived at the first Spanish village the locals offered them oranges. The Guardia Civil asked them about German troop movements they might have seen as an invasion of the Iberian Peninsula by Axis forces still was a possibility. Next they were asked for their papers and when they said they had none the answer was reassuring: 'Don't worry; we will fix that small problem in no time. Just come along to that big building down the street.' The big building turned out to be the local jail, where their fingerprints were taken, forms filled in and from where they were taken later to the Miranda del Ebro camp, where Raymond V. spent eight months until released and taken to the Belgian embassy in Madrid.

Spain had just come out of its Civil War and was dirt poor. Some of the soldiers guarding the camp had shoes with no soles. Being there against their will, the detainees refused to get up in the morning to attend the hoisting of the flag. The Belgian embassy paid for their meals, brought from a local restaurant. Since most other nationalities did not benefit from similar arrangements and had to make do with the repulsive camp 'soup', the Belgians were at first in serious danger of becoming extremely unpopular. To avoid this they would invite in turn groups of French, Dutch, Polish or other prisoners to share their meals.

After the Normandy landings it did not make any sense to try to send Allied pilots back to Britain with all the risks, including being caught in the fighting, this entailed. So they were briefed to hunker down until liberated by Allied troops. But this meant they had to be sheltered and fed for a longer, unpredictable time, increasing the risks for those who hid them.

Guerrillas and sabotage
Unlike southern France, Greece, Yugoslavia or the Ukraine, the Belgian territory, heavily built-up, does not lend itself to hiding bands of partisans roaming in the woods for long periods. If some groups did in fact hide in the Ardennes towards the end of the war, they were an exception. This does not mean armed interventions and sabotage were not possible. Armed resistance based in the cities could and did operate hit-and-run operations – say, the assassination of known collaborators who had denounced people to the Germans. Arms were cleverly concealed. To be found in possession of firearms would inevitably earn you a death sentence, usually carried out. Rarely were German military personnel deliberately targeted because of the severe reprisals against the local population this always attracted. Taking out Belgian collaborators was not only easier and less risky but more profitable because of its dissuasive effect.

The largest and best organized group was the Armée Secrète (AS), which was largely composed of officers and men of the 1940 Belgian army who had either been liberated or escaped from POW camps. Commanded by General Pire, whose unit had rubbed shoulders with Montgomery's at Louvain in May 1940, and numbering about 55,000, it was well structured and disciplined and had close contacts with the government in exile in London. They would probably have given a good account of themselves if circumstances had been different. Indeed, contrary to expectations, there was little fighting in Belgium in September 1944 and by December most armed guerrilla groups had been disarmed and many fighters had joined the regular Belgian Army being reconstructed around the Belgian Brigade which had arrived with Montgomery's troops.

Other important groups which, with the AS, totalled about 150,000 members were the Armée belge des Partisans, Mouvement national Royaliste, the Milices patriotiques, Fidelio and the Witte Brigade in Flanders and the Front de l'Indépendance/Partisans armés which, by blowing up about thirty pylons caused the 'Grande Coupure', a large power cut over most of Wallonia in January 1944 that paralysed many of the factories making products for the Wehrmacht. Bridges and trains were blown up in the summer of 1944 when the Germans were sending troops to Normandy. Several hundred brave men and women lost their lives while involved in such sabotage, either on the spot or by later execution. Others attacked post offices to get their hands on money to fund operations, pay for food for persons in hiding and so on.

By early August 1944 and until the arrival of the Allied troops, the armed resistance had become a mosaic of organizations, initiatives and individual actions that strove to paralyse the Nazi war machine in Belgium and succeeded to a point.

Repression

Again, the harsh methods used to repress dissent, sabotage, espionage or attempts on the lives of members of the German armed forces in Belgium were no different from those used in other western European countries occupied by Nazi Germany.

Not far from Mechelen on the motorway from Brussels to Antwerp, is Fort Breendonk which had served as GHQ for Belgian forces in 1940 and this had now become a political prison. Resistance fighters, freemasons, communists, Jews, or others who displeased the occupiers were detained, forced to work, tortured or executed here, either by hanging or firing squad. Some were ordinary workers, others university professors, priests, former Belgian army officers and even a former general of the Tsarist army, most probably no friend of communism. Among the 3,457 inmates detained in the fort during the war was communist leader Grippa, who had already been jailed by the Belgian police in May 1940. Guards, torturers and executioners were German or Belgian. A visit to Fort Breendonk is well worth the short drive north from Brussels for those who care to understand more about what human beings can do to one another. The small room can be seen, where the prisoner was suspended from his wrists, which were tied behind his back, gradually dislodging the arms from their sockets and causing excruciating pain. The torture chamber has been maintained intact, exactly as the SS left it, with the pulley hanging from the ceiling and the stove where irons were heated red hot. A little gutter conducted blood and urine to a sewer. The torture chamber was situated close to where the other inmates were locked at night, in cots three deep; they could clearly hear the screams of the tortured.

Clad in old Belgian army uniforms, these other inmates were forced to cart away the tons of earth that originally covered the fort, a backbreaking, completely useless work, only designed to wear out underfed men, who could expect severe beatings with heavy sticks or long whips at the least sign of being tired. Several post office workers from Charleroi, who had intercepted letters denouncing people to the Germans were worked to death like this, the guards sometimes competing to see who would be first to kill a prisoner on a given day.

The execution posts and gallows have also been preserved. An Austrian army chaplain has testified of the courage of the Belgians about to be hanged or shot: 'How they knew how to die!' Sometimes the firing squads, usually young German soldiers from a nearby garrison, were nervous and missed their aim. An SS soldier then took his time delivering the *coup de grâce* and would later proudly show his blood-spattered uniform to the assembled inmates. Care was also taken that those being hanged would take some time to die. Among these were three who had shot dead a Belgian collaborationist journalist, Paul Colin.

Both the Dossin Barracks and Fort Breendonk were turned into memorials/museums after the war and can be visited. Reading the last letters to their families of those about to be executed is a poignant experience.[66]

Other executions took place at the Tir National firing range in Brussels, where most victims are buried, and at the Liège Citadel. The big Fort de Huy, halfway between Namur and Liège also served as a prison, as did ordinary jails across the country.

The Germans usually went through the motions of a trial and Belgian lawyers were allowed to assist the accused. The fact that the hearings were held in German however severely handicapped the defence.

Allied aid and support

If trust and a satisfactory relationship usually existed between London and the different intelligence gathering networks in Belgium, it was mistrust of communist infiltration/control in the armed resistance groups that led the British and later the Americans to be extremely cautious when sending arms or other military supplies to Belgium. With some exceptions the Belgian Resistance only ever received radios, money and so on by parachute drop. On the other hand, in the brief period over the summer of 1944 when it was feared the Germans would make a stand in Belgium, Belgian and other SAS units were dropped to take control of armed resistance groups which would have been used in the Ardennes to disrupt German communications and supplies. On 6 September 1944, a small group of Belgian SAS under the command of Lieutenant Van der Heyte was dropped by mistake beyond the intended point, in Germany, which made them the first Allied unit to penetrate German-held territory armed and in uniform, five days before US ground reconnaissance troops did so. However, since the German troops all retreated to their own border in September 1944, these preparations had been unnecessary.

Who resisted?

It has been stated there was more resistance in Wallonia than in Flanders and vice versa for collaboration. This may be true statistically but is an oversimplification. The number of executions of *résistants*, of spies caught, and especially of acts of sabotage was much higher in French-speaking Belgium, including Brussels. In proportion, more Flemish civil servants usually (but by no means always) coming from the nationalist VNV party helped the Germans, and young Flemings joined the SS in far higher numbers than did Walloons. But economic collaboration, for instance selling supplies to the German Army or even producing small arms, was far more developed in industrialized Wallonia than rural Flanders. And if resistance was strong among the socialist and communist coalminers and steelworkers of Wallonia, there certainly was a lot of espionage activity in Flanders, along the coast and the Atlantic Wall and many Jews were hidden in Flemish homes. The Flemish nationalist ideology, often mixed with strong Christian convictions, tempted more young Flemings (in proportion as well as in absolute numbers) to go and fight 'to defend Europe against godless Bolshevism' than the more industrialized and de-Christianized Walloons. But then the most famous Belgian collaborator was Degrelle, who was as Walloon as they come. And the Liège police helped the Germans arrest Jews quite as much as did their colleagues in Antwerp. Furthermore, it is sometimes difficult to establish to which language group some people belonged and many were bilingual, especially in Brussels and in Flanders.

Three groups of the Belgian population were overrepresented in the Resistance in proportion to the general population. The communists were very active, mainly in the industrial basins of Wallonia (Mons, Charleroi, Liège), where 'class consciousness' and the Marxist creed were quite prevalent. Well-organized cells of the Belgian Communist Party sprang into action as soon as the word came from Moscow, and that word (only) came after Germany invaded the Soviet Union in June 1941. Until then the communists had either been neutral or had even helped the Nazis to some extent. Communist propaganda, from the summer of 1941 quite predictably supported the Stalinist views about the war, triggering strong British and American mistrust. Interestingly some Soviet Army POWs brought to Belgium by their captors escaped and, together with local *Verzetstrijders* (Dutch for resistance fighters) created small armed resistance groups in the Flemish coalmining areas of Limburg, in the north east of the country.

One of the largest groups of armed resistance fighters, the Patriotes armés/Front de l'Indépendance was definitively communist-led and orientated, even if not all of its members belonged to the Party. Some were veterans of the International Brigades in the Spanish civil war or Spanish Republican refugees.

Another over-represented group in relation to the population was the Belgian nobility. If the communists (and socialists) were mainly active in sabotage, especially of the railways in 1944, armed resistance and propaganda, the Belgian aristocrats were often engaged in intelligence gathering or the hiding of Jews. Though its role has declined since 1945, the Belgian nobility have played an important role in maintaining the cohesion of the country throughout its history under many foreign rulers. Some families of Belgian nobility can trace their lines many centuries back and, as in Britain, the king each year confers titles of baron, count or viscount to meritorious politicians, academicians, diplomats, sportsmen or sportswomen, or elevates them to nobility without a title. It is one of the few countries were nobility is especially mentioned in the constitution, though the relevant article also states that no special privilege can be attached to it. Use of titles and coats of arms is controlled by a government agency and abuses can be punished. Often landowners, in 1940 the nobility still played an important role. Most of the diplomats, many army officers, senior civil servants and a few cabinet ministers belonged to it. When the occupation began many members of the Belgian nobility were in the armed forces and several managed to make their way to Britain. A study of the last names of members of the Belgians in the RAF and in the Belgian Brigade reveals a higher proportion of them than in the population as a whole. Usually sharing similar ideas about patriotism, sense of duty and religion, having lived through or been raised in the remembrance of the first occupation, during which their elders had usually played a role in the army, often knowing each other since childhood, being related, or educated at the same schools, when joining the Resistance they knew exactly whom they could trust among others of the same background when they needed help – whether for recruitment to espionage networks, or when themselves needing to go underground. A study of the last names of those who lost their lives either by execution or in German camps again shows a high number of members of the Belgian aristocracy, since working for these networks meant paying a high price indeed when caught. A curious incident happened when one of these families, later to lose several of its members who were executed for resisting, and who owned several horses, was asked by a German officer if he could ride one of them. It was difficult to say no and it would have been unwise too, seeing the activities they were already engaged in. But patriotism is perhaps not only felt by humans, because the horse the German chose to ride immediately threw him off, something that particular stallion had never done before, having previously always been very calm and patient.

Nevertheless, some members of very prominent aristocratic families were Rexists and some of those did choose to collaborate with the occupiers.

Last but not least, a third group was extremely active and over-represented in the list of Belgians or foreigners who lost their lives fighting Nazism. Either organized into defence groups for their own preservation, or in resistance groups with people of other backgrounds, the Jews wrote pamphlets or articles for the clandestine press, organized the hiding of fellow Jews and took part in attacks against Germans. Among others, this included young Dr Livshitz whose heroism and tragic fate are described in Chapter 8.

There was a high proportion of women in the Belgian Resistance. Bearing in mind the propaganda use the Allies had made of the executions of Edith Cavell and Gabrielle Petit in the previous war, the Germans as a rule did not shoot women in Belgium. However Marguerite Bervoets, who was caught whilst taking pictures of the anti-aircraft guns protecting the Chièvres Lufwaffe base was taken to Germany and guillotined there in August 1944, and the same fate befell Louise Hénin, decapitated at Plötzensee near Berlin in June 1944. Germaine Arents was luckier. Being pregnant when arrested she was taken to a Liège maternity ward. There her colleagues, posing as nurses and ambulance drivers, simply came and took her away in a 'liberated' vehicle suitably disguised. Many other Belgian women died at the infamous Ravensbrück camp.

It could be said that with the exception of sabotaging railways in 1944 and delivering the Port of Antwerp intact, armed resistance was a far less effective contribution to the Allied effort than espionage and 'exfiltration' of flyers. But this could also be attributed to the very fast withdrawal from Belgium of the bulk of German troops back behind the Rhine and into the Netherlands, and the subsequent speedy arrival of Allied troops, so that the planned guerrilla actions in the Ardennes behind German lines in the autumn of 1944 became unnecessary.

The Belgian Resistance as a whole paid a high price: 350 of its members were executed in Belgium and 1,570 put to death in Germany, while 4,000 were deported or detained in Belgium for periods ranging from some months in a Belgian jail to several years at Dachau, Ravensbrück or other Nazi concentration or extermination camps.

Of 5,266 agents who were recognized after the war as Action and Intelligence Agents (Agents des Services de Renseignement et d'Action or Agents, SRA for short) 1,815 did not survive the war. About 12,500 individuals were recognized as auxiliaries and 10,000 as occasional agents by the Belgian government.

Jean V., Raymond's younger brother, aged 19, was taken to the large Saint Gilles jail in Brussels, where he was thoroughly interrogated. Having established it was a serious case of espionage the Gestapo took over from the Feldpolizei. When his mother came to visit him she would take away his dirty linen, but he did not tell her why there were bloodstains. His morale declined. He already had problems with his eyesight and when he asked to see a doctor about it, the German tricked him by feigning he was giving him a slap in the face. Since Jean still could see somewhat, he winced. The German doctor concluded he was faking it and sent him back to his cell. One of his cellmates, who had killed a German soldier, was still under 18 so they waited until the morning of his birthday to execute him. Another time a whole group, including Jean, was told they were about to be shot but then a German officer rechecked his list and sent him back to his cell adding his turn would come soon enough. After a few 'thorough' interrogations, and with information from other sources, the Germans realized the real courier was Raymond, and that Jean might not have known much of what his brother was doing. He was kept in detention however 'just in case'. His mother did everything she could think of to have him freed. At the Bruges English Convent where she had been a pupil before the First World War, she had been friends with German girls who had returned to their country and to whom she had sent food parcels during the famine years of the early interwar period. She wrote to them all and they in turn wrote to General Geyer von Schweppenburg, former military attaché in Belgium, who now held a senior command in the Wehrmacht. The Red Cross was also approached. Eventually, after five months, Jean was set free, but the young man would bear the after-effects for the rest of his life. His sight was severely impaired and his nerves affected. He had to give up studying history since he could only read a few words at a time with a magnifying glass, and he had some therapy.

After the war he received the Croix de Guerre, the Médaille de la Résistance and the Médaille des Prisonniers politiques. He became a conference interpreter and worked for the Belgian government and the fledgling Common Market. One of the languages he studied was German and he eventually became a firm supporter of European integration.

Chapter 7

Collaboration

The economy

If the payments imposed on the Belgian economy were a very heavy burden, war circumstances also had beneficial effects, at least for some. The coalminers had their quite low salaries raised when they went on strike after the working hours were increased and inflation started to bite. The pay raise came at the Germans' insistence – it was obviously in their interest to keep the mines running since they took most of the output away. Factories producing small arms like FN outside Liège and their numerous subcontractors were made to produce rifles, pistols and sub-machine guns for the Wehrmacht, usually German models. The ERLA factory in Antwerp revamped German aircraft engines. Occasional acts of sabotage, mostly committed towards the end of the war, were very severely punished when discovered. The Wehrmacht and Todt Organisation were also important clients for food, fuel, construction materials, cement, logs, the use of railway rolling stock etc. As was to be expected and as in other occupied countries, Belgian firms fulfilled the orders. After the war most of the bosses concerned were to say they had no choice but to comply, since refusal would inevitably be followed by requisition, jailing of the recalcitrant bosses and loss of jobs for the workers. This was true to a point and had been allowed for in the legislation passed just before the war. But the overzealous according to the Galopin doctrine, or those who had illicitly enriched themselves, were brought to justice after Liberation.

Political collaboration

Contrary to the situation in France, where the local government openly and repeatedly advocated collaboration (the Vichy government was in fact the legal, constitutional government, where the neutrals sent their embassy representatives – including the United States until Pearl Harbor), there was no legally constituted government in Belgium that could collaborate with the Germans, since the principal ministers had gone to London. This does not mean there was no collaboration of course, but as we shall see it took different forms.

Though it is a completely separate language from German, Dutch Flemish belongs to the Germanic group of languages and is closer to German than say, English or the Scandinavian group. Already during the First World War occupation, inspired by the nineteenth-century Pangermanist doctrine,[67] the Germans had pursued an active *Flamenpolitik* (Flemish policy) encouraging the desertion of Flemish soldiers on the stabilized Yser Front, administratively separating Wallonia and Flanders and creating a Flemish executive body, the Council of Flanders (*Raad van Vlaanderen*). They deported recalcitrant burgomasters in Flemish cities and replaced them with more pliant ones, exchanged the French language for Dutch at Ghent University and generally encouraged Flemish national feeling and separatism. Far from all Flemish nationalists fell for this obvious trap but some did, like August Borms, about whom more later. Not unnaturally, repression after the war of what was seen as high treason to Belgium radicalized the Flemish movement and some sanctions incensed moderate Flemings, whose attitude had remained irreproachable and who found it hard to accept the harshness of some of these measures or statements. Many Flemish reserve officers in the Belgian Army had also given the matter a lot of thought during the long war years and after it was over became more active in the movement to obtain linguistic equality for Flanders, if not outright independence. In the interwar years a belief had also developed, as stated earlier, that Flemish soldiers had been killed or even executed for not having understood orders given to them in French by their officers during the first war. This has since been disproved by Flemish historians, but myths endure.

The most important Flemish political movement existing in the interwar years was the Vlaams Nationaal Verbond (VNV), the Flemish National Alliance. Already between the wars the German embassy in Brussels had financed *Volk en Staat* the paper of Staf De Clercq, who headed VNV and encouraged defeatist propaganda in the Flemish units of the army. Hendrik Elias, Burgomaster of Ghent, succeeded De Clercq when he died of cancer during the occupation.

The Verdinaso movement was left without its leader, Van Severen, when he was assassinated by the French in May 1940, as we have seen. The other movements sought to recruit its orphaned members. Some of his followers, like the French-speaking Louis Gueuning wisely decided to wait and see and only became politically active again after 1945. Others joined various extreme rightist movements, Jef François, René Lagrou and Ward Hermans even enlisting in the SS. And there were some who actually enlisted with the Resistance, which might have been the most consistent attitude with at least some of Van Severen's ideas. Endless speculations were made during and after the war as to what the leader of Verdinaso would have done, some saying he would have become a Belgian Quisling. We will never know.

Jef Van de Wiele was Mayor of Deurne, a suburb of Antwerp. He had studied and taught Germanic languages and become quite proficient, corresponding with professors in German universities. He founded *DeVlag*, Dutch for 'the flag' and also an acronym for the German/Flemish Work Association. Having declared in favour of outright annexation to the Reich he actively recruited young Flemings to join the SS. They could do this in different ways, by joining the Flemish Waffen SS, about which more later, or a more politically oriented institution based in Belgium, the Algemene SS Vlaanderen, founded by ex-Verdinaso members René Lagrou and Ward Hermans and taking its orders from Reichsführer SS Himmler's representatives in Belgium, SS officers Kammerhofer and later Jungclaus. The Algemene SS Vlaanderen's influence waned however, DeVlag proving the stronger.

Van de Wiele from DeVlag and Elias, leader of the VNV, would be among the last to be freed in the 1960s, after many years in jail, their death sentences having been commuted to life imprisonment.

Reimond Tollenaere was not so lucky. Fighting with the *Flämische* SS in Russia he was killed by 'friendly fire', when an artillery shell shot by the Spaniards of the Legion Azul, the Spanish contingent sent by Franco to fight communism, hit his command post.

August Borms

By far the most important and charismatic Flemish nationalist leader who wholly and unreservedly embraced collaboration in both occupations was August Borms. Born in 1878 into a fervent Catholic family he became a teacher of Germanic languages after studying in mainly Roman Catholic schools and at Leuven (Louvain) University. In the years 1903–6 he lived in Peru with a few other teachers, at a Lima school, seconded there under an agreement between the Belgian and Peruvian governments. He kept fond memories of his stay in South America but his wife hated the place (and the sea voyages) and he had to send her home. After his return he continued teaching at schools in Flanders and embarked on a quasi-religious political struggle for the cause of the Flemish people and their language, oppressed as he saw it by the '*franskiljons*', the French-speaking Flemings. Meeting followed meeting all over Flanders but also in the Netherlands and in the north-west of France, where Flemish had once been spoken. When the Kaiser's troops invaded Belgium he first called upon the Flemish soldiers in the Belgian Army to fight like lions, and upon King Albert to restore the Flemings' rights after the war. But after some time he changed his mind and turned wholeheartedly towards the German occupiers. Although the latter mistrusted him and his friends, who themselves were far from united, he was instrumental in seeing one of the Flemish Movement's longstanding aspirations realized: in 1916 the University of Ghent became Dutch speaking, though the number of teaching staff and alumni remained minute. It was quickly dubbed 'the von Bissing University', after the name of the German military governor. Famous historian Henri Pirenne, who had taught (in French) at Ghent University, refused collaboration and was deported to Germany, as were some Belgian magistrates who briefly arrested and detained Borms for high treason under Belgian legislation.

Being a devout Catholic did not stop Borms from denouncing a parish priest who had criticized the German occupiers from the pulpit and was then arrested and deported. Infuriated by reports he had read about the poor treatment Flemish soldiers in the Belgian Army were receiving from their officers and NCOs at the front in the trenches, he started touring POW camps in Germany to try to recruit volunteers for a new police force. He was received with catcalls and cries of 'traitor'. He went so far as to try to block the exchange of sick Belgian soldiers for German ones through Switzerland, as this would have lessened the success of his recruiting drives. The exchange went ahead anyway.[68] An unelected executive body, the Raad van Vlaanderen (Council of Flanders) was also set up. This was dubbed the Verraad van Vlaanderen by his opponents (*Verraad* means 'treason'). Borms became its 'Minister for Defence'.

Other acts by Borms shocked many Belgians including Flemings, such as when he justified both the invasion of Belgium in 1914 and the forced deportation of Belgian (including Flemish) workers to Germany, or when he made a trip to Berlin with other activists and was wined and dined there by the political establishment. The trip was supposed to be kept secret but German papers made it public, to the great scandal of many who were near starvation in occupied Belgium. On this occasion he told a member of the German National Assembly (the future Reichstag) Mathias Erzberger,[69] that he realized only a very small number of the Flemings, about 5 per cent, were behind him. Indeed a large number of the Flemish-feeling militants thought it unwise to stake so much on Germany; the outcome of the war was far from certain and indeed they would not go as far as he did in declaring for a total separation of Flanders from Belgium, and in general disapproved of Borms' actions. After the German retreat in 1918, he fled to Germany with his family for a brief period and then returned to Brussels where he lived under an assumed name. In February 1919, he was arrested and stood trial for treason, subversion and rebellion. A (Flemish) jury found him guilty on the two last charges and he was condemned to death, his sentence being commuted to life imprisonment. The Vatican at first intervened on his behalf but was told in no uncertain terms by Foreign Minister Hymans that this was an internal Belgian matter. The Papal Nuncio reported this to the Holy See and the 'fatherly' intervention of Benedict XV, who many thought had not been wholly neutral during the conflict and who had been accused of sympathy for Catholic Austria-Hungary and partially Catholic Germany, was withdrawn. Eventually, thirty-nine death sentences were passed, but nobody was executed after the First World War either for collaboration or treason.

Borms sat for ten years in the Leuven jail for serious offenders but benefited from the political detainees regime. He was allowed visits, letters and newspapers, as well as a daily walk in the prison courtyard. Flemish activists raised funds for him, as both his salary as teacher and his pension had been cancelled (as was the decoration of the Order of Léopold II, which he had been awarded for having taught in Peru). This saved his incredibly devoted and patient wife and six children from destitution and paid for the latter's studies.

A campaign to free him was set up, but he steadfastly refused the offer to be freed on condition he renounced all political activities, a condition most other condemned activists accepted. 'Borms vrij!'(free) became the rallying cry of the Flemish nationalist movement, and he himself a symbol for the Flemish struggle, while his partisans gradually made a martyr of him, going so far as to depict him with a saint's aura and comparing his plight with that of Jesus ... When he was eventually freed without conditions in 1929, he was the last still detained for treasonable activities. Having put on some weight through lack of exercise in jail, he at once resumed his political activities, now becoming the most prestigious Flemish nationalist politician by far. He did not lack enemies among the Belgian nationalists, who strongly opposed Flemish separatism, or among Belgian Army veterans. His foes recalled what he had done during the late war and compared him unfavourably with the hundreds (including Flemings) who had been shot by the Germans, among them Gabrielle Petit, a young Belgian woman executed as a spy in 1916, or the well-known Edith Cavell.

When the Germans invaded again in May 1940, Borms unhesitatingly resumed his attitude and activities of the previous occupation, though in the meantime his influence had decreased. A new generation of hard-line Flemish nationalists like Staf De Clercq, leader of the Vlaams Nationaal Verbond or Jef Van de Wiele of DeVlag had come up in the meantime and considered Borms old hat, but they treated him with respect and tried to win him over since he still commanded a considerable following.

Borms presided over a commission created by the Germans which awarded compensation the Belgian state was made to pay to those (including himself) who had lost jobs, pensions and so on, because of their activities during the 1914–18 occupation. He expressed unreserved support for Hitler. This was something many other Flemish nationalists disapproved of. They had worked actively for the Flemish cause during the First World War and in the interwar years, but refrained from doing so during the new occupation because they sensed how different the Nazis were from the Kaiser's men and also because they realized the Germans would not grant Flanders the independence they craved. Borms, on the other hand, consistently encouraged young Flemish men to join the SS and fight against Bolshevism, and travelled repeatedly to Germany to visit young Flemish SS recruits in training. On one such trip in Munich he fell off a tram and was visited in hospital by no less a person than Rudolf Hess. More serious was a traffic accident he suffered in Belgium in early 1943. It left him crippled, on crutches for the rest of his life. With the Allied troops approaching in August 1944 he took refuge in Germany with his family, where they were all arrested and were brought back to Belgium in 1945 to face trial, his wife and children being progressively freed over the following months or years.

Military collaboration: the Flemish SS

In *Hitler's Flemish Lions* British author Jonathan Trigg (see bibliography) writes that out of 137,000 West Europeans who volunteered and served in the Waffen SS, the Walloons contributed 15,000 and the Flemish an 'unbelievably high number of 23,000 [...] out of a total [Flemish] population of 5 million'. By comparison he gives the numbers for the Netherlands as 50,000 and for France as 8,000 but does not quote his source. Another source[70] quotes a more credible 10,000 for the Flemings alone, including a large number of recruits from northern France with a Flemish family background and many who did not fight in Russia.

Most of the Flemish volunteers were members of the Flemish nationalist parties, VNV and later, in growing numbers, DeVlag, the two groups having great difficulty getting on together at first because of party rivalries. There were fisticuffs between them at a training camp in Germany.

For the most part they came from poor miners' families with many children, which their pay it was hoped would help feed. If idealism was not the main motive for volunteering, it certainly played a part, as did the Catholic convictions of most. Indeed the number of volunteers increased steeply after the German attack on the Soviet Union, having been static at a paltry 800 until then. The average age was 23 and 70 per cent of them were unmarried. That the number of recruits remained constant until the end of the war instead of dwindling in proportion with Germany's chances of winning can only be explained by the fact that many who had been deeply involved in collaboration found joining the SS a convenient way of making themselves scarce in Belgium, a country they did not see as their own but whose inevitable retribution towards 'traitors' they had every reason to fear.

First merged with the Dutch volunteers of the SS Brigades Westland and Norland, they later formed a dedicated Flemish unit, the Legion Flandern which was transformed into successively the SS Sturmbrigade Langemarck[71] and later the 27 Freiwilligen Grenadier Division Langemarck (Flämische Nr 1). They wore the standard SS black uniform with a Flemish lion on the sleeve (a black lion on a yellow field). At first they did not wear the SS runes on the collar but a three-pronged 'sun wheel' or 'trifo' swastika. Later this was changed to the regular well-known SS sign. Contrary to what recruiting posters suggested they were never equipped with tanks or antitank self-propelled guns but only as infantry. With a few exceptions their officers were all German, which caused disappointment, even resentment, as did the fact that though many were devout Catholics, few facilities were made available for religious practice or comfort.

Not all were unconditional supporters of Germany, because when it was decided in 1943 to transform the *Vlaams Legioen* (Flemish Legion) into an SS unit several members refused and would not take the oath of allegiance to Hitler, compulsory for all members of the SS.

The first recruits were sent to Debica in Poland, where they received a very tough training. In fact the training the Waffen SS received can be reckoned among the hardest of any soldiers in any army ever. Many could not stomach it and were sent home to take up less demanding roles in the different auxiliaries the Germans had set up. In September 1941, they were transferred to Arys in East Prussia where the training was, if anything, even tougher and lasted from 0500hrs till late in the evening, sometimes with night exercises as well. Those who had been officers in the pre-war Belgian Army went to Lauenburg for an adaptation course in German procedures and language.

Finally, in the winter 1941–42 the gruelling infantry training was followed by bitter fighting in the marshes south of Leningrad, on the banks of Lake Ladoga and the Volchow River, both against the regular Soviet Army and the partisans. The Flemish Legion fought with undisputable bravery and lost heavily to the enemy. SS *Sturmmann* (Corporal) Juul Geurts won an Iron Cross 1st Class near Lake Ladoga and so later did anti-tank gunner Rémy Schrijnen for destroying twelve enemy tanks in Estonia. A large number of the Flemish SS (about 5,000) lost their lives in Russia.

There are no reports that they committed atrocities but it is well known that the war on the Eastern front was bitter and merciless. On a few occasions they fought alongside the Spanish Legion Azul, and got on very well with them, exchanging olive oil and Spanish *chorizo* for Flemish delicacies like *speculoos* biscuits received from home.

Some individual Flemings also served in other SS or regular German Army units like the Dutch of the Freiwilligen Legion Niederlände, the 5 SS Panzergrenadier Division Wiking and the SS Panzer Division Das Reich.

Robert S. attended a memorial service for the prominent Flemish politician Reimond Tollenaere who had been killed in Russia. When he came home he announced he had decided to join the Waffen SS to do his bit for Flanders and also to help his parents cope with feeding his five brothers and sisters. His mother cried and would have none of it but his father who had strong nationalist feelings and had always subscribed to Wij *the VNV newspaper, approved. His uncle, a parish priest in the neighbouring village, also approved. Robert went to the nearest recruitment post and filled in forms, among others one which asked for any party affiliation and where he duly mentioned belonging to the VNV, and passed the physical tests which were at that time still very demanding. On 31 July 1943, he boarded a train at Ghent Sint Pieters station together with about 150 other volunteers on their way to the Debica training camp. Most of the families were there to see them off, as well as a few dozen uniformed girls belonging to the Party's young women's association. Enthusiasm was high and all gave the Hitler salute. A few months later he was fighting on the Leningrad front, in snow and ice. The conditions were terrible but the tough training he had received paid off. When the lakes and marshes they had been fighting in eventually thawed in the spring, the stench of all the corpses that had been lying unburied was so strong his unit was given a large provision of vodka to be able to endure removing the now decomposing bodies. With spring came the mosquitoes, myriads of them.*

One evening a German Fieseler Storch light observation and liaison plane was seen flying over the German lines and certainly unintentionally crash-landed in no man's land. Neither the German lines nor the Russian moved, because that would have started an escalation of fire no one wanted at that time. The pilot and lone passenger were left to their own devices but the next night the Flemish advance observation posts saw two men approaching, obviously without any hostile intentions. The Flemings, by now old 'front rats', held their fire thinking them to be Russian deserters of which there were always plenty. Lo and behold they were the former occupants of the plane who had patiently waited for 24 hours in a shell hole.

A few weeks later Robert and his comrades were surprised to hear music coming from loudspeakers in the Russian lines, followed by appeals to them to desert, in Dutch language with a perfect Flemish accent. They were told that those not prepared to walk over and partake in the comfortable life the Russians assured them they would have, would be mercilessly massacred by the victorious Soviet armies which numbered 50 million soldiers, 85,000 tanks and 110,000 planes. This was met by a general opening of fire from the Flemish-held positions. The Russian propaganda also claimed they would never be granted home leave, only their German officers, but Robert found out this was not true, as he actually was sent home for two weeks. After being deloused and issued a new, clean uniform and bread and sausage for the long train trip, he was also provided with a whole lot of papers and stamps, which he had to show several times to the ever inquisitive and unpopular Feldgendarmes. These officials with their typical gorget plate were always looking for deserters and caught many on the Eastern front, and were therefore aptly nicknamed 'die Kopfjägern', the headhunters or 'Kettenhunde', collar dogs (they were the same ones the Belgians referred to as 'Cognacs').

Back at the front Robert was slightly wounded when his company, commanded by Flemish Obersturmführer SS M. and supported by tanks, reconquered a position the Spanish Legion Azul had lost a few days before. For this feat of arms, the Flemish unit was mentioned in the communiqué of OKW, the German High Command, as was to happen at least twice more.

In another form of military collaboration a Flemish *Fabriekswacht*, a unit to guard factories, railway stations and bridges as well as farm crops against saboteurs, was set up under the command of a certain Poddevyn who was then assassinated by *Verzetstrijders* (resistance fighters) in October 1942. He was succeeded by Christiaan Turcksin and the name of the outfit changed to *Wachtbrigade* and then again to *Flakbrigade*. Their total number seems to have been around 6,000. Their uniform closely resembled that of the Luftwaffe and the plan was for them to man Flak guns. Some were killed by the Resistance while guarding a Luftwaffe base. They originated mainly from the VNV, with some from Verdinaso. They refused to take an oath of allegiance to Hitler and Turcksin seems to have refused to force draft 1,500 former reserve officers of the Belgian Army, as prompted by von Falkenhausen. According to some sources[72] Leopold III discreetly thanked him for it through an intermediary. Stationed in northern France, about half the force deserted in 1944 and the rest, some 2,500 men, were withdrawn to Germany. After the war a few of those with blood on their hands were executed, the rest were given prison sentences for treason.

Rex, Léon Degrelle and *Légion Wallonie*

If the Flemish SS wore a Flemish lion on their cuffs and would not have dreamed of wearing the hated Belgian tricolor, the Walloon SS on the contrary did so, and felt Belgian. The constant excuse made by Léon Degrelle for wearing the uniform of the SS was that by doing so and being seen by the Germans to have contributed to the extirpation of Bolshevism, Hitler would reward him politically by restoring the Greater Netherlands or the Burgundian States he dreamed of .[73] Whatever the promises made (or not made) by different German authorities like Hitler or Himmler to Flemish and Walloon leaders, they were to say the least vague, and it is far from certain that any of those wholly contradictory promises would have been honoured had they won the war. Indeed for Flanders to have been given independence from Belgium would have been absolutely irreconcilable with a restoration of the old Netherlands, which included Flanders, Wallonia and Holland as well as Luxembourg and northern France.

Born in Bouillon in the Ardennes into a Catholic family and with a French grandfather, Léon Degrelle became politically active when studying at Louvain's very ancient Catholic university. Hired by a religiously oriented publishing house called Christus Rex, he gradually worked his way to its top echelons, occasionally writing articles himself. The name Rex was thus adopted by a group within the traditional political Catholic Party, consisting of young men who gradually became more anti-establishment and were especially prone to denounce corrupt practices they said were part and parcel of the parliamentary regime. Support for them grew rapidly, since many people in the middle classes felt let down by the nineteenth-century style parliamentary system that had been unable to avoid the great financial crash of the early 1930s while, so they believed, the politicians lined their pockets. Though the economic credo of the

Rexists was extremely vague, their insistence on the denunciation of corruption scandals and advocacy of strong rule rather than the regime of politicians who, again and again, formed unstable, inefficient and short-lived governments, won them a resounding electoral victory in 1936. That year the Rexists took 21 seats in Parliament out of 212. The link with the Catholic Church, at that time very strong in Belgium, remained and many clerics expressed their sympathy, sometimes even wearing a little broom-shaped brooch on their cassocks, the household implement being the obvious means to 'sweep away corruption'.

At this point Degrelle, the undisputed and charismatic leader of Rex, who meanwhile had broken with the Catholic party, started making mistakes. He visited both Hitler and Mussolini whom he admired and got them to help him financially. By no means all of his supporters cared for these leaders, especially the Führer. In character with his boisterous, blustering style, Degrelle publicly boasted that Monsignor Van Roey, the Belgian Cardinal and Catholic Primate would support him in a coming by-election, where he was to stand against veteran politician Van Zeeland, the Prime Minister and a longtime prominent member of the Catholic Party. This was not entirely without basis, but was a silly thing to say openly because the senior Catholic in the land obviously could only support the established Catholic Party. So the ambitious but blundering Degrelle felt the full weight of Van Roey's subsequent denial and support for Van Zeeland, which struck him like the heavy blow of a crosier. As a result, Van Zeeland, enjoying the support of all the established parties, even the communists, thoroughly trounced Degrelle, winning 80 per cent of the votes. Again in the general election of 1939, his party suffered a crushing defeat, losing all but four of its seats in Parliament. As a result, at the outbreak of war, Rex was only a shadow of what it had been in the mid-1930s. So when Germany invaded in May 1940, after having first prudently condemned the invasion as a crime in his newspaper *Le Pays Réel* (obviously no one knew at first who was going to win and Rex had been an ardent supporter of the neutrality policy), Degrelle saw the momentous events of the early summer of that year as a new opportunity. This was after he was released from the detention camp in southern France, where the French police had locked him up after he had been delivered to them by their Belgian colleagues, as we have seen.

Having lost weight in jail, 'le beau Léon' (he had handsome features) began talking to Germans in authority, who at first had no real use for him and indeed even despised him as an opportunist, Goebbels forbidding any mention of him in the press at this early stage of the occupation.

Unlike Mussert in the Netherlands or Quisling in Norway, he was not put at the head of a collaborationist government, which in any event never materialized in Belgium, partly because the Germans realized it could not be done without the King, who remained on Belgian soil. Nor could Degrelle really see what he could do for the Germans. On 22 June 1941, Barbarossa, the German invasion of the Soviet Union changed all that, and he and about 750 of his followers asked to join the 'European crusade' against 'Judeo-Bolshevism' – they had been among his principal declared enemies – with the aim, as he himself explained in his writings, of ingratiating themselves with the Nazis. They were hoping a grateful, victorious Reich would accord Belgium very favourable treatment when peace eventually came. It should be mentioned that Degrelle and the men who joined him in wearing the German uniform did so under the express condition they would never have to fight against the Western Allies, a promise the Germans kept. At some point in the Reich's collapse the zealous *Gauleiter* of Kassel had sent Walloon recruits to fight the invading Americans but Degrelle managed to have them withdrawn in time.

Reading Léon Degrelle's *La Campagne de Russie* (see Bibliography) it is interesting to see how enormous courage, sacrifice and suffering can be expended in vain on a wrong cause. Writing in very florid French, the author, at first a simple private soldier in the Wehrmacht, marvels at the beauty of the flora and fauna of the Russian countryside, at the warmth of the Russian peasants who welcome them, ply them with food and flock to the orthodox religious services he has reintroduced, whilst noticing that portraits in uniform of the boys of the house who are serving in the Red Army hang in the *isbas* (wooden huts), alongside a picture of Hitler. He regretted the harshness with which some Germans stupidly treated these 'simple souls', who had welcomed those who had (temporarily) saved them from communism and blessed them and the black and white crosses painted on their tanks. (He also dwelled on the 'disgusting habits and lack of hygiene of some locals who relieve themselves anywhere'.) Fighting in the Caucasus Mountains, his unit takes enormous numbers of prisoners who, left starving by the Germans, take to eating rotting flesh from long-dead cows or even turn to cannibalism. On one occasion his fellow Walloon soldiers discover there has for some time been a cadaver in the well they have all been drinking from. All acquire persistent lice. He is harshly scornful of the Mongol, Kalmyk, Kirgiz and other Asiatic 'hordes' who fight in the Red Army and whose cruelty and barbarian habits he delights in describing. Fighting becomes severe in the Donetz region and a high proportion of his fellow Walloons are killed in action. Exhausted, the Légion Wallonie is reorganized and reinforced with 2,000 new recruits, including 200 French and some regular officers of the Belgian Army, freed from their Oflags (POW camps for officers). On the whole though, in proportion to their numbers, very few Belgian POWs joined him. About 800 Belgian workers, forcibly drafted into German industry, also volunteered after having been addressed by Degrelle. Because far fewer Flemings had been regular officers in the Belgian Army before the war, the Flemish SS were mostly commanded by Germans and resented it. On the other hand, Belgian French-speaking SS were commanded by compatriot officers who had usually been officers already. The Commanding Officer, 29-year-old SS Lieutenant Colonel (*Obersturmbannführer*) Lucien Lippert, had been first in his class at the Royal Military Academy in Brussels before the war. Another one, a former captain who had fought against the Germans at the Battle of the Lys, always exchanged his German steel helmet for a khaki Belgian army forage cap before going into action and was killed while wearing that headgear, in a Russian forest.

After a political meeting at the Brussels Palais des Sports the SS Sturmbrigade Wallonien entrained again in November 1943 to head East. There they saw outright Dantesque fighting when eleven German Divisions including the Walloon SS Brigade, were surrounded in the Ukraine because of an express order by Hitler, who forbade a retreat from a salient along the Dniepr River which Heeresgruppe Süd (Southern Army Group), commanded by von Manstein, had already (and more wisely) decided on. At the end of January 1944, Soviet General Zhukov sent two armies, commanded by Koniev and Vatutin, to encircle the salient around Khorsun, east of Tcherkassy, the town on the Dniepr River that would give its name to the bitter, terrible battle that followed. In minus 20°C the breakout from the Tcherkassy cauldron or pocket was made after three weeks of incredibly harsh fighting. Only about half of the surrounded Germans and Walloons manage to escape and only 630 out of the 1,700 Walloons who stood as the rearguard survived. Degrelle describes the prolonged and savage hand-to-hand fighting of the exhausted men, how Russian prisoners who had agreed to serve in the German Army turned coat again and led their compatriots against the German positions they knew well. How also, now the tide was turning, it became very difficult to take prisoners to interrogate and how Russian tanks deliberately crushed carts laden with wounded men under their tracks. Without bridging equipment the retreating Germans and Walloons had to swim through a half-frozen river with a strong current, under direct Russian fire. Lippert was killed by an explosive bullet in the chest. Degrelle, who had showed initiative and leadership in the retreat, was made *Obersturmbannführer* (Lieutenant Colonel) and given command of the Walloon Brigade. When the breakthrough column reached the German lines Hitler had him called to his wolf's lair in East Prussia, awarded him the Knight's Cross of the Iron Cross and had a conversation with him.

Hitler now gave orders that they should support Degrelle, 'the only useful Belgian'. Spurned at first, he had become a highly valuable propaganda asset for the Nazis, who could demonstrate that even in a time of declining fortunes, non-Germans supported them. His picture with the Iron Cross appeared on the cover of *Signal* and other German-controlled papers and the SS generals who were his superiors were given strict orders by Himmler to prevent him from taking risks. His motives were utterly to be condemned and his actions highly treasonable towards his country, which had been invaded and was being oppressed by the country he was now fighting for, yet it is undoubtedly true that Degrelle was competent in military terms and was both brave and very lucky. It has been said (though there is no proof) that Hitler remarked that if he had had a son he would have wanted him to be like Degrelle.

On 1 April 1944, there was a parade of the Walloon SS who had survived Tcherkassy through the streets of the Belgian capital, riding on Panzers that had been lent to them by a locally stationed unit – a unique event in any capital city in occupied Europe.

Coming back from Belgium where his brother had been assassinated by the *Résistance*, Degrelle was looking for his unit outside Dorpat (today called Tartu), the second city of Estonia, when he stumbled upon German auxiliary and administrative troops in full retreat in speeding lorries. The Soviet tanks and infantry had turned and overrun the weak defensive line protecting the city and were only 500m behind the fleeing Germans. Degrelle was well known by now to all in the German camp because of so much press exposure. Rallying a mix of Estonian soldiers and German cooks, medics and bureaucrats, he managed to control the panic and stem the Russian flow until German tanks and anti-tank guns arrived. For this new feat Hitler gave him the Oak Leaves for his Iron Cross. Several of his men were also decorated for bravery by the Germans, two of them, by an almost incredible coincidence, called Rommel and Montgomery!

Degrelle's private life was not unproblematic. While he was away fighting in Russia his wife had had an affair with an Austrian Luftwaffe officer stationed in Belgium. Passionate letters were exchanged, but when the cuckolded husband came home on leave his wife tearfully told him what had happened. Quite in character, Degrelle called the Austrian out, but duels had been forbidden by the Führer for the duration of the war. The Luftwaffe officer seemed to realize he had done wrong and spoke of suicide. How far he went with this plan is not clear, but some days later it was Degrelle who reported that the Austrian had indeed committed suicide and his body had been found. The German police, however, concluded from the multiple head and heart gunshot wounds that these could not possibly have been self-inflicted. Moreover, a man had been seen fleeing from the scene so it is probable someone in Degrelle's pay had 'suicided' the Austrian. The Nazi hierarchy in Berlin decided the whole affair would be better hushed up and so it was.

In the autumn of 1944, the SS Brigade Wallonie, once again decimated, was withdrawn and reorganized. Hundreds of Rexist party members who had fled to Germany with their families when Belgium was liberated, now joined up. The new 28th SS Division Wallonie was sent to the west, in anticipation of the German offensive which would eventually lead to the Battle of the Bulge. When the offensive started, Degrelle and his men (re)entered Belgium. They were not involved in fighting in their homeland, but were supposed to organize the 'peaceful' reoccupation and political reorganization of the country. However the military situation prevented them from leaving the small villages in the Ardennes where they had been confined. In his book Degrelle strenuously denies his men were involved in the massacres at Bande, which occurred during the brief reoccupation of a part of Belgium by the Germans. This however is disputed. The fact is that thirty-four young men, including two brothers and one boy of only seventeen were summarily executed in that village on 24 December 1944, by men wearing German uniforms – either Germans, Belgians or men of other nationalities speaking French, not German.[74] Canadian and British paratroopers, accompanied by a troop of Belgian SAS, found the bodies when they liberated the village for the second time. A second massacre of about twenty Belgian civilians took place outside the small city of Stavelot. This was clearly done by German SS, who were later identified and tried.

Degrelle, whilst paying homage to the tenacity and courage of the Allied soldiers, 'which any soldier would recognize', attributes the German defeat mainly to the massive bombings by Allied aircraft, which progressively made all roads in the Ardennes impassable for the German columns. These, having failed to conquer the Aachen–Liège and Trier–Arlon main roads at the outset, had to resort to ever smaller pathways in the thick pine-tree woods, considerably slowing their advance and especially their logistics. It is a fact that lack of fuel stopped the two main armoured thrusts towards Liège at La Gleize and towards the Meuse River at Celles, close to Dinant. And another fact, not mentioned by Degrelle, is that by denying access to a vital crossroads at Bastogne, the American 101st Airborne Division also considerably slowed the Germans and disturbed their plans and supplies.

Back in the east in early 1945, though realizing by now the war was lost, Degrelle's Walloons fought desperately in Pomerania, defending small villages against the overwhelmingly more numerous and better equipped Soviet Army. In his book he described how one of his platoons, not knowing a certain village had already been taken by the enemy, just marched through it in retreat with rifles slung over their shoulders, the Soviets not recognizing them in the darkness, while the blond German soldiers hanged as deserters from the girders of one of the bridges over the Oder River, swung gently in unison as the concussion of artillery fire reached the bodies. The Walloons fighting in the east were joined by Major Hellebaut. This Belgian officer joined the Walloon SS, rather surprisingly, at the time of the Normandy landings. His decision was the more remarkable in that both his father and grandfather had been Belgian generals and even ministers for war. Not expecting someone with such a background to volunteer to fight for Germany (and this in June 1944), one of his friends had told him in confidence he was a member of the Resistance. Upon hearing of Hellebaut's decision the friend in question of course feared the worst, fled from his home and went into hiding – however, Hellebaut did not betray him to his new masters. He went to fight on the Eastern Front and soon, bizarrely, would be entitled to wear an Iron Cross alongside the British Military Cross he had won in 1918. He was to be the last commander of the Walloon SS.

When German resistance completely collapsed, Degrelle and some of what was left of his men made their way to Denmark. He himself managed to take ship to Norway, which was still occupied, in a German naval minesweeper. There the local German commander put Armaments Minister's Albert Speer's personal plane at his disposal, to make good his escape.

According to Degrelle, out of a total of 6,000 who joined the Légion Wallonie under its different and successive names, 2,500 were killed, 80 per cent wounded and, of those who had joined at the very beginning only 3 men survived, including he himself. He was wounded five times.

Spending most of his time in the east, Degrelle had progressively lost interest in Rex, the party he had founded, and staked more and more on the Légion Wallonie, which he hoped to use for his own political ends after the war and which was transferred from the Wehrmacht to the SS in June 1943, a sign of Degrelle's gradual but irreversible evolution towards total collaboration. The party declined and the creed of the Rexists was transformed from one of Belgian unitary nationalism, with a strong Catholic input, to outright adherence to Nazism and the bizarre idea that the Walloons were a sort of lost tribe of the Germanic nation and that their only hope lay in a German victory. Having entered on this path by concluding one of his speeches with a loud 'Heil Hitler!' in January 1941, by 1943 Degrelle was advocating outright annexation of Wallonia into the Reich – which in effect meant the whole country, since Flanders would obviously not be left out, and thus the disappearance of Belgium as an independent state. This when the eventual defeat of the Reich appeared ever more probable! In fact it was Degrelle himself who asked Himmler for the incorporation of his soldiers into the SS. Yet, according to his best biographer, Degrelle never learned to speak German.[75]

Back in Belgium, during Degrelle's long absences his deputies steered the party uneasily along the lines he had defined, and when between the end of 1943 and the summer of 1944 it became obvious to all that an Allied landing in north-west Europe would precede a German defeat, the situation in Belgium became downright chaotic. This was especially the case in Wallonia, where attempts at the lives of Rexist officeholders, usually by communist inspired *résistants*, were answered with reprisals by them often on persons who were not directly involved like François Bovesse, a respected former justice minister, or like the banker Galopin. The Germans also started executing Belgian hostages in reprisal for the assassination of Rexists. Support for the latter dwindled, either because everybody could see the writing on the wall or because of the erratic course the party had taken and the outright support for Hitler which not everybody approved of.

When he heard of Hitler's death, Degrelle says in his book, he thought of the pure, frank look in the leader's eyes, his simplicity, intelligence and strength, as well as the sadness he was sure all Germans felt at the news and how faithful they had all remained to him to the end. Not a word of criticism is there for a man who had brought untold suffering and destruction to his own people as well as to the whole of Europe. Just as remarkably the word 'Jew' does not appear a single time in Degrelle's memoirs, except in reference to a political commissar whose testament, found on his dead body in Ukraine states that 'being Jewish, he wanted to avenge the Jews'. Degrelle's only comment is simply that 'men's passions know no limits'.

Chapter 8

A tale of two trains:
The fate of the Jews in Belgium

Rounding up and deportation of Jews

It is fair to say there has been less anti-Semitism in Belgium in the last two centuries than in most other European countries. It would be inaccurate to state there has been none. The hitherto small Jewish community started growing in the nineteenth century with immigration from Eastern Europe, and communities developed mainly in Antwerp and Brussels with smaller ones in Liège and Charleroi. The Antwerp Jews, many of them involved in the diamond business, were usually more religious and the Brussels community more secular, though a large synagogue was inaugurated in central Brussels in 1878 and visited by King Léopold II, who had many Jews among his close associates and friends. Then, Jews attained prominence in all walks of life, the academic and judiciary worlds, in banking, business, the arts, politics, and so on. Even in a country where pre-Vatican II Council conservative Catholicism was prevalent indeed, it was very rare that being Jewish was held or used against anyone and there certainly was nothing comparable to the Dreyfus affair which rocked France during these years, or the anti-Semitism then prevailing in the Austro-Hungarian Empire, let alone in pogrom-prone Tsarist Russia. Two Belgian Jewish generals held senior commands during the First World War. When in 1939 Nazi minister Goebbels sought a propaganda coup, by making the liner *Saint Louis* go from port to port (including in the United States) without their German Jewish passengers being permitted to land anywhere, it was ultimately in Antwerp that the ship was allowed to dock. A quarter of the Jewish passengers were allowed to stay in Belgium. Tragically, this was exactly a year before the German invasion and most of them eventually ended up in extermination camps.

During the 1930s, large numbers of Jews fleeing Nazi and Polish anti-Semitism sought refuge in Belgium and this was the occasion of the only serious upsurge of anti-Semitism. It came from one sector of Belgian public opinion, influenced by the extreme right movements then thriving in France and Germany which had amalgamated Jews and communism, their worst enemies. 'Judeo-bolshevism' was a concept largely held in Europe at that time, even in England among Mosley's followers, and certainly by some Flemish nationalists who had studied in Germany. General Bernheim, who had commanded one of the six Belgian Infantry divisions at the end of the First World War, was made president of the Belgian Jewish *Consistoire* to try to remedy this by reminding everyone that the Belgian Jews had done their patriotic duty during the late conflict. In 1939 the Belgian budget, even though shorn of many other expenses because of the very heavy military effort, included a substantial sum to help the 10,000 destitute Jews in Belgium at the time, mostly refugees from Germany, Austria and Poland.

The 6 million European Jews who were killed by the Nazis during the Second World War included about 25,000 from Belgium, of whom half were Belgian nationals and half were Jewish refugees who had come to Belgium from other countries. Against all, the German occupiers were not slow in implementing their anti-Semitic policies. First they tried to have all Jews expelled from the public services, but being told this was clearly against the Belgian Constitution, which expressly forbade discrimination on the basis of race or religion, they progressively resorted to more radical means. By June 1941, Jewish shops were to be clearly advertised as such, Jews could no longer sit on the boards of businesses, and they were even told to hand in their radio sets. They were to live only in four designated cities where the largest communities already were, and a curfew was imposed exclusively for Jews. Compulsory wearing of the yellow Star of David was introduced one year later but Queen Elisabeth managed to gain an exemption for Belgian Jews who had served in the armed forces.[76] The Brussels burgomasters and aldermen having refused to distribute the fabric stars, and the occupiers unwilling to dismiss them all, it was eventually the *Kommandanturen*, the German military local commanders, who had to do so. The compulsory wearing of these symbols had a strong impact on public opinion and if it was the Germans' idea thus to hold the Jews up for public opprobrium, they certainly failed: one woman remarked that since she had been wearing her star, people had started giving up their seats to her on trams, something that had never happened to her before!

Synagogues were closed down and the Germans took control of some Jewish-owned assets including luxury accommodation, works of art, and bank accounts. Two Belgian banks, Philippson and Lambert, were owned by Jewish families. The Philippson family entrusted the business to an authorized representative, Jean Degroof, who ran it during the occupation. It is still known today as Banque Degroof. Banque Lambert was sequestrated by the Germans. The chairman of the board, Baroness Lambert resided in the UK during the war and later in the US. The bank restarted after the war but was later merged with others.

From August to October 1942 most Jews were systematically arrested and after a variable time in transit at a central collection point at the Dossin Barracks, Mechelen,[77] a city between Brussels and Antwerp, they were deported by successive trains to Auschwitz-Birkenau.

At the Dossin Barracks a ragdoll can be seen in the exhibition. It belonged to Charlotte Hamburger, who was born in Amsterdam in 1907 and moved to Antwerp with her parents. She married a non-Jew, Louis De Houwer in 1937 and became a Belgian citizen. Little Albertine was born to them. Both were active in the Front de l'Indépendance and were caught in 1942. Louis was executed at Fort Breendonk. Charlotte, who was pregnant when arrested, made the little doll herself in jail before being taken to Mechelen and there being put on a train to Auschwitz in August 1942. She was probably gassed on arrival. Her daughter Albertine escaped being deported and survived the war.

In another glass case one can see, surprisingly, a German Iron Cross Second Class medal. It was given for acts of bravery and had been awarded to a Jewish German Max Cohen, fighting for his country in the First World War – an example of how integrated the Jews were in pre-Nazi Germany. Cohen received another medal, which can also be seen, sent to him in 1935 for his service as a front veteran, in the name of the Führer and Chancellor of the Reich, Adolf Hitler! In 1938 he fled to Belgium from Lower Saxony, after practically all he owned had been confiscated before he was allowed to leave with his family. Almost destitute, he found work in a leather factory. In June 1943, his whole family was taken to the Dossin barracks and his medals were taken away, before the family were all put on Train XXI to Auschwitz. None survived.

Belgian help in rounding up the Jews came in many forms. As early as April 1941 a pogrom took place in Antwerp, a city where the largest and most visible Jewish community lived, during which a synagogue was sacked. This was perpetrated by extreme nationalist Flemings among whom anti-Semitism was rampant, but it was instigated by the Germans, as evidenced by the presence of a filming crew of the *Propaganda Staffel* being on hand to record and publicize the event, certainly no coincidence.

When the Germans demanded the lists of Jews from the local regis-
ters, most city administrations refused, notably those in Brussels, again
arguing that this would be against the Belgian Constitution. But some
cooperated. When the Germans asked local police to help to arrest Jews
who had not presented themselves voluntarily, as decreed, most police
forces would not, but again there were some who did, notoriously the
Antwerp police force. But then again some Jewish families were saved
when individual policemen came to them discreetly the night before, to
warn them to get away before they arrived next morning with their colleagues and superiors. One Antwerp policeman refused outright to par-
ticipate and as a result lost three days' leave and was given a reprimand.

The Belgian government officially recognized in 2005 that 'the fact that
Belgian citizens collaborated with the occupying forces and played a part
in that horrific episode remains a blemish on the country's national record
that no one can erase.' In 2007 the then Burgomaster of Antwerp officially
apologized for the help the police had given to the Germans.

Efforts to save Jews
Notwithstanding these incidents of collaboration, Belgium was one of the
few countries occupied by Nazi Germany where a majority of the Jews
(about 56 per cent) who were resident when the occupation began, escaped
deportation and annihilation mainly thanks to the help and devotion of
many Belgians. Yad Vashem, the official Israeli institution studying
the Holocaust, following strict criteria has identified over 1,500 Belgian
'Righteous among the Nations', mostly Belgian nationals or others who
were active in Belgium (out of a total of 20,000 for the whole of Europe)
and who were honoured thus for having saved one or more Jewish people.
Prominent among them was the mother of King Léopold III, Queen
Elisabeth, widow of King Albert I, one of the very few members of a royal
family in Europe to openly intervene on behalf of Jews,[78] whose successful intercessions with the German military command, indeed with Hitler
himself, resulted in several hundred Jews, mostly of Belgian nationality,
being released after arrest and saved, though some were rearrested and
deported later.

Numerous Catholic priests and nuns hid and helped Jews out of
Christian mercy, as we shall see, as did families of the Belgian nobility
inspired by a sense of duty. Groups led by political, humanitarian or social
ideals, clandestine Jewish groups and ordinary people from all walks of
life listened to the voice of their conscience and goodness of their heart
and acted accordingly. Though, unlike in Eastern Europe there was no

specific law against it or official punishment for hiding Jews, being found to have done so could, according to the circumstances bring dire consequences, like being jailed as a hostage, sent arbitrarily to a concentration camp or even worse.

Feeding hidden and therefore undocumented Jews was a problem, in part solved by the black market. The different movements in the Belgian Resistance also often provided them with money or counterfeit ration coupons. In the case of children taken into homes for orphans or boarding schools, the rations were just spread a bit thinner. Some of these institutions were in the countryside and grew their own vegetables and so on, which helped.

Several of those deemed Righteous among the Nations were leaders of the Catholic or Protestant Churches, such as the bishop of Liège, Monsignor Kerkhofs, who urged the clerics in his diocese to save Jews from deportation. The Cantor and leader of the Liège Jewish community and his family sought refuge at the residence of the prelate, who welcomed him as a colleague and gave his family shelter until suitable hiding places could be found, to which he drove them himself. The Cantor stayed for a while and became his 'secretary'. Father Joseph Peeters, who followed Mgr Kerkhofs' prompting, hid Jews and forged papers but was eventually betrayed and executed by the Germans at the Liège Citadel in August 1943. Father Reynders (who was known in religious circles as Dom Bruno) was a Benedictine monk and a priest who sheltered or found shelters for literally hundreds of Jewish children, more often than not taking them there personally. The case of Father Hubert Célis, who was also a padre in the Belgian Army, is quite astounding: arrested for hiding pilots and Resistance fighters as well as Jews, he was taken before a German interrogator. With considerable *chutzpah* he readily admitted to the last of the 'offences' so as to give credibility to his denial of the others. He then asked the interrogator if he was a Catholic. On hearing this was the case he progressively inverted their roles, appealing to the German's Christian beliefs, reminding him there was no law in Belgium against sheltering people or helping Jews, and eventually talking the man into releasing him!

Count René de Liedekerke and his wife (née the Countess d'Oultremont) sheltered hundreds of needy children at their château, within the network of the Léopold III camps set up for that purpose in various parts of the country. Among them were a number of Jewish children and they later raised some of them as their own after hearing their parents had not come back from the extermination camps. Another member of the Belgian aristocracy, Prince Eugène de Ligne and his wife née de Noailles, took in Jews at their imposing and beautiful Château de Beloeil outside Tournai, which they had turned into a shelter for all those hunted by the Germans. They made sure the children received proper education and healthcare, calling upon the King's personal doctor when they fell ill.

René Ransquin was a high-ranking police officer in Brussels. Together with a Polish Jew who had been an officer in his country's army they forged papers for other Polish Jews, combining their respective skills. Two very senior civil servants in the justice ministry were also recognized as Righteous among the Nations, and, surprisingly, their counterpart in the German administration Wilhelm Baron von Hahn assisted in releasing hundreds of detained Jews.

Also named were some intrepid women like the remarkable Yvonne Nèvejean. Few did as much as she in finding shelters for a huge numbers of Jewish children, using her position as head of the Oeuvre Nationale de l'Enfance (National Children's Welfare). It has been estimated that she and her helpers may have saved between 3,000 and 4,000 children, a feat not many could boast of in history. When the Germans raided a Jewish children's home in October 1942, she persuaded Queen Elisabeth, the Queen Mother of Belgium (who was German born), to intervene with Military Governor von Falkenhausen on their behalf and the children were released. She was active at fundraising to pay for the children's upkeep and also managed to have the London government in exile send money clandestinely. On one of these occasions the following incident took place. Allowed by a special *Ausweis* (permit) to drive about at night because of her official activities at the Oeuvre Nationale de l'Enfance which served as her cover, she went to a road close to Bruges to pick up a Belgian who had been parachuted in from England with diamonds to buy back arrested Jews and buy food for hidden children. She concealed parachutist Jean Stasse under a blanket in the back of the car and was on the way back, when from a distance she saw the blue flashlights of German Feldgendarmes manning a checkpoint. She stopped right there, told her passenger to hide in the bushes and drove on. The German police looked in the now empty car and asked her if she had seen any 'parachute terrorists'. She said no but added she was very scared of 'saboteurs' when driving at night. Could they hang on a minute while she drove back a few metres and went behind a bush to satisfy nature's call? On hearing they would she went back and retrieved her passenger and the unsuspecting Germans even provided her (or rather them) with a motorcycle escort all the way to Bruges! Rumour spread by word of mouth about what she was doing and Jews began to seek her out and ask her to save at least their children, so she had the delicate and dangerous task of finding families who would welcome them or looking for other hiding places. Madame Nèvejean, who died in 1987 and probably also worked for British Intelligence during the war, had done an internship in Berlin before the war with the German Nazi Girls' Association (Bund Deutscher Mädel). She got to know high-ranking SS officers at that time, which perhaps saved her when she was called in under suspicion of hiding Jews. The Belgian Post Office made a special stamp bearing her image, after she died.

Many Jews were also hidden and saved by clandestine organizations linked to the socialist or communist parties, or Jewish underground groups or organizations like the Comité de Défense des Juifs (CDJ). This organization, close to the Front de l'Indépendance and the communists and where Andrée Geulen, Fela Perelman and Yvonne Jospa all worked, managed to feed about 5,000 Jews in hiding. It sent a non-Jewish sociologist and professor at Louvain Catholic University, Victor Martin, to Eastern Europe to discover what was really happening to the deported Jews. Martin did indeed find out and report the truth, venturing within a short distance of Auschwitz. The CDJ enjoyed excellent relations with the Belgian Catholic hierarchy, including those like Mgr Kerchofs who helped them considerably, especially in saving Jewish children.

In many cases, Jewish parents had to part with their children for one reason or another and entrust them to non-Jewish families, often complete strangers. In other cases, the parents had been arrested but the children had escaped. Many of these *enfants cachés* (hidden children) went to Catholic boarding schools for boys or girls, or camps in the countryside organized by charitable organizations for the benefit of urban children. Usually only the abbot or mother superior, headmaster/headmistress, or the camp manager knew exactly who they were, even if others had their suspicions. Denunciations occurred but were rare. Though the extent of the Holocaust was not known at the time there were rumours and deportations were widely known as fact. Very few approved of what the Nazis were doing to obviously innocent people, let alone children, even if many or most looked the other way.

After the war another problem crept up as to the future of these children. In some cases they were badly treated, indeed even abused by their foster parents or used as cheap servants. But in most recorded cases the exact opposite was true. The luckier ones went back to their original families after the war, but some of these children had never known or had only vague memories of their real parents. In many cases a bond of affection had formed with the adoptive parents and parting was difficult if not heart breaking ... In other cases the parents did not come back to claim them. Many of these orphans were taken to Israel by the agents of the immigration agencies of the fledgling Israeli State.

Often, 'hidden' children renewed contact with their saviours after the war and showed their gratitude.[79] One Israeli general I interviewed spoke of going back to Antwerp many years after the war, ringing the doorbell at the house of the family where he had found shelter as a little boy, everyone pretending at the time he was just one of the sons of the house, recognizing his 'sister' at first sight and falling into her arms. Many recalled having to strictly observe the Catholic religious rites (Sunday mass, communion and so on) so as not to arouse suspicion. Though many forged baptism certificates were issued, the Cardinal Archbishop of Belgium, Mgr Van Roey, who when consulted on individual cases approved of giving shelter to Jews, gave strict instructions that in no case were these children to be baptized or otherwise forcibly converted, though there were some attempts at this. Indeed, in some cases Christians taught the children the rudiments of the Hebrew language, Jewish religion, the history of the Jewish people, and so on.

The official report on Belgium published by Yad Vashem in 2005,[80] in which the known individual cases are related, also writes, 'It is fair to say [...] that the majority of the Jews who survived the Nazi occupation in Belgium did so thanks to the devotion of [those] many individuals.' It is impossible to recall all the individual cases and those interested should consult this publication, which makes fascinating reading.[81]

One case concerning the Rosenfeld family, as personally related to the author by a friend now living in Brazil and which follows here, can serve as a good example:

My parents had been married for a year when war came to Belgium in 1940. I was born on February 16, 1941. My father had German nationality and lived in Belgium representing German firms. My mother became German by marriage. In May 1940, when the Nazis invaded my father was arrested by the Belgian authorities as an enemy citizen and sent to France in a prison camp. In October he was transferred to Gurs (Basses Pyrenées), where he managed to escape from in May 1941 and came back to Belgium. By the time he escaped only the Jews were still detained in Gurs because the non-Jews had been freed in accordance with the armistice agreement signed between France and Germany. All the Jewish inmates were later sent to extermination camps.

Meanwhile, my mother, grandmother and a sister of my grandmother, all with German nationality had to register at the Jewish registry the Germans had instituted. In April 1942, a German decree forbade Jews to work in independent businesses and my parents decided to go underground and live at the home of an old lady, Mrs Van Melle, 32 Rue du Bourgmestre in Brussels. They survived by selling belts they manufactured clandestinely. Leather had to be found on the black market as well as clients for the finished belts. No easy task.

There are two reasons why my family managed to survive during the war in Belgium. The first was the decision of my parents to go into hiding. Such a decision was not easy to take because without contacts or funds, speaking bad French or with a strong foreign accent meant you had to trust people you didn't know with your lives, and live with the danger of being denounced and caught with tragic consequences. My mother told of a cousin who had gone through a fake conversion to Catholicism and to whom she confided of her intention to go into hiding. Her answer was: 'What worse fate can happen to us than being sent to a working camp?' Neither her husband nor she came back from Auschwitz. The second reason was the extraordinary support, both moral and material we got from the Belgian population. To these factors a dose of luck should be added.

Mrs Van Melle, with whom we were hiding, allowed from time to time Resistance fighters or other persons sought by the Germans, to take refuge at her house. Because of this, two members of a collaborators' militia invaded her house one day. The person they were looking for wasn't there but instead they stumbled upon a complete Jewish family! Very few people knew where we were hiding but by sheer luck, a friend, a Monsieur Moreels, who was a butcher, had come to visit us that day. I can remember my father telling me Moreels just bought off the two collaborators for 7,000 Francs, quite a sum at the time. I have kept a picture of Moreels ever since. However our hiding place was now compromised and we had to leave at once.

My parents wanted to move away to the Ardennes but it was dangerous to do so without fake papers because the Germans checked passengers at railway stations and on trains. Thanks to a certain Lommel, who worked as a clerk at Brussels Town Hall we got the necessary fake documents. My father became Pierre Alphonse

Speeckaert, my mother Mariette Van Daelen-Speeckaert and I changed my name to Jean-Michel Joseph Marie Speeckaert. In our wedding booklet an elder sister was also mentioned, because the document wasn't really a fake but a real wedding booklet the rightful owner had forgotten at the registrar's office and Lommel doctored it to add a boy my age.

It was a Catholic organization who arranged for us to reside in Gembes, a village in the Ardennes, under our new civil status. The tip about this organization had been given to us by a friend already detained at the Dossin Barracks and even from inside he had managed to let us know about it. Unfortunately, he himself did not profit from it and did not return from Auschwitz.

Once settled in at that village and like they had in Brussels, my parents tried to work to make a living. My mother would spin wool and barter a kilo of spun wool for a kilo of flour. The village people were very nice to us and knew of our problems. The local butcher would always add a few marrowbones to the little meat we could buy, so we could put them in our soup. Farmers would sell us milk at very cheap prices. We got the same ration of firewood as the locals. I went to the village school and it was in fact the first time I ever saw children my own age. There is absolutely no doubt that all of the 300 inhabitants of the village as well as most people of the neighbouring villages knew exactly who we were. After the war we used to go back there for our holidays and I was nicknamed 'Jean-Jean amon les Juifs' (Jean-Jean from among the Jews). When the war was over we moved back to Brussels and my father went to the local police station to get proper papers, with a written statement signed by Mrs Van Melle that we had resided with her. When everything was in order and my father was about to leave the head constable called him into his office and told him, 'We at the police station here knew all along you were hiding there.'

The tales of two trains also merit special mention:

Train XX

The deportations out of the Dossin Barracks soon became known to various Resistance movements. Some studied the feasibility of an attack on a train but rejected the idea as too risky. So three brave, one could say foolhardy young men decided to take matters into their own hands and were allowed to do so by the leader of Groupe G, who provided them with a single pistol and seven rounds, to have a go. On 19 April 1943, by coincidence the same day the Warsaw ghetto revolt started, Train XX was slowly being pulled by its steam locomotive up a hill near the village of Bootmeerbeke, not far from Brussels, on its way to Germany. The conductor saw a red light and immediately stopped. He was later to say he realized at once it could only be a fake, because he knew there never had been lights at that spot. It was a flashlight being shined through a red rag. As the convoy screeched to a halt, Robert Maistriau, Jean Franklemon and George Livschitz, the only Jew of the three, jumped up to the locked wagons, started prying them open and yelled at the passengers to quickly get out. To their consternation most passengers were unsure, and only 231 Jews (one in seven) had saved themselves by the time the German escorts realized what was going on and started firing, far fewer than would have been possible. Some were recaptured but most made it to safety, provided in some cases with a small sum of money by their intrepid saviours (who got away themselves) so as to be able to survive. The train resumed its fateful journey and most of the occupants were gassed immediately after arriving at Auschwitz. The attack on Train XX, with just a single firearm, was the only such case in Europe and has inspired at least two films. George ('Youra') Livshitz, a doctor and undoubtedly a brave young man, went on fighting Nazism, was later betrayed in unrelated circumstances by a Russian posing as a fellow *Résistant*, managed to escape by wounding a guard, was betrayed and arrested again and at last executed at the Tir National shooting range in Brussels. His last letter to his parents was in recent times displayed at Fort Breendonk. His brother met the same fate.

The last 'phantom' train
By September 1944, the Nazis had managed to round up most of the Jews in Belgium that they could find, and these had already been sent to their deaths. With the Allies fast approaching, the SS who had now replaced the military government decided to load a train with about 1,500 Resistance fighters, Jews who for one reason or another had not yet been deported and other persons they had detained and whom they now gathered from jails in Brussels, Mons, Tournai and even Lille in northern France. The plan was to send them in one go to Germany before retreating. The train duly departed but never made it to the German border as it was successfully stalled by railway workers, who sent it back and forth from station to station under different pretexts, like lack of coal, disruption of the lines, faulty equipment, (real) red lights turned on, etc. Eventually the train was abandoned in a Brussels station by the Germans, who

panicked and fled, and it was taken into the protection of diplomats of neutral countries until the Allies arrived. All those on board were saved, among them a member of the Comet line.

Conclusion

Of the 25,257 Jews, together with 351 gypsies, sent from Belgium to the extermination camps, mainly Auschwitz, between August 1942 and July 1944 in 28 trains, only 1,200 survived. Among the Belgian Resistance fighters who were killed or executed were 244 Jews.

The exact number of persons involved with saving Jews in Belgium will never be known exactly. It is difficult to compare with the situation in the neighbouring countries as circumstances (these could include the existence of a government or not and its attitude towards the Jews, what percentage of the Jews were citizens of the country, were integrated and knew people who might help them as compared to recent refugees who often did not master the local language, closeness to neutral countries like Spain, Switzerland or Sweden and so on) were variable and certainly very different in Eastern Europe. In Belgium, unlike France for example, there was no legal government in place locally and the civil servants or police were, on the whole far less compliant than in France in these matters. Yet the percentage of Jews saved in the Netherlands, where a very large majority were from families long established in the country and holding citizenship, was much lower (24 per cent) than in Belgium (56 per cent), though in France survival was higher still (76 per cent). There, the proportion of Jews who were recent immigrants was far greater than that of Jewish families who had been in France for several generations, but other factors came into play, like the fact that part of France was not occupied until November 1942, also the particular cases of the large Jewish communities in Alsace and North Africa, and so on. The record survival rate as is well known, was in Denmark, where almost all of the circa 6,000 Jews in the country were shipped by the Resistance on a single night, in dozens of boats, across the strait and into neutral Sweden. This aspect of the Holocaust has been studied in depth by Yad Vashem.

Chapter 9

Liberation

There exists an abundant literature on the campaign of the Allied armies led by Eisenhower, Montgomery and Bradley in north-west Europe from June 1944 until the end of the war. This includes the liberation of Belgium. It seems therefore superfluous to dwell on that campaign as a whole, so what follows focuses rather on aspects of the liberation of Belgium that are less known.

Chaos before Liberation
In the period between the German withdrawal (or just before it) and the arrival of the Allied troops, resistance activity took many forms, some far from pretty, like the hunt for Rexists, of whom about 700 were killed, sometimes with their families, and other collaborators, or the shooting dead of women who had slept with Germans and even, in some cases outright banditry, like kidnapping for ransom. These actions were in many cases as foolish and useless as they were cruel, sometimes targeting people who had not collaborated in any way. Coupled with reprisals, the situation degenerated into a small civil war in the Flemish province of Limburg which left tens if not hundreds dead on both sides. One senseless example took place on 21 August 1944, when three men invaded the house of a Doctor Neven, living in a village in Limburg, who had never been known for German sympathies. They threw the patients out including the one he was examining, took him and his wife to the courtyard and summarily executed them. The cleaning woman was killed by a ricochet bullet.The perpetrators fled to Liège where they probably had come from, passing a German checkpoint with fake papers. About 15,000 people fled from Flanders to Germany.

Things were no different in Wallonia.The assassination of the Rexist burgomaster of Charleroi, with his wife and son, caused one of the worst outrages: Rexists from Brussels came down to avenge this, rounded up nineteen ordinary citizens including doctors, lawyers and pensioners, one priest and several women, and summarily shot them at Courcelles on seventeen and 18 August 1944. In 1947, twenty-seven Rexists were executed for their part in this massacre.

Arrival of the Allied troops
Severe bombing of transport infrastructure by the Allies caused serious loss of life during the spring of 1944, which some estimates have placed as high as 10,000 people. On 2 September, the first Allied troops crossed the French–Belgian border and on 4 September the Irish Guards entered Brussels, followed by the Piron Infantry Brigade which had been reassembled for the purpose, the armoured squadron, who were already outside Brussels waiting for the rest. The Palais de Justice, a famous Brussels landmark, was set on fire by the retreating Germans but otherwise the Belgian capital was spared serious destruction. General Crerar's Canadians conquered the First World War battlefields in west Flanders and liberated Bruges and most of that region on 12 September,[82] whilst a Polish armoured unit under their command was the first to enter Ypres. Everywhere the Allies were given a rapturous welcome. Between 6 and 12 September a German paratroop unit specially sent in from Germany made a stand at Hechtel in north-east Belgium, to block the road to the Dutch city of Nijmegen, and the Irish Guards had to turn the enemy, who also executed 36 Belgian civilians without trial. US troops under Bradley liberated most of Wallonia. The XXXth British Corps fought its way into Antwerp and then had to fight the German XVth Army which was still occupying the Island of Walcheren, which meant that the capture of Antwerp intact was useless as the ships sailing up the Scheldt River to that port still had to run the gauntlet of German artillery on the northern bank. General Brian Horrocks, general officer in command of XXXth Corps candidly admits in his memoirs: 'It never entered my head that the Scheldt estuary would be mined and that we would not be able to use Antwerp until the channel had been swept and the Germans cleared from the coastlines on either sides ... Napoleon would, no doubt, have realized these things, but Horrocks didn't.'[83]

After the ill-fated battle for Arnhem the Allies stopped, unable to cross all three of the large rivers that flow through the Netherlands to the sea. Thus the stage was set for Battle of the Bulge: the British and Canadians to the north, that is northern Belgium, and the southern Netherlands and the Americans to the south, all the way to the Swiss border, with a French contingent in their midst in a wide arc roughly following the Rhine. The strong offensive the Germans unleashed on 16 December had as its principal objective the reconquest of the valuable port of Antwerp. The principal effort led by a strong armoured column under command of Lieutenant Colonel SS Peiper and supported by parachute drops, was not towards Bastogne and the south-west but descending the Amblève and

Ourthe River valleys north-west towards Huy and Liège, hoping to capture the Meuse bridges there. This was in fact meant to be the main German thrust, and behind Peiper the whole 6th Panzer Army (Sepp Dietrich) was supposed to follow. However, this attack petered out because Peiper's men ran out of fuel. They were supported by the new super heavy Königstiger tanks, one of which still stands at La Gleize village, which is as far as Peiper got. There they were surrounded and stopped by the tenacious resistance of the Americans. Further south, the German attack by the 5th Panzer Army (von Manteuffel) was more successful in the axis from Dasburg at the Luxembourg–Germany border to Bastogne and the Meuse River bridges at Dinant. But unlike in 1940 the Panzers never arrived at the banks of that river, reaching only the village of Celles, some 10km short. A German Panther tank still stands there. And a Sherman appropriately stands on the main General McAuliffe Square of Bastogne, heroically defended by the 101st Airborne, trucked in just before the town was encircled by the Germans, until relieved by Patton's troops at 1600hrs on Boxing Day 1944.

The fighting was bitter, like the cold. American author John Toland wrote that after Peiper's men had massacred 125 American prisoners (and some Belgian civilians as well) at Malmédy, infuriated US troops rarely took prisoners and at Chenogne 60 Germans were summarily executed after surrendering. The Belgian civilians also paid a price. The Belgian towns of Malmédy and Saint Vith, annexed by Germany in 1940, were heavily bombed by the US Army Air Corps with heavy loss of life. The latter was 95 per cent destroyed. When Stavelot and Bande were occupied again by the Germans during their offensive, civilians were massacred. Belgian SS men were blamed for the Bande outrage.

During and after the Battle of the Bulge, about 1,500 V-1s and V-2s fell on Liège and Antwerp without causing the serious disruption of the Allied logistics intended, but resulting in hundreds of civilian casualties in both cities.

Raymond V. was given a few days leave and rushed to Bruges to see his mother and brothers for the first time in years. The Germans, however, still held Bruges and the Canadian officer he spoke to said that a large-scale artillery bombardment on the city would take place next morning to 'soften' them in preparation for an attack. He told him he hoped his family would be spared but it was likely that not much would be left of the city. Fortunately, the Germans withdrew during the night and the Canadians entered without firing a shot, to Raymond V.'s immense relief. His family was quite surprised to see him in British uniform.

His mother and friends had spent the night sewing together British and American flags which now hung from the windows. The family silver that had been buried in the garden was dug up, as was Berthe's journal from the First World War occupation, which contained very unpleasant comments about the Germans.

The Belgian Brigade in action from Normandy to Germany

The Belgian Brigade, 'over trained' and by now with excellent morale was very eager to go into combat in early June 1944, but had to wait in growing frustration during the weeks immediately following D-Day. Finally, marching orders to the Tilbury embarkation camp and port arrived and in the first days of August pay was no longer received in sterling but in French francs, a sure sign of what was coming. At the very last moment, at Hildersham outside Cambridge, American-built Staghound armoured cars were added to their inventory and these each packed a powerful punch of two .50in. anti-aircraft machine guns, rendering the old Beccles AA guns the Belgians were equipped with completely superfluous. Not knowing what else to do with them, the Belgians buried them on the grounds of the château where they were billeted. (They might still be there.)

On 7 and 8 August, the 2,500 Belgians were landed from a Liberty Ship at Gold Beach and only days later were in action in northern Normandy, hugging the coast towards Le Havre.

The armoured reconnaissance squadron, equipped with Daimler Mk 1 armoured cars, Daimler Scout cars and jeeps transporting the 'winklers', commanded by Major de Selliers de Moranville was placed under command of the British 6th Airborne Division to act as its Recce unit, a task normally entrusted to three full squadrons.

Raymond V. was one of the 'winklers', the foot soldiers transported in two jeeps driven between the two scout cars and two armoured cars of a troop and tasked to disembark, cover the armoured cars against enemy anti-tank weapons with their small arms and to extend observations to places off road or beyond the reach of the vehicles. He belonged to the 2nd Troop of the armoured squadron, under command of Lieutenant Dewandre.

Late August brought rain and drizzle and more often than not their vehicles became bogged in mud, while mosquitos were a constant nuisance. The winklers from the whole squadron were sometimes regrouped together and told to reconnoitre a farm or wood. In one such instance, at the large Buisson Farm they had just moved into, Raymond V. fired his Bren gun through a window, then, as trained, withdrew inside. At that precise moment a burst of enemy machine-gun fire spattered the wall behind him, missing him by inches. He was later slightly wounded when a small piece of shrapnel hit him in the chin.

In Normandy some farmers were slightly hostile because of the destruction and slaughter of their cows the invasion brought with it, but usually the Belgians were plied with fresh eggs and calvados, the local liquor made with apples. The first prisoners were taken during the last days of August. A Polish deserter from the Wehrmacht gave useful information, and a *Feldwebel* (senior NCO) was bicycling down a road with his rifle carelessly slung over his shoulder when suddenly, coming round a bend, he found two Lee Enfield rifles pointed directly at his stomach. Nothing useful could be pried from this fellow, who was angry and dismayed at having been taken prisoner in such a stupid way. Others, led to expect by Nazi propaganda that they would be shot on the spot, began crying, offered their watches and wedding rings and showed pictures of their children, not realizing the great bursts of laughter from the Belgians did not mean there was anything more sinister in store for them than being put on lorries and sent to the rear, and captivity. In one French village, the parish priest seeing the Belgians had lined up the Germans facing a wall so that they could search them, thought he was about to witness a summary execution. He started noisily pleading and hectoring the Belgians, who had no such intention. Since he was not to be convinced and was making a nuisance of himself they had to remove him from the scene by force.

The crews of armoured cars were sometimes used in ways they had not been trained for, like giving fire support for small infantry attacks. But generally the five troops progressed, as directed, on different parallel itineraries, finding out what roads or bridges were passable, extricating themselves from ambushes either by withdrawing in good order behind a smokescreen, with the Daimlers fanning out to fire in every direction, or, if the enemy was thought to be weaker and devoid of anti-tank guns, by pressing on and firing like hell, the different drills to each effect being signalled by coloured rockets fired from a pistol by the officer in charge.

In one such instance, at a crossroads, Raymond V. joined in the general covering fire by using his small mortar.

More than once when engaged by German anti-tank guns, the armoured cars became stuck in mud or in the roadside gutters, making things somewhat trickier. The British paras who fought alongside them did not hide their satisfaction at fighting on foot rather being confined in the Daimlers they referred to as 'rolling coffins'. At some places the Germans withdrew after only token resistance but more serious fighting was sometimes encountered along well-prepared defensive lines, often along railway embankments, the bridges of which had usually been blown. Salenelles, Doluzé, Pont-L'Evêque, Deauville, and Pont-Audemer were the small Normandy cities the Belgians liberated on their way. The Belgians stayed close to the banks of the Seine River and at one point stumbled upon an Allied flyer they almost mistook for an enemy sniper. Having stayed hidden for weeks on end during the day and only venturing out at night, his face had become deathly pale.

At the end of August the Germans suddenly and quickly withdrew from France and Belgium and the Belgian Brigade joined the rush in hot pursuit. After a long drive the Franco-Belgian border was reached and on 3 September Brussels was finally entered via the suburb of Anderlecht and the Midi railway station. Enthusiasm for the liberators was overwhelming and they were plied with drinks, flowers and more. Not without risk to life and limb, girls were climbing the vehicles to kiss the soldiers. Some were thought to be wounded in the face when in fact lipstick was to blame for the red stains. The drivers had to be careful not to run over the massed crowds lining the streets of the capital and all but blocking the way. Not knowing there were Belgians wearing British battle-dress they usually were mistaken for Britons. 'Look at that British officer over there!' Lieutenant Dewandre's mother said to a friend, 'Doesn't he look like my son?' When recognized as Belgians, the crowd's cheers grew even more rapturous. Driving along the main streets of Brussels the Belgian soldiers saw the Palais de Justice, set ablaze by the retreating Germans. They stopped to pay their respects at the Unknown Soldier's grave and then drove to Laeken Palace to greet the only member of the Belgian royal family present, Elisabeth, the Queen Mother, to whom Lieutenant Dewandre introduced General Brian Horrocks. On hearing that the men of the Belgian armoured squadron whose families were not living in Brussels were to fight on without home leave, the Queen offered to have their families called by phone to give them the good news. That night Lieutenant Dewandre went to sleep in his mother's home in Brussels and, getting up next morning, found a fellow trying to steal the spare wheel of his jeep...

On 5 September, the regrouped Brigade complete with the armoured squadron, entered the capital officially. Some months later, on 10 March

1945, Field Marshal Montgomery, escorted in by the Belgian armoured squadron, paid an official visit to the reinstated Burgomaster Vandemeulebroek and a medal parade was held on the Grand Place in front of the Town Hall, Monty handing over two Military Crosses and two Military Medals to members of the squadron.

During the following days in September 1944, the armoured squadron was told to clear the region south-east of Brussels of small pockets of enemy troops. They then moved northwards to the Belgian Army training grounds of Leopoldsburg, an area well known to all pre-war Belgian officers in the Brigade. One Daimler Mk 1 was lost and two men killed in action. The Belgians were involved in clearing both banks of the Wessem canal, close to the Dutch border, which was reached on 19 September. A Boeing B17, hit by flak, was seen flying low with sputtering engines over the canal and suddenly the crew bailed out. As the northern bank was still held by the enemy, the Belgians shouted at the parachuting Americans to try to come down on the southern bank, but maybe distrusting their foreign accents half of the crew came down on the wrong side, where the waiting Germans took them prisoner.

The Belgian Brigade was made to hold the hinge between the British and American sectors during Operation Market Garden and was held in reserve. After that it was ordered to train new recruits drafted in Belgium and was reorganized, with several new officers. However, the war ended before the revamped 'Brigade Piron' was sent into action again. The Americans also trained and equipped several Infantry Battalions.

Raymond V. finished the war with the Belgian Croix de Guerre with two clasps and battle honours ('Normandie' and 'Canal de Wessem'), the 1940–45 Volunteer medal, the Médaille de la Résistance and the Croix des Evadés for having been in the Underground and escaped to Britain. He was made a Knight of the Order of Léopold II and also held the British France and Germany Star and VE Medal. He was also recognized as Agent Service Renseignement et Action.

The Belgian Resistance prevents destruction of the Port of Antwerp

When General Brian Horrocks' XXX Corps entered Belgium on 3 and 4 September, he left the Guards to capture Brussels and ordered – quite sensibly – Major General Roberts, Commander of the 11th Armoured Division, to 'run like hell' towards Antwerp. This Roberts did and his leading elements, four reconnaissance tanks led by Major Dunlop, early on 4 September, whilst speeding along the main motorway leading from Brussels to Antwerp, suddenly saw a civilian in a beige raincoat signalling them to stop. Dunlop, suspicious at first, kept the civilian covered with his pistol but wisely allowed him to speak. The man turned out to be Belgian *Lieutenant du Génie* (Engineers) Vekemans of the Antwerp Resistance, a former POW who had been freed by the Germans.

Along with a few hundred other *résistants* coming from different groups, including communists and conservatives under the overall command of Lieutenant Reniers, also a Belgian Army engineer, they had realized many months ago the importance of delivering the great port of Antwerp intact into Allied hands. So indeed had the Belgian government in London, which had pointed this out to the relevant Allied authorities even before D-Day. And it had become even more crucial because the Atlantic and Channel ports like Cherbourg, Le Havre or Dunkirk, in the parts of France or Belgium the Allies had liberated so far, were either still held by German pockets, precisely to deny their use to the British and Americans, or had been completely destroyed before surrender. The enormous logistics needed to supply the Allies, who by now had about a million soldiers ashore, thus was still entirely dependent on the artificial ports build on the Normandy beaches just after D-Day. And these logistics lines were now, given the distances covered and speed of the Allied advance during the last months, close to choking point. Early in 1944, the Antwerp Coordination Committee was formed and different groups of the *Weerstand* ('resistance' in Dutch) were tasked with monitoring the port's accesses and German arrangements in the docks, at the sluice gates, at the electrical generation plant powering them, the floating cranes and tugs, the oil storage facilities, the tunnels under the Scheldt River and so on. Close contact was kept with London, to which the German engineers' preparations for demolition were reported, like the arrival of several barges laden with explosives and equipment to dig holes in the docksides to blow them apart. Five Belgian harbour pilots were designated by the Germans to help sink blockships, but told the Resistance what they knew, made themselves scarce the day the Germans needed them and were helped to go into hiding with their families.

During the same months, as the Allies were known to be approaching, several sabotage actions disrupted railway traffic in and around the port to disturb the German preparations for destruction. On 2 September, a coded message was given on the BBC: 'On s'amuse bien à l'école' (Kids have fun at school). This was an order to cut the telephone lines to the port. Plucky 20-year-old Gilberte Lenaerts, who already had quite a history in the Antwerp Resistance for hiding Jews, Allied pilots and young Belgians dodging compulsory work in Germany, was sent across the lines on her bicycle by Reniers to contact the headquarters of the advancing British troops and inform them of the situation in Antwerp. She was later to marry British Major Roger Brunsdon, who was (literally) on his way to meet her. Having delivered her message she was asked to go back across the lines to gather intelligence about the German troop dispositions beyond Antwerp and to return with a report. She carried out that risky mission also, and later on even helped Allied paras to exfiltrate, after the failed Market Garden operation at Arnhem.

The Germans had placed an observation point overlooking the main Brussels–Antwerp motorway, to give the signal for the demolition charges in the port to be ignited when the Allies were arriving and this had been observed by the Resistance.

The morning of 4 September was the crucial moment, when the combination of a fast advance by the British Army and preparatory action by the Belgian Resistance saved the port of Antwerp. Just in time, Lieutenant Vekemans managed to persuade Major Dunlop to stop the leading tanks from proceeding as planned along the main road to Antwerp, where they would have been spotted by the German observation post and would have been stopped by mined bridges anyway. He instead led them along another route which he had reconnoitred earlier and from which they could not be seen, taking them across unmined bridges and straight into Antwerp port, where they caught the German defenders unprepared. Together with the waiting Belgian Resistance groups, who knew exactly where to go and what to do, they neutralized the mines in the docksides and saved all the sluices except one, as well as 40km of intact docks, wharves, dry docks, rolling stock, cranes, oil tanks, grain storage facilities, generators and other installations in one of Europe's largest ports. General Roberts, whose 11th Armoured Division tanks had covered about 350km in just five days, was able to report this very important development to his superiors. His troops were utterly exhausted and in dire need of rest and regrouping, but all the same it is unfortunate that, from Eisenhower down the whole chain of command, nobody told him to go on for just a few extra miles to cut off the German troops which were now retreating into the Dutch island of Walcheren on the north bank of the Scheldt estuary. Here, they were able to deny access to the port of Antwerp for several more weeks. The island was finally cleared of their presence, at great cost, in November, and during the period from 26 November until 8 May 1944, V-E Day, 1,240 Allied ships landed 5 million tons of supplies – thus shortening the war in spite of the 483 V-1 and 1,341 V-2 missiles that rained down on Antwerp (London's share of V-2s was 1,150).

A large screen of hundreds of anti-aircraft guns was set up to try to protect the vital harbour against bombers and V-1s.

Lieutenant General Brian Horrocks later wrote that the fall of Antwerp was not his victory but that of the Belgian Resistance, without which he could not have advanced so fast. Reniers later made it to the rank of general in the Belgian Army and Gilberte Brunsdon-Lenaerts was made an OBE, and awarded a Grand Cross of the Order of Léopold II and other Belgian decorations including the Croix de Guerre, as well as a commendation for bravery from Eisenhower. She lived in London until her death in 2012.

Eight Belgian Commandos also received the Croix de Guerre for their fighting on the Island of Walcheren, while Lieutenant, later General, Pierre Danloy got a British Military Cross.

Liberation of prisoners and recovery of works of art

As the Allied armies moved into Germany, they liberated the inmates of the Belgian POW camps and these were promptly brought back to Belgium and reunited with their families, as were those who had been forced to go and work in Germany. Rebuilding their shattered lives was the first priority. The lot of surviving Belgians from the Nazi concentration and extermination camps was sometimes far worse. The Belgian non-Jewish ex-Resistance fighters usually could go back to their families, but many of the Jewish ex-detainees had no surviving relatives. Jewish orphans were often taken care of by the different Jewish organizations and spirited away to what was then British-mandate Palestine. Those Jews who had come to Belgium as refugees in the 1930s, from Germany or Eastern Europe and had become stateless because their country of origin had withdrawn their nationality, were given Belgian nationality and, under certain circumstances awarded pensions or compensation payments from the government.

Apart from opening the horrifying Nazi camps and forcing the local population to visit them, the US and British Armies also found about 5 million artefacts and objets d'art that had been pillaged all over Western Europe, including some 5,000 church bells. Many of these had come from Belgium and were gradually shipped back after identification. In salt mines in Silesia and Austria hundreds of works of arts were found stored, including ancient Flemish tapestries, the Bruges Michelangelo *Madonna with Child*, and the *Lamb of God* from Ghent Cathedral by Jan Van Eyck. They had a narrow escape because one of the last orders from the Nazi hierarchy was to blow up the salt mine at Altausee, in Austria, where most of them were stashed away. The local miners, realizing that blow-ing up the mine would cause them to lose their livelihood, took matters into their own hands and used only a controlled explosion to block the entrance, thus saving the priceless treasures inside. The works of art were gradually retrieved and found their way home.

Recovery of the archives the Germans had taken away proved far more protracted, because in 1945 the Russians took them all away to Moscow. There they stayed for as long as the Soviet Union lasted. Even after its collapse it took the Belgian government long years of negotiation (and a lot of money) to get back from the Russian Federation what was after all Belgian property, but was considered there to be war booty and repar-ations. Finally, in 2000, ten Belgian army lorries eventually brought the 60 tons of paperwork back to Brussels, to the great satisfaction of historians.

Chapter 10

Aftermath

Return of the London government

On 8 September 1944 an RAF Transport Command Dakota flew the Belgian government back from London to Brussels – where it was met, it should be said, with indifference, contrasting with the enthusiasm with which the British and Belgian liberating troops had been welcomed. However, it immediately set to work. Economic reconstruction of the country began at once and two factors positively aided it – the Marshall Plan for aid from the USA, and the relative affluence of the country thanks to its having retained the Congo, its African colony. The destruction caused by the war was also less than after the First World War and less than in many other parts of Europe.

There was a need to limit the amount of paper money in circulation, since the occupiers had liberally printed great quantities of it, and the London government had done the same, in order that it could be dropped to the Resistance. Finance Minister Gutt now strictly controlled the money supply to reduce inflation. To this end, and also to catch economic collaborators who had illicitly enriched themselves during the occupation, in October 1944 he ordered an immediate, unannounced change of the currency notes. A huge stock of new notes, printed secretly in England, arrived overnight and was distributed, up to a certain limit, in exchange for old ones. Significant differences between accounts for 1940 and 1945 had to be explained when notes that had ceased to be legal tender were traded in, to catch those who had profited from the black market or supplying the Germans. Lieutenant Dewandre and his men, exchanging fire with the Germans across a canal, saw two clerks from the finance ministry who had donned old Belgian army helmets arriving at his command post. They had braved the bullets and shrapnel to deliver, complete with signed receipts, freshly printed banknotes and to take away the old ones his soldiers had in their possession. Who says bureaucrats are lazy and risk averse? Pierlot addressed the Belgian Parliament, thanked the Allies, paid homage to the Resistance and its dead and also thanked all those countries (mainly in Latin America) which, by maintaining diplomatic relations with the government in exile, had never doubted that Belgian sovereignty would one day be restored.

Repression of collaboration and lasting scars

About 87,000 people were prosecuted for high treason, war crimes, for having denounced resistance fighters or Jews with fatal results, or for having aided the enemy in some other way. Of those found guilty about 4,000 received death sentences, and 242 were actually carried out. Among those executed were Flemish nationalist ideologue August Borms, who had already received a death sentence for collaboration after the First World War,[84] Lucien Eickhorn, the collaborationist Burgomaster of Arlon, and Leo Vindevogel who was a former VNV member of Parliament. José Streel, the ideologue of Rex who had broken with Degrelle, was also executed despite many pleas in his favour, including some from former *Résistants* and from Foreign Minister Spaak's wife (he had warned her of impending arrest during the occupation and thus enabled her to save herself by going into hiding). The case of one executed woman, Irma Laplace, who was a Flemish nationalist accused of having denounced to the Germans (with fatal result) Resistance fighters who had killed her son, caused controversy. When the case was recently reopened, there were found to have been mitigating circumstances and she was rehabilitated. Execution (always by firing squad, sometimes in the back) was carried out in almost equal numbers on Flemish- or French-speaking Belgians. Some non-Belgians (Germans, Austrians etc.) also faced firing squads for acts committed during the occupation, including the German commandant of Fort Breendonk, Philipp Schmitt, who was shot in August 1950.

A number of other Belgians and a few more German, Austrian, French or Spanish citizens received more or less lengthy prison sentences, but most had been released by 1955. One, Jef Van de Wiele, who headed a short-lived Flemish government in exile in Germany in 1945, and had been originally sentenced to death, was only freed in 1963. The same fate befell Gérard Romsée, Secretary General for Home Affairs appointed by the Germans, who was freed in 1954. Former Belgian Army Major Hellebaut, who had commanded the Légion Wallonie during its last year, was also sentenced to death but reprieved and freed in 1959. He died in 1984.

By comparison, in the Netherlands at the end of the Second World War only thirty-nine persons were executed, including the head of the collaborationist government Anton Mussert, and Seyss Inquart, the Austrian-born Gauleiter, and one woman. In Luxembourg there was a total of eight (excluding Gauleiter Simon, who was found dead in his cell), all Luxembourg citizens. The Germans had executed 700 people in the Grand Duchy during the occupation.

Other notorious collaborators like Staf De Clercq and Reimond Tollenaere died during the war or fled abroad, like Father Cyriel Verschaeve and Robert Verbelen. Both died in Austria, the latter after having worked for the American and Austrian espionage services and having been condemned in absentia for murder in Belgium. Some others made their way to Ireland or South America, usually living under assumed names.

As for the most famous of all Belgian collaborators, SS Obersturmbannführer and Volksführer der Wallonen Léon Degrelle, holder of the Knight's Cross 1st and 2nd class, was to die peacefully in a Spanish hospital aged 87, in 1994. He had fled to German-occupied Norway during the last days of the Reich. Outside Oslo, armaments minister Speer's Heinkel was put at his disposal, filled to the brim with fuel and flown right across Europe, including Belgium, with Degrelle and a few others on board. The date was well chosen as the whole of Europe was celebrating VE Day and air traffic control lax. The former SS lieutenant colonel later described how the plane, its fuel spent, landed on a beach, with the crew and passengers being unsure whether they were in France or Spain. As they struggled against the surf, in the distance they saw men striding towards them. If they were French it meant certain extradition and eventual execution, if Spanish they were (relatively) safe. To their immense relief they saw the typical Spanish Guardia Civil shiny black leather hats. The Franco government considered handing Degrelle over but eventually did not, having seen former Vichy Prime Minister Laval being executed after having been extradited by them.

Under a death sentence given in absentia in 1945, attempts (some say halfhearted, because he knew a thing or two about Belgian politicians who were by now back in power) were made to kidnap him, but never got far beyond the planning stage. So Degrelle stayed in Spain, married a rich Spanish heiress and became a Spanish citizen (thus forever escaping extradition), went into the real estate business, helped to build US Air Force bases and attended his daughter's wedding in a 'summer SS uniform' he designed himself, since the SS never served in regions like North Africa. He freely gave interviews to Belgian journalists and historians.

The end of the war found Robert S. in a Soviet Army prison camp outside Mecklenburg in eastern Germany, where what was left of his 27th Volunteer SS Division Langemarck had finally surrendered after many months of fighting in the Ukraine, in Estonia, in the Curland pocket – where they fought alongside the Walloon SS – and finally, inside Germany in Pomerania and along the Oder River. All foreign volunteers who had fought with the Germans were sent to their

countries of origin. The British also sent back to the Soviets those Cossacks and
Russians who had fought against them under turncoat General Vlasov.[85] *Robert S.*
was taken with a few others to the British occupation zone in the west of
Germany, there to be handed over to the Belgian Army and brought back home. In
January 1946, in a visiting room of Brussels Saint Gilles' jail, he met the young
lawyer who was to defend him in court martial, Raymond V. Robert S. drew a
severe sentence but other factors besides his having joined the SS were taken into
account.

Raymond V. married in 1946. His father-in-law was a former diplomat who
had saved Jews during the war.

Of the 87,000 prosecuted about half were found guilty. Some for offences
which might seem trivial today, but were not so in the heated climate after
four and a half years of increasingly hard occupation. Georges Rémy, alias
Hergé, the creator of that immortal Belgian icon Tintin, was prosecuted
for having continued to publish his comic strips during the occupation in
two newspapers controlled by the Germans, *Le XXème Siècle* and *Le Soir*.
Some of his drawings were outright anti-Semitic. He was exonerated.

Georges Simenon, the prolific Liège-born writer of thrillers translated
into practically all languages and also the author of anti-Semitic articles in
the pre-war *Gazette de Liège*, spent the war in France and after that went to
the United States for ten years to avoid trouble. His brother had joined the
Légion Wallonie, fled the country and following Georges' advice, joined
the French Foreign Legion, only to be killed in French Indochina. Their
mother never forgave Georges, writing to him that she would rather have
seen him die...

Immediately after Liberation, some collaborators were locked up in the
animal cages of the Antwerp zoo for a while, others at the sinister Fort
Breendonk, pending trial. Some women who had 'collaborated horizon-
tally' with Germans had their hair shaved and in a few cases a swastika
carved on their scalps. Other collaborators, confirmed or supposed, had
their houses sacked by riotous mobs. One Rexist was lynched by an angry
mob. These practices did not last long, but many real or alleged collaborators thought it safer to move away to another town or part of the city.

It should be mentioned that with a few exceptions, due process of law
took place, even though too harshly in the eyes of some. Most summary
executions occurred during the Liberation days, like that of a brother of
Gérard Romsée, Paul Romsée, but there were almost no kangaroo courts
in the following weeks – these being usually followed by immediate

execution, perhaps by means of gruesome methods, as happened in some places in France.

Von Falkenhausen, the former German military governor, obviously could not be called a collaborator, but neither could he be let off scot free. He had fallen foul of the Nazis because of his close connections to some of the Stauffenberg conspirators, mainly Goerdeler, the former mayor of Königsberg and Leipzig, who was executed. He had been locked up by them at Buchenwald. Freed in the confusion during the last days of the war, he was prosecuted in Belgium for having ordered executions, among other charges, but escaped the death penalty when his lawyers produced posters in court dating from the 1923 Ruhr occupation, which stated that the Belgian military authority there had had Germans executed. He was found guilty of deporting 25,000 Jews and 43,000 non-Jews and was given a stiff prison sentence of twelve years' hard labour – though he served only a small part of it, being freed in 1951. He was later to marry a woman much younger than himself who had been in the Resistance, and died peacefully in 1966.

His more Nazi-oriented deputy Eggert Reeder, who had stayed on after von Falkenhausen was replaced by a 'civilian' SS administration, also only served one third of a twelve-year jail sentence for having deported Jews and executed hostages.

Impact on Belgian politics after the war
The most lasting aftermath of the Second World War in Belgium remains the lingering unease in both Flanders and Wallonia about the past. To this day, the theme of total amnesty is often brought up in an antagonistic debate. This means, since nobody has been in jail since the 1960s, that pensions, compensation or other rights which were forfeited as part of a punitive sentence should be reinstated. When even Flemish moderates propose this (it was voted for by the Regional Government of Flanders), former Resistance fighters, mainly in Wallonia, are up in arms.

It would be an oversimplification to trace back the opposition between French and Dutch speakers in Belgium to the two occupations as it pre-dates the First World War. But it is undisputable that ill feeling was exacerbated. The two long occupations, each lasting four years, have left lasting scars. Bloodshed has always been avoided but Belgian politics are to this day dominated by the squabbles between Flemings and Walloons. Creative strategies have been developed over the years and successive con-stitutional reforms transformed Belgium into a federal state, giving each of the two language communities a large degree of autonomy in economic and financial matters and even total political independence of decision for education, culture, local transport and so on, complete with legislative and executive bodies. Total political independence for Flanders is still the goal of a significant part of Flemish opinion (and striven for by the largest political party in Flanders), though how this could be achieved while tackling the problems of, first, dividing the national debt, and second, resolving the status of largely French-speaking Brussels, claimed by Flanders as its capital, remains open. Though they may be a minority among the Flemings, many of those who want total independence claim to be the spiritual heirs of Borms and similar idealists. As noted earlier, an amnesty, the wiping out of any judiciary or financial consequences of penalties incurred because of collaboration remains a controversial claim. But on the whole Flemish nationalists do admit that those among them who sided with the Nazi occupiers made a mistake and were naïve.

One theory goes that if it were not for the two cycles of occupation, with collaboration by some Flemings, followed by (harsh) repression and also the no less important revival of Belgian national feeling after both wars, the 'Belgian problem' would have been solved one way or another. It is dangerous to rewrite history with 'ifs' – if Germany had won either world war, if Napoleon had won at Waterloo, and so on. They didn't. In recent decades economic factors and the question of the role and future of the monarchy have also played an increasing part, as some situations like the larger prosperity of one region over another or the popularity of the royal family have gone through curious inversions. Service-based Flanders is now richer than heavy-industry-based Wallonia, while some in Flanders now see a king, for whom the Flemings overwhelmingly voted in the 1950 consultation about the future of Léopold III, as an obstacle to a Flemish Republic, whereas the Walloons (and the French-speaking majority in Brussels) see the monarchy as a bulwark against the dismantling of the country itself and also of the federal government, through which financial benefits flow towards their depressed region. The royal family, though not spared scandal and criticism in recent years, is still very popular with many Belgians north and south.

The Communist party
At the onset of occupation, the strong Belgian Communist party, mainly concentrated in the mining regions of Wallonia, kept quiet, in line with the Ribbentrop-Molotov Pact. That changed with Barbarossa, the German attack on the Soviet Union in June 1941, after which they received, like the other Communist parties in Western Europe, orders from Moscow to

inflict maximum damage on the Reich. This they did and it is fair to say they played an important role in the Resistance, though usually keeping aloof from other movements. They had collected large amounts of arms and rioted in Brussels a few weeks after Liberation, suffering thirty-four wounded in their own ranks, facts that worried Pierlot, Eisenhower and Montgomery, who took swift action to relieve them of their arms in case they should prove a menace to the reinstated government.

During the occupation, the communists, who sometimes hid in the coal mines, paid a heavy price – the Germans showed them little mercy when they were caught. Very strong politically at the Liberation, when they had up to 25 seats in Parliament out of 212, they played an important role in the opposition to King Léopold's return. Their wartime paper *Le Drapeau rouge* (the Red Flag), between May 1940 and the invasion of the Soviet Union a year later, blamed the City of London (and Wall Street) for the war and for all the evils of this world, just like German propaganda, and then abruptly stopped following that line in late May 1941 when their patrons found themselves in alliance with London (and later Washington). The paper continued to be printed after the war, but the political influence of the communists was to dwindle fast in the post-war years and has practically disappeared since the fall of communism elsewhere.

Opposition to King Léopold's return
The first elections since before the war were held as soon as practicable and Pierlot stayed on for a while as prime minister. Internal disagreements caused the government to fall, however, and he was replaced in February 1945 by a Flemish socialist, Van Acker. Women were given unrestricted voting rights in 1949. Until then only war widows had had these rights.

Between 1945 and 1951 the *Question Royale/Koningskwestie*, a quasi-civil war raged about whether Léopold III should resume his reign. He had been freed by American troops in 1945 from confinement in Austria, where the SS had deported him the day after D-day, apparently after considering killing him. The Catholic Party supported him, while the Socialists and Liberals opposed his return because of his attitude during the war. The debate became very embittered, many demonstrations and political meetings were held and no compromise could be found despite repeated visits by Belgian politicians of all hues to Léopold's temporary retreat in Switzerland. In the meantime Prince Charles of Belgium, his younger brother, acted as regent of the realm, a duty he discharged to the satisfaction of most. 'J'ai sauvé le brol,' he used to say, which can be loosely translated as, 'I saved the shop.' His elder brother, however, never forgave him for what he saw as an excess of eagerness to replace him.

After a referendum-like consultation in 1951, in which a majority of Belgians voted for Léopold's return, it was noted that support was not spread evenly between Flanders, which voted overwhelmingly in his favour, and Wallonia, where the majority was very slim – indeed non-existent in some districts. Léopold III eventually came back to Belgium after waiting five years in Switzerland but riots, with some loss of life, broke out in Wallonia. On 1 August 1950, he decided to abdicate in favour of his young son Baudouin, who went on to reign for forty years.

Years of internal peacemaking and reconstruction then set in. King Baudouin, a considerate and humane man, did an invaluable job in helping to turn the page. The Marshall plan was put to good use to restart the economy and rebuild infrastructures. Credits were allocated for the reconstruction of factories, private dwellings, or farms destroyed or damaged. Many unemployed were put to work reconstructing the railways, bridges, stations, etc. that had been bombed or blown up. After the troubled 1940s and early 1950s, the late 1950s and the 1960s were years of renewed prosperity.

Conclusions

For many years afterwards, few books were written about the Second World War in Belgium, partly due to a general agreement to let bygones be bygones and to avoid reopening wounds once the deeply divisive question of King Léopold's return had finally been settled; reconstruction and normal political debate became the priorities. These debates could sometimes become very passionate when the future of the educational system was discussed, or in 1960 when a general strike that brought some rioting broke out in Wallonia. Political instability continues to plague major institutions and rarely has a government managed to stay in power for the full duration of their legislature after general elections. Forming a new coalition, in which the monarchs have so far played an important role, is almost always difficult and protracted.

The badly prepared proclamation of independence of the Congo in 1960, resulted in that unfortunate country's slide into complete chaos and civil war. Thousands of Belgian settlers had to be airlifted and repatriated, causing anguish in the home country. The suffering of the misruled Congolese people was to last several decades. The two United Nations mandate territories administered by Belgium, Rwanda and Burundi, were also granted independence a few years later and they too went on to suffer long and bloody civil wars, especially Rwanda.

Ex-King Léopold, a passionate nature and science lover, travelled to exotic places like Amazonia and New Guinea, wrote a book defending his controversial wartime decisions (it was only published after his death) and encouraged others to write also, raised the children he had with Princess Lilian, his second wife, and died peacefully in 1983, the same year as his brother, the former Regent Charles.

When King Baudouin died childless of a heart attack in 1993, his brother Albert succeeded him. Both had accompanied their father into captivity in Germany and then temporary exile in Switzerland. Albert II abdicated in 2013, aged 79, after reigning to general approbation for twenty years and was succeeded by his son Philippe.

Pierlot was made a count, but because his Catholic Party sided with Léopold during the controversy over the King's future and his declarations in 1940, he was ostracized and lived on as a bitter man in his native Ardennes until his death in 1963. For the sake of reconciliation, the Catholic party eventually stopped supporting the restoration of King Léopold.

Spaak went on to become one of Belgium's most brilliant politicians in the post-war years, chairing the first General Assembly of the United Nations and the Council of Europe, becoming Secretary General of NATO and playing a very important role in launching what is now the European Union. His chequered career included remaining Foreign Minister of Belgium for many years and into the 1960s, in the aftermath of the Belgian Congo's catastrophic collapse following independence. We know he was much saddened by Britain's hesitation in fully committing itself to a more integrated Europe, a cause he worked very hard for. He died in 1973.

Colonel Piron and Lieutenant Dewandre both made their career in the post-war Belgian Army and attained the rank of general, the latter holding a senior NATO command before retiring. Many other officers and NCOs did the same, in an army that to this day uses English expressions like battledress and service dress, Regimental and Company Sergeant Major (RSM and CSM), Quartermaster (QM), padre, kitbag, parade ground, and many others, a direct link with the First Belgian Brigade. An infantry battalion took over its traditions and battle honours, called Libération/ Bevrijding. The battle honours of the armoured squadron and artillery batteries awarded by the British Army are now inscribed on the modern tanks and guns of today's Belgian Army. And Belgian paratroopers of the 1st Bataillon, whose predecessors were British SAS, use red berets, cap badges and Pegasus shoulder patches identical to those of their British colleagues.

One of the main crossings in Brussels is named after Field Marshal Montgomery and there is an 'Avenue Winston Churchill', as well as an 'Avenue Franklin Roosevelt'.

Belgium lost approximately 88,000 dead in the Second World War. That was more than 1 per cent of its global population in 1939. The human suffering from wounds, lasting mental scars, lost or absent loved ones, separation, destruction, material loss etc., cannot be quantified.

The decades of peace that followed thanks to NATO, and the prosperity Belgium has enjoyed thanks to European integration and peaceful collaboration with and between its neighbours, has no precedent in that country's history. Active support for those two international organizations which have their seats in Brussels, as well as for the United Nations, has been the basis of its foreign policy since 1945.

In 1966, the author was studying at Paris University. His father Raymond and his uncle Jean, then in their mid-forties, came to visit and all three went for a meal in a quiet restaurant outside Paris. Jean, perhaps because he was almost blind, had a strong voice. 'Well,' he asked his nephew, 'how old are you now?' Upon hearing I was 19, he commented loudly: 'Ah! That was the age I was when I went to jail!' Complete silence suddenly fell over the restaurant and the other patrons, not knowing in what circumstances he had been detained, glanced across at our table …

Notes

1. All times given are Belgian time which was one hour behind German time.
2. Eben Emael is pronounced 'Aben Emaal' (double 'a' is sounded as in 'far'). Named after the village close to where the Fort was built, it is written without an umlaut above the last 'e', as some do. This final vowel is not pronounced.
3. The hollow charge, invented by the Chicago gangsters to pry open safes, works by concentrating the blast into an incandescent molten metal jet that deeply penetrates steel. It is still widely used in anti-tank shells. Until then, armour piercing shells were made with a very hard metal core like tungsten (wolfram) only mined in Spain and Portugal.
4. Those interested in a visit to Eben Emael and other forts in the Liège area, most of which have been restored and opened to the public should consult the plentiful information on visits, history of the different forts etc. that is available on the internet, including 'Fortified Position of Liège' and www.fort-eben-emael.be/en/
5. It should be noted that the language spoken in Flanders and in the Netherlands (Holland) is the same. It is called *Nederlands* ('Netherlandish'). The way it is spoken in the Netherlands differs from that of Flanders in the accent and a small proportion of the vocabulary – rather like Oxford English and American as spoken in the South.
6. This myth was invented in the years after the First World War, possibly by August Borms (see Chapter 7), but to this day many still believe it to be true. However, to anyone who has served in any regular armed force it is evident that no army unit is ever sent into combat unless the trained men are known to understand the orders of their officers or NCOs. It is unlikely the Belgian army would have been able to withstand four years of intermittent assaults alternating with quieter periods as happened in 1914–18 if such had not been the case. It has also been disproved by serious Flemish historians such as Sophie De Schaepdrijver of Penn State University (see bibliography), basing their conclusions on contemporary sources.
7. B.H. Liddell Hart, 1941 *The Current of War*, Hutchinson and Co.: London.
8. German firms did some earth-moving work under contract but that does not mean they were made privy to real confidential data like firing plans, range and calibre of guns etc. Much more could be (and was) deduced from aerial reconnaissance anyway.
9. French and British flights in Belgian airspace, which was officially closed, were usually left unmolested, but Luftwaffe ones always intercepted, sometimes resulting in shooting incidents. In one instance a Belgian pilot was shot down and killed. Some RAF planes had to land in Belgium for lack of fuel. French ones were usually refuelled and discreetly sent on their way, but British ones used a different octane gasoline to the Belgian variety.

10. Venlo is a small town just on the Dutch side of the border with Germany. On 9 November 1939, British Major Stevens and Captain Best, working for SIS in The Hague, together with a Dutch intelligence officer, were lured there 'to make contact with the German resistance.' It was in fact a trick by the Gestapo and *Sicherheitsdienst* (Intelligence) and they were dragged over the border to be thoroughly interrogated. The Dutchman was killed during the incident but amazingly both British officers survived the war. From that moment London and Paris, once burned, twice shy, became very suspicious of any advances by the genuine German resistance.

11. A small monument has now been erected at the place of the crash. Having fallen ill, Majors Reinberger and Hoenmans were returned to Germany later during the war in an exchange, but curiously did not incur serious penalties. The pilot could plead ignorance of the briefcase's contents but the staff officer could not. Not surprisingly, as his marital indiscretions became known to his wife, Reinberger's marriage broke up.

12. Since Belgium was not at war, the official mobilization situation was *Pied de paix renforcé* (Enhanced Peacetime Situation) as opposed to *Pied de Guerre* (War Situation).

13. On MV *Aboukir*, on which the British military mission to the Belgian GHQ, later embarked when the Belgian Army surrendered. The *Aboukir* was torpedoed with heavy loss of life, including the mission.

14. The Cointet barriers (see photo) were steel contraptions made of pieces of rail welded together and when solidly fastened to concrete walls or made fast together end on end made an effective anti-tank barrier, as had been proven by trials, including firing at it with artillery. Of course, as every military person knows, an obstacle has to be kept under fire to prevent its eventual removal. In another instance, hundreds of railway wagons were tied together to form an anti-tank barrier. A large part of the Cointet barriers were reused by the Germans in the Atlantic Wall. Some call them 'Belgian Gates'.

15. Paul Reynaud, who was to preside over the worst military defeat of his country since Waterloo because of the unpreparedness of his army, had the gall to later write a book with the title *La France a sauvé l'Europe* (France saved Europe)! He further disgraced himself when the car he was fleeing in crashed, killing his mistress. In the car were found bars of gold and a large sum in cash he had taken from the secret funds for his own uses.

16. Dutch manufacturer Fokker gave the German Empire its best planes, the Dutch Government allowed some retreating German troops to use Dutch territory around Maastricht in November 1918, and the Kaiser went into exile in Holland, the government adamantly refusing to extradite him. It should be added that thousands of Belgian refugees were very well looked after in the Netherlands during the first occupation.

17. An unexpected consequence of Hitler's decision to invade the neutral Netherlands, thus pushing it into an alliance with Britain, was to deprive Japan of its main source of oil in the Dutch Indies (Indonesia) and precipitating the attack on Pearl Harbor and the conquest of the large Dutch colony.

18. The most likely theory about Weygand's parents was that he was the son of Empress Charlotte of Mexico and Belgian General Van der Smissen, commander

of the Belgian Army contingent sent by her brother, King Léopold II to help her husband Emperor Maximilian, an Austrian Archduke and brother of Emperor Franz-Josef. Napoleon III of France tried during the American Civil War to create an Empire of Mexico and sent troops to support it but eventually France left Maximilian to his devices, to be executed by the Mexicans under Benito Juarez. Charlotte, named after Charlotte, Princess of Wales (+1817), of whom her father Léopold I was the widower, went mad and died at an advanced age. Others say she was raped by a Mexican. Weygand probably died without knowing himself.

19. When the German troops occupied the Netherlands, Hitler had guards posted outside Doorn Castle where the old Kaiser was residing, officially to honour him but in fact to prevent old school officers entering to pay their respects. Nobody was allowed in.

20. *Bedingungslose Waffenschtrekkung* means literally 'unconditional laying down of arms'. Unconditional surrender was exactly what the Allies later demanded from Germany at Casablanca. German moderates would claim this reinforced the Nazis because it discouraged any hope of a compromise peace with the Western Allies, but Germany itself had created a precedent, at least in Europe. Von Reichenau's chief of staff, who welcomed Derousseaux and took him to the conference room was General Paulus, the same man who was to surrender (unconditionally) his VIth Army to the Soviets at Stalingrad.

21. The Brussels Royal Military Museum (Musée Royal de l'Armée et d'Histoire militaire) is certainly worth a visit for those interested in the 1940 campaign and for anyone interested in military history. In addition to many memorabilia about Belgian military history since the eighteenth century, it boasts a remarkable collection of tanks and military planes, including rare First World War German aircraft. (www.klm-mra.be)

22. The name 'Holland' is in fact a misnomer, as it is the name of only a part (two of its provinces) of the Netherlands, but since it played a central role in that country's history the name has stuck.

23. Had Charlotte, the daughter of King George IV of England, not died in childbirth, Léopold would have been her Prince Consort. As it was, Victoria, her first cousin, became heir to the throne. Léopold and his niece Queen Victoria (she was the daughter of his sister) were very fond of each other and they exchanged many letters. He advised her when she was young and he arranged her marriage to one of his nephews in Germany, Prince Albert. For political reasons Léopold remarried, the daughter of King Louis-Philippe of France, but he never forgot his first English wife, Charlotte – he gave her name to his daughter (who became Empress of Mexico for a short time), and died with her name on his lips.

24. Léopold I's son and heir, of the Belgian Congo fame. It is alleged he asked Paris for the Belgians who had joined the French Foreign Legion to be excused from fighting against the Prussians so as to avoid giving Bismarck the slightest pretext of attacking Belgium. This however gave the Belgians Legionnaires a lasting reputation as shirkers, reflected in the lyrics of the Legion march Le Boudin: '... some blood sausage / For the Alsatians, the Swiss, and the Lorrains / For the Belgians, there's none left / They're lazy shirkers.'

25. 'C'est bien fait pour la gueuse!' (The bitch got what she deserved!) was often heard over the summer of 1940 in French right-wing circles who had never fully

accepted republican and parliamentary institutions and linked them to corruption. The official form of government instituted by Pétain was *Etat français* (French State), a way of avoiding the word 'Republic'.

Characteristically the motto of his *Révolution nationale* was *Travail, Famille, Patrie*. Churchill may have had good reasons to attack the French fleet at Dakar and Mers-el Kébir but there is no doubt many more French military and young men would have rallied to de Gaulle if (a lot of) French blood had not been spilled there. A few Belgian officers including General Van Overstraeten, also mistrusted the British because they remembered the many attempts by London to annexe the Belgian Congo, and the negative propaganda about Belgian colonization that went with it (and still lingers to this day). Furthermore Van Overstraeten had been in the German East African Campaign during the First World War and had had problems with the British there.

26. Léopold III did realize the French were irremediably beaten as soon as 15 May, when old General Galet, who had been his father's military adviser, and whom he had sent to Gamelin's headquarters at Vincennes outside Paris, reported to him in that vein. Galet also accurately predicted that the Dutch Army would not last long either. Contrary to what some believe, many French units fought very bravely in May and June 1940 and their losses were significant. But the French Army (and nation) of 1940 was not that of 1918. The incredible bravery, tenacity and resilience of the French soldiers in the First World War had resulted in astronomic losses (almost 1.5 million out of a population of 39 million) and this had left its mark. In 1939–40, the French as a whole did not have the stomach or motivation for a repeat performance. Unlike propaganda-fed Germans, bent on revenge, the French had a free press and part of it criticized the decision to go to war. Apart from the terrible memories of 25 years before, and widespread antimilitaristic propaganda that had fed on it in the interwar years, there were current political reasons for the reluctance to fight: the right had lost faith in the parliamentary system and saw communism as a far greater danger than Germany. The communists, quite a strong force at the time and allied to the Germans by virtue of the Molotov/Ribbentrop pact, were writing in their media that it was useless 'to be killed for Danzig', when not committing outright sabotage of weapon production.

27. Nothing eventually came of this, but the impression was enhanced when Léopold III asked his ministers via the embassies in London and Paris for 'blank decrees', which could be filled in to dismiss them and call for other ministers. This was denied him by the government.

28. Conventional wisdom has always had it that Albert would never have left Belgian territory but recent documents point to the fact he considered withdrawing the army into France in October 1914, but that French General Foch convinced him to make a (successful) last stand on the Yser River and promised (and duly sent) him reinforcements. To leave the army to its devices and go into exile on his own would be an entirely different matter though.

King Léopold was 38 years old in 1940: so was his father in 1914. Skilful Allied propaganda had made a hero of Albert, the *Roi-Chevalier*, the (brave, chivalrous) knightly King. It is this author's opinion that King Albert was made more heroic than was warranted (at least from the Allies' point of view) and Léopold III far more of a villain than he deserved. Quite naturally both saw their duty first and foremost in the welfare and interests of the Belgian people and took the French and British interest to heart only insofar as Belgium had legal or moral obligations towards them which coincided with the good of their own country. This is illustrated in Albert I's case by his refusal to sacrifice Belgian troops needlessly in massive Allied infantry offensives (like the Somme or Passchendaele), whose success he did not believe in, and by the several enquiries he made through emissaries who contacted his (German) wife's relatives on the possibilities of a negotiated peace with Germany and Austria-Hungary, and of which he duly informed the Allies but which got nowhere and were eventually stopped. In fact the points discussed did not differ very much from Wilson's eventual Fourteen Points.

29. The French words 'a capitulé en rase campagne' carry additional opprobrium because they reminded French hearers of General Dupont who, during the Napoleonic wars, surrendered his army in the field to the Spanish at Baylen, incurring everlasting shame in his country. His surrender is usually described in those same words Reynaud now used. Never again would a French General behave so. 'This is a deed without precedent in history,' Reynaud commented, with obvious exaggeration.

30. This was done both through the French embassy in London and the British embassy in Paris, as well as by means of the ubiquitous General Spears.

31. The *Daily Mirror* had attacked Keyes: 'What were you up to in Leopold's Palace? Didn't you smell a rat?' The paper printed an apology to the Admiral and a financial arrangement was made. The chronological account, day by day, of events in May 1940 gave the lie to the accusations that King Leopold had not given warning of the impending surrender. This was sent to all Belgian embassies abroad to be disseminated to the local press, especially in the neutral countries. Prominent American diplomats, including the ambassador to Belgium Cudahy, as well as his naval attaché Commander Gade USN, defended Léopold III, and former ambassador to London Joseph P. Kennedy even wrote a short book in similar vein. It is a pity Churchill never recognized his mistake, though prompted by many to do so, and indeed repeated this view in his post-war memoirs.

32. It has been said but never proved that the Royal Marines Commandos' green beret was a homage Lord Keyes paid to the bravery of the Chasseurs Ardennais, whom he had seen in battle wearing large green berets.

33. Admiral Keyes's eldest son Lieutenant Colonel Geoffrey Keyes died in a commando raid in North Africa, trying to assassinate Rommel. He won a posthumous VC.

34. Today these cities are referred to as Menen and Kortrijk.

35. The French merged the Belgian 'suspects' with their own and a virulently anti-communist Degrelle at one time found himself in the same cell as nine communist members of the French parliament. VNV leader Staf De Clercq was freed after the intervention of his fellow Flemish Nationalist members of parliament with Prime Minister Pierlot. Considering his behaviour during the occupation he might well have been executed after the war, but died of illness in his bed in 1942. May be it would have been better for his image in history had he shared Van Severen's fate.

36. The French officer responsible was later court-martialled and executed by the Vichy government.

37. www.museespitfire.be

38. Aristides de Sousa Mendes was declared Righteous among the Nations by Yad Vashem in Jerusalem, for having issued literally thousands of visas allowing Jews to go to Portugal. The Spanish government would not allow refugees in unless they had visas for other countries beyond, so they would not stay in Spain. Because of this, securing a Portuguese visa was extremely important, the US or other consulates being far less accommodating. Since Sousa Mendes acted against the express orders of the Salazar government he was recalled to Portugal and dismissed. His pension was cancelled and he died destitute. His courage and humanity was only recognized officially by the Portuguese government after the Carnation Revolution in that country on 25 April 1974, which toppled the regime installed by Salazar. Only then was he officially rehabilitated. Sousa Mendes also gave visas to members of the French branch of the Rothschild family and to many non-Jews who had reasons to fear the Nazis, like the Grand Ducal family of Luxembourg, the last Empress of Austria-Hungary and her son Otto of Habsburg, among others. Sousa Mendes was a devout catholic, with several children and a complicated family life. When in extreme poverty he would have meals at the Lisbon Jewish welfare house.

39. The newly installed French Vichy regime even stopped some cables sent by Ambassador de Cartier de Marchienne, encouraging Pierlot and Spaak to come to London, from reaching them.

40. It should be noted that thousands of Jewish refugees took refuge in Portugal, and were welcomed there, some staying until the end of the war, some making their way on to North or South America, and some settling there for good. In Portugal and in Portuguese Mozambique, Allied and Axis diplomats and seriously wounded or crippled prisoners of war were exchanged. The country, through which the Duke and Duchess of Windsor also passed, was awash with spies from both sides. Trade with all belligerants continued until the end of the war.

41. The famous British actor Leslie Howard lost his life when one of these flights was shot down by the Luftwaffe, apparently unintentionally. (See *Flight 777* by Ian Colvin, Pen & Sword: London)

42. It still serves as official Residence for the Belgian ambassadors. Both Baron de Cartier de Marchienne, who died in 1946, and his wife are buried in the Belgian war cemetery in Brookwood, along with other Belgians who died in Britain during the war.

43. The building at 105 Eaton Square is no longer used by the Belgian embassy but a plaque, unveiled by HM The Queen Mother Elizabeth, widow of King George VI, and by the future King of the Belgians, Albert II, still adorns its façade. It reads: *Here many Belgians volunteered during World War II to fight with their Allies on land, at sea and in the air to liberate their country. Those who gave their lives in the cause of freedom shall not be forgotten.* With so many Belgians greeting each other every morning by shaking hands, something the English at the time didn't do, Eaton Square was nicknamed 'shake hand square' by the locals.

44. Some of those who had come through Spain or Portugal and about whom the British were in doubt sat out the rest of the war at the internment centre on the Isle of Man. A few others were convicted and executed as spies.

45. An important, indeed seminal event was a football match played on 11 October 1941 at Wembley stadium, between teams from Belgium and the Netherlands,

attended by Spaak, Prince Bernhard of the Netherlands and Spaak's opposite number Van Cleffens. The match was drawn, but personal contacts made there most probably helped start the negotiations.

46. Count Louis d'Ursel, the Belgian Minister in Bern, proved the most recalcitrant and for a while in 1940 sent his own 'instructions' to several of his colleagues in Romania, Portugal and so on, in the form of 'circulars'. They were the points of view of King Léopold about the events of May and June 1940 and the attitude that should be adopted by Belgium after the ceasefire with Germany. Belgian diplomats meeting their German counterparts at social functions in neutral countries should now greet them courteously, etcetera. The government now sought a rapprochement with the King, who had made d'Ursel his mouthpiece, but it could not however accept that the embassies would not obey the foreign ministry, based in London. So d'Ursel's replacement was contemplated but only became effective later because it was feared the Swiss, under German pressure would not give their *agrément* to a successor. This is a request to the receiving government for a new head of a diplomatic mission to be accepted and always precedes a formal appointment.

47. There was a hare-brained scheme by some in the Belgian government to send a lone agent, member of the Belgian Parliament and Naval Captain François Truffaut, on his own and armed with just a single 9mm pistol, to recover it. He was not told how he was supposed to transport some 200 tons of gold from West Africa to Britain, if he could get hold of them. James Bond might have achieved it, Truffaut didn't.

48. Reference Cab/66/15/2.

49. An American author has claimed that 10 million people lost their lives, thus making Léopold II guilty of worse mass murder than Hitler's of the Jews, and a death toll almost comparable to the total for military deaths in the First World War! The 'projection statistics' made by this person however do not sustain scrutiny as there were no census operations held in the region until much later in the 1920s and the entire population of the Congo River basin at the time of Léopold II's Congo Free State might not have attained that total number. The figures used were based in part on mathematical errors made by explorer Stanley and projection on the whole country of loss of life sustained in riverbank villages that had been visited and which were more populous than the rest of the country inland. Léopold II's agents present in the region at the time were far too few to commit or even organize a massacre of such scale, that would have deprived them of a large part of their valuable working force. However, even if the number of 10 million deaths is based on sloppy research and vastly exaggerated, it is indisputable that native populations in central Africa as a whole suffered heavy loss of life, lack of immunity against imported diseases also playing a very important role. It should be noted that on the whole, and judged by modern eyes and minds, these were very hard times indeed for African, Asian or native American populations. British repression of the Indian Mutiny or of the Zulus and Boers, French interventions in their African colonies (like the now forgotten Voulet-Chanoine 'infernal column' in Chad) and Madagascar, German repression of the Herero revolt in today's Namibia or the Portuguese destruction of Gugunhana's kingdom in Mozambique

were all contemporary, as was the gradual disappearance of the native North American nations, or expeditions by the Argentinian and Chilean armies against native populations – to name only a few examples. (See *The Scramble for Africa* by Thomas Pakenham.)

50. There were unsubstantiated reports that Sengier also worked for the Soviets. Seeing his background, it seems unlikely.

51. North Korea trained one of Congolese President Mobutu's elite army brigades in the 1970s. Mobutu, a former NCO of the Force Publique, (mis)ruled the Congo for more than thirty years (1965–97).

52. At the Atlantik Wall open air museum at Raversijde, close to Ostend. A quick Google search will find a good description and several relevant links. The domain with bunkers and gun emplacements, and which also includes a First World War coastal battery, remained practically intact because it was part of the estate where Prince Charles, Regent of Belgium and Léopold III's younger brother lived after his regency and until his death. His cottage can also be seen.

53. They were future Kings of the Belgians Baudouin and Albert and their elder sister Joséphine-Charlotte, who would marry Grand Duke Jean of Luxembourg.

54. That he had sent his children and important papers away to France was given as proof that, contrary to what some said, Léopold certainly had no intention to surrender his army prematurely, even less to betray his homeland.

55. François De Kinder, Pierlot's brother-in-law, came to Brussels and duly delivered his message, to which a non-committal answer was given by other, quicker means. On his way back through France he was taken hostage by the Germans and executed.

56. The Bellevue Museum, dedicated to the history of Belgium, is located in Place des Palais, just next to the royal palace in central Brussels. (www.belvue.be/en)

57. The invasion of Greece, which Hitler eventually had to support because the Italians could not cope, is said by some to have got in the way of plans for the invasion of the USSR. The Germans had good reason not to tell the Italians too much, because the Italian general staff was stuffed with royalist generals who told the Allies all they knew. This might have contributed to Rommel's defeat in North Africa. Even Il Duce's son-in-law Ciano was not entirely loyal to the Axis as we have seen, and later paid for it with his life, being executed in January 1944 by Mussolini at the Germans' insistence.

58. King Léopold spoke fluent German (as well as French, Dutch and English) but in all interviews with Germans in authority during the war insisted on speaking French through an interpreter for reasons of dignity and of protocol, as he was head of state. This also gave him more time to prepare his answers. The same ploy is often used by polyglot politicians to this day.

59. Provinces in Belgium are the equivalent of a French *département*. They have recently lost much of their relevance because the regional governments of Flanders and Wallonia have taken over most of their powers, but are the regional administrative entity between the central Brussels government and the city administrations, which are very powerful. There is a central federal police (the former Gendarmerie and Police judiciaire who were recently merged), but local police forces in Belgium report to the local mayor.

60. He claimed he had been trying to find the Interior Minister, his superior, whom he thought had gone to France, but that he had been the victim of a road accident near Dunkirk that prevented him from returning to his post in Bruges.

61. Linen bags that had contained foodstuffs and were stamped accordingly were embroidered by grateful Belgian ladies with Belgian and American flags and sent back as tokens of gratitude.

62. The rest of the history of this particular painting makes fascinating reading. One of its panels (the *Righteous Judges*) was stolen in 1934 and held for ransom, but never paid for or found. A copy was then made from pictures of it, but with one of the characters having King Léopold III's head painted in instead of the original so as to make it clear to future generations it was a twentieth-century copy. Many theories have been written about who stole it and where it might (still) be hidden. Some say inside the Cathedral itself, a sacristan guilty of the theft dying without having had time to say exactly where it was on his deathbed.

63. During the first months of occupation some networks, knowingly or not, worked for Vichy France or the Polish government in exile.

64. Much to their surprise the Zéro network thus found an unlikely ally in the form of a member of the Abwehr who warned them of impending arrests, gave them useful information and so on. Some Belgian jailers also worked for the Resistance and passed messages to and from arrested agents.

65. Queen Mathilde, wife of King Philippe of the Belgians, is a member of the d'Udekem d'Acoz family.

66. www.breendonk.be/EN/

67. Pangermanism was a political and philosophical movement born in Germany in the nineteenth century as a reaction to the ideas of the French Revolution brought to the country by Napoleon's troops. It aimed at the unification of all Germanic people in Germany, Austria, Scandinavia, Flanders, the Netherlands etc.

68. Borms' younger brother had volunteered for the Belgian Army before 1914, was made a corporal but during the war deserted an incredible seven times, each time being sent to disciplinary units. Borms' biographer Christine Van Everbroeck, rightly remarks that one can only be amazed at the clemency of the Belgian military courts. Just one desertion committed in the British Army at the time would have brought him face-to-face with a firing squad, 'blindfolded and alone'.

69. Erzberger signed the 1918 Armistice for Germany and paid for it with his life, being assassinated later by German nationalists.

70. De Vlaamse Oostfronters. See Bibliography.

71. Langemarck, today written as Langemark, is a village in Flanders where there was heavy fighting in the First World War, including by Corporal Hitler. A large German military cemetery is located there.

72. *De Fabriekswacht – Vlamingen in 'Die Luftwaffe'*, (see Bibliography) Dries Timmermans Uitgeverij De Krijger.

73. The flag of the Walloon SS was adorned with a red St Andrew's cross which was the emblem of the medieval Burgundian States and is also to be found in the Spanish Army flag, since the Spanish Habsburg kings like Philip II were direct descendants of the dukes of Burgundy through Habsburg Emperor Charles V (born AD 1500 in Ghent), who was also King of Spain.

74. After the war, one of the perpetrators was identified and turned out to be a Swiss citizen, who was given a 20-year sentence. Some sources speak of a special unit sent by Himmler to weed out *Résistants*.
75. Martin Conway. See Bibliography.
76. Jews in the Belgian armed forces, many of them prisoners in Germany, were left alone and not discriminated against in relation to their fellow prisoners.
77. These former Belgian Army barracks in Mechelen have been turned into a memorial dedicated to the victims of the deportation, and a large educational museum on the deportation of Jews and gipsies from Belgium has been built next to it. The Dossin Barracks website is: www.kazernedossin.eu/EN
78. The only other case I am aware of is that of Princess Alice of Greece, the mother of Prince Philip, Duke of Edinburgh.
79. For a long time after the war, Israelis saved by Belgians named Righteous among the Nations would invite a number of the latter to Israel every year. They would then hold a reception at the Belgian embassy in Tel Aviv. Most of the Righteous having died or reached old age, the habit of inviting them has been discontinued, but the yearly reception in homage is still held.
80. *The Encyclopedia of the Righteous among the Nations* (Rescuers of Jews during the Holocaust), Belgium (see Bibliography).
81. Israeli author Sylvain Brachfeld, who was born in Antwerp and was himself saved by being hidden in a Catholic boarding school, has also written several books on the subject. They are mentioned in the Bibliography. His father was beaten to death by the SS in a German prison camp.
82. The Germans blew several bridges around the medieval city of Bruges. A new reconstructed bridge is adorned with two bronze bisons and is called the Manitoba Bridge, honouring the XIIth Manitoba Dragoons.
83. Horrocks's recollections are quoted in Cornelius Ryan's *A Bridge Too Far*. See Bibliography.
84. The fact that Borms was 70 years old and crippled, so that when deprived of his crutches he collapsed while being tied to the execution post, shocked many including some of his enemies, and some have made propaganda from it. He died bravely.
85. See *The Last Secret* by Nicholas Bethel (see Bibliography).

Bibliography

Acknowledgements

The main sources for this work were as follows:

- Churchill's and Spaak's memoirs, as well as those of Pierlot's chief of staff in 1940, the late Pierre d'Ydewalle, who was a relative of the author and went on to serve many years as Governor of West Flanders after the war.
- *Outrageous Fortune* by Lord Keyes (the son of the hero of Zeebrugge, whom I had the privilege to meet in the late 1990s) was also very helpful and especially so were the various works by Van Welkenhuysen. Simon Sebag Montefiore, whose other works I also find excellent is one of the few British authors I know to have accurately described the Belgian Army's role in 1940 in his *Dunkirk*.
- José Gotovitch and Jules Gérard-Libois' *L'An Quarante* is a classic account of the occupation and Jean Stengers' books remain the authority on the role of the monarchy in Belgium.
- I would like to mention two Flemish historians, Sophie De Schaepdrijver and Christine Van Everbroeck, also authors of excellent books. If I had not read them this work would have been quite incomplete and unbalanced.
- Martin Conway's *Degrelle* is I think the best study of that complicated personality, whose own work on the Russian campaign I also read. I am indebted to a fellow retired diplomat who sent me two interesting studies on the Flemish SS in Russia. The Israeli author of Belgian origin Sylvain Brachfeld has made very thorough studies of the persecution of the Jews in Belgium during the Second World War, which was also studied in depth by Rudi Van Doorslaer and Ludo Saerens.
- I would like to mention also General Geyr von Schweppenburg's book, which I found fascinating to read (especially his experiences as a military attaché in London before the war). It is interestingly prefaced by no less than Leslie Hore Belisha. I do not know of any other case of a British Jew and (prominent) former member of cabinet agreeing to write a foreword for a book by a German general who had served Hitler! This German (but not Nazi) general intervened to have my uncle released, when the Gestapo had arrested him instead of my father. After the war my father, a former member of the Resistance, and the General, who were related, corresponded until the latter's death.
- Jan Velaers and Herman Van Goethem probably wrote the definitive book on the Second World War in Belgium and I hope their work is translated into English one day. The latter is director of the Dossin Barracks Memorial.
- I should also mention as sources private conversations I had with members of the Belgian and British diplomatic corps and defence forces who had first-hand experiences of some of the events described, as well as with historians mentioned in the Word of Thanks.

To make it easier for the reader who would like to check the sources used by the author, general references are given first below, followed by references under the chapter title in which they have been used.

General sources

1914–1945 Lectures on RTBF (Belgian French-language radio) given by Prof. Francis Balace.

Bullock, Alan *Hitler, a Study in Tyranny*. Odhams, 1952.

Churchill, Winston S. *Memoirs of the Second World War*. Houghton Mifflin: Boston, 1959.

Coolsaet, Rik *België en zijn Buitenlandse Politiek*. Van Halewyck: Leuven, 1998.

Dictionnaire d'Histoire de Belgique, Editorial Director Prof. Hervé Hasquin. Didier Hatier: Brussels, 1988.

Gilbert, Martin *Atlas of the Second World War (2nd Edition)*. Routledge: London/New York, 2009.

De Launay, Jacques *Histoires Secrètes de la Belgique 1935–1945*. Alain Moreau: Paris, 1975.

Marks, Sally *Innocents Abroad: Belgium at the Paris Peace Conference of 1919*. The University of North Carolina Press, 1981.

Shirer, William L. *The Rise and Fall of the Third Reich*. Fawcett Books: Greenwich, Conn., 1959.

Spaak, Paul-Henri *Combats inachevés (De l'Indépendance à l'Alliance)*. Fayard: Paris, 1969.

Speer, Albert *Erinnerungen*. Ullstein, 1969.

Trausch, Gilbert *Histoire du Luxembourg*. Ministère de la Culture Luxembourg, 2011.

Velaers, Jan and Herman Van Goethem *Leopold III (De Koning, het Land, de Oorlog)*. Lannoo: Tielt, 1994.

De Visscher, C. and F. Vanlangenhove *Documents diplomatiques belges 1920–1940: La Politique de Sécurité extérieure*. Palais des Académies: Brussels, 1964.

De Vos, Luc *La Belgique et la Seconde Guerre mondiale*. Racine: Brussels, 2004.

Van Zuylen, (Ambassador) Pierre *Les Mains libres: Politique extérieure de la Belgique 1914–1940*. Desclée De Brouwer: Brussels, 1950.

Chapter 1. They knew it was coming

Fest, Joachim *Plotting Hitler's Death (The German Resistance to Hitler)*. Weidenfeld and Nicolson: London, 1996.

Vanwelkenhuyzen, Jean *Neutralité armée: La Politique militaire de la Belgique pendant la 'drôle de Guerre'* La Renaissance du Livre: Brussels, 1979.

Vanwelkenhuyzen, Jean *Ces Avertissements qui venaient de Berlin 1939–1940*. Duculot: Paris-Gembloux, 1982.

Vanwelkenhuyzen, Jean *L'Agonie de la Paix*. Duculot: Paris-Louvain La Neuve, 1989.

Von Schweppenburg, General Baron Geyr (former Military Attaché in London, Brussels and The Hague) *The Critical Years*, Preface by L. Hore-Belisha. Wingate: London, 1952.

D'Ydewalle, Pierre *Mémoires 1912–1940 (Aux avant-postes)*. Editions Racine: Brussels, 1994.

Chapter 2. Invasion

Bloch, Marc *L'étrange Défaite*. (1946) New edn, Gallimard, 1990.

Ceux du Fort d'Eben Emael Published by the Veterans' Association, Flemal Liège.

Coenen. E. and F. Vernier *La Position fortifiée de Liège*. De Krijger: Erpe, 2001.

De Decker, Cynrick and Jean-Louis Roba *Mei 1940 boven België: De Luchtstrijd tijdens de Achtiendaagse Veldtocht*. De Krijger Erembodegem, 1993.

Destrebecq, Guy and P. Marchand *La Chasse belge 1939–1946*. Editions d'Along: Le Muy, France, 2003.

Dunstan, Simon *Fort Eben Emael: The Key to Hitler's Victory in the West*. Osprey, 2005.

De Fabribeckers, Edmond *La Campagne de l'Armée belge en 1940*. Rossel: Brussels, 1978.

Georges, Commandant e.r. Roger *De Bastogne à Exaerde: Campagne du 2e Chasseurs Ardennais*. Schmitz: Bastogne, 1991.

Hautecler, Cdt Georges *Le Combat de Bodange le 10 mai 1940*. Ministère de la Défense nationale, Imprimerie des FBA, 1955.

Hautecler, Cdt Georges *Le Combat de Chabrehez le 10 mai 1940*. Ministère de la Défense nationale, Imprimerie des FBA, 1957.

Hiance, Roger *Wonck Mai 1940*. Edn Hiance: Wonck, 2007.

L'Histoire de l'Aéronautique belge: La Campagne des dix-huit Jours. In Memo Revue historique N° 12–84.

Jacoby, A. *Derrière les Barbelés 1940–45: Colditz, Prenzlau (. . .)* Edn L. Bourdeaux Capelle Dinant, 1998.

Kemp, Ian *Eben Emael*. Ian Allan: London, 2006.

De Lannoy, François 'Felsennest 12 Mai 1940: Les Vainqueurs d'Eben Emael décorés par le Führer' in *39–45 Magazine*, January 2009.

Mai-Juin 1940: Les Panzers Historica Magazine, special issue 39–45 May 2012.

Mrazek Col. James E. AUS *The Fall of Eben Emael* Presidio Press, Novato CA, 1991.

Montefiore, Hugh Sebag *Dunkirk (Fight to the last Man)*. Penguin: London, 2006.

Oublié . . . L'Aéronautique militaire belge en mai-juin 1940 in Wing Masters Hors Série 8.

Pacco, John *Het Militair Vliegwezen 1930–1940*. J.P. Publications: Aartselaar, 2003.

Papeians De Morkhoven, (Dom) Christian, OSB *L'Abbaye de Saint André-Zevenkerken*. Desclée De Brouwer: Bruges, 1998.

Polderman, Fabrice *La Bataille de Flandre*. Atlantica Editora: Rio de Janeiro, 1943.

Saunders, Tim *Fort Eben Emael*. Pen & Sword: Barnsley, 2005.

Schmidt, George *L'Aéronautique militaire belge 1914–1940*. Rossel Editions: Brussels, 1975.

Shepperd, Allan *France 1940: Blitzkrieg in the West*. Osprey Publishing: Oxford, 1990.

Taghon, Peter 'L'Aéronautique militaire belge en mai-juin 1940' in *Avions Hors Série* 18 Lela Presse.

Taghon, Peter *Mai 1940: La Campagne des Dix-huit Jours*. Duculot: Louvain la Neuve, 1989.

Vanwelkenhuyzen, Jean *1940: Plein Feux sur un Désastre*. Racine: Brussels, 1995.

Verhaegen, Général Hre Baron *Le Rôle de l'Armée belge en 1940*. Presses du 12ème de Ligne, 1948.

Vliegen, René *Fort Eben Emael*. FEE Wagelmans Visé, 1990.

Chapter 3. All the King's men

Aron, Robert *Léopold III ou le Choix impossible*. Plon: Paris, 1977.

Crahay, Lt Gen. A. *Le Général Van Overstraeten, 'Vice-Roi' en 1940*. J.-M. Collet (ed.) Braine l'Alleud, 1990.

Giscard d'Estaing, Antoine *Léopold III: Un Roi dans la Tourmente*. Racine: Brussels, 1996.

Kennedy, Joseph P. *The Surrender of King Leopold*. J.P. Kennedy Memorial Foundation: New York, 1950.

Keyes, R., Lord of Zeebrugge and Dover *Outrageous Fortune (The Tragedy of Leopold III of the Belgians 1901–1941)*. Secker Warburg: London, 1984.

Kirschen, Gilbert *L'Education d'un Prince (Entretiens avec Léopold III)*. Didier Hatier: Brussels–Paris, 1984.

Léopold III *Pour l'Histoire: Sur quelques épisodes de mon règne*. Racine: Brussels, 2001.

De Man, Henri *Cavalier seul*. Editions du Cheval Ailé: Geneva, 1948.

Van Overstraeten, General R. *Dans l'Etau*. Plon: Paris, 1960.

Moureaux, Serge *Léopold III: La Tentation totalitaire*. Editions Luc Pire: Brussels, 2002.

Roegiers, Patrick *La spectaculaire Histoire des Rois des Belges*. Perrin: Paris, 2007.

Stengers, Jean *Léopold III et le Gouvernement (Les deux politiques belges de 1940)*. Duculot: Brussels, 1980.

Stengers, Jean *L'Action du Roi en Belgique depuis 1831: Pouvoir et Influence*. Duculot: Louvain-la-Neuve, 1992.

Vanwelkenhuyzen, Jean *Quand les Chemins se séparent (Aux Sources de la Question royale)*. Racine: Brussels, 2001.

Chapter 4. The innocents abroad

Baete, Hubert (ed.) *Belgian Forces in the United Kingdom*, Comité 1944–94. Defence: Ostend/Brussels, 1994.

'Belgian Airmen decorated in RAF', *Aero Journal* No. 46.

Capron, Freddy *L'Aviation belge et nos Souverains*. Editions J.M. Collet: Brussels, 1988.

Cornu, G. *Le Drame de l'Or belge* (Transport of Belgian Gold back from Dakar to France). In: *Fana de l'Aviation* September 2005, and www.anac-fr.com/2gm/2gm_77.htm

'Dans l'Oeil du Typhon: Pilotes belges sur Hawker Typhoon', *Aero Journal* No. 36.

Delcorde, Raoul *Les Diplomates belges*. MardagaWavre (Belgium), 2010.

Delmelle, Joseph *Histoire de la Navigation et des Ports belges*. Paul Legrain: Brussels, 1982.

Destrebecq, Guy *La Chasse belge 1939–1946*. Editions D'Along: Le Muy, 2003.

Dieu, Maj., e.r. G.N. *La Victoire de Saïo – 3 Juillet 1941* In Memo 6-81.

Van den Dungen, Pierre *Pierlot*. Conference given at CEGES Brussels, 28 January 2011.

Dutry-Soinne, Tinou *Les Méconnus de Londres*. Racine: Brussels, 2008.

Gérard, Hervé *Les As de l'Aviation belge*. J.M. Collet, Braine l'Alleud, 1994.

Gérard, J., Gérard, H. and Rens, G. *Se Battre pour la Belgique 1940–1945*. J.M. Collet: Brussels, 1982.

Gunther, John *Inside Africa*. Harper and Brothers: New York, 1953.

Hendy, John *The Dover Ostend Line*. Ferry Publications: Stapelhurst, 1991.

Irving, David *Churchill's War*. Focal Point, 2003.

Irving, David *Hitler's War*. Focal Point, 2002.

Kestergat, J. *Quand le Zaïre s'appelait Congo*. Paul Legrain Brussels 1985

De Laveleye, Valentine *Victor de Laveleye: Un Destin inachevé*, 2003.

Pakenham, Thomas *The Scramble for Africa* Abacus new edn, 1992.

Plissart, Etienne *Souvenirs de Guerre 1942–44.* See www.librarything.com/author/
plissartetienne

La S.A. Armement Deppe dans les deux guerres mondiales. Anvers (Antwerp), 1946.

Secret War Cabinet Paper of 10 February 1941 (Belgian Loan to the British Government), National Archives Ref: cab/66/15/2.

Thomas, Nigel *Foreign Volunteers of the Allied Forces 1939–45.* Osprey Publishing:
London, 1991.

De Vos, Luc 'The reconstruction of Belgian military forces in Britain', in : M.C.
Conway and J. Gotovitch (eds), *Europe in Exile.* Berghahn Books: New York/Oxford,
2001.

Chapter 5. Occupation

Amouroux, Henri *La grande Aventure des Français sous l'Occupation.* Robert Laffont:
Paris, 1978.

Balthazar, Herman *Het dagelijkse Leven in België* ASLK-Galerij: Brussels, 1984.

Butler, Rupert *Legions of Death: The Nazi Enslavement of Europe* Pen & Sword: Barnsley,
1983.

Delandsheere, Paul and Alphonse Ooms *La Belgique sous les Nazis* L'Edition
Universelle: Brussels, 1941.

Jours de Guerre. Series on RTBF (French-language Belgian television), 1980–85.

Kesteloot, Chantal *Bruxelles sous l'Occupation.* Luc Pire-CEGES: Brussels, 2009.

Libois, J.G. and J. Gotovitch *L'An Quarante (La Belgique occupée).* Brussels, 1970.

Martin, Dirk and Lieven Saerens *Anvers sous l'Occupation, 1940–1945.* Renaissance du
Livre, 2010.

Paxton, Robert O. *Vichy France, Old Guard and New Order, 1940–1944.* Columbia
University Press, 2001.

Raskin, Evrard *Princesse Lilian (La femme qui fit tomber Léopold III).* Luc Pire: Brussels,
1999.

Taghon, Peter and Jean-Louis Roba *Brussel 1940–45.* Uitgeverij De Krijger Erpe, 2000.

Triffaux, Jean-Marie *Arlon 1939–45(De la Mobilisation à la Répression).* Arlon, 1994.

Verhoeyen, Etienne *La Belgique occupée.* De Boeck University, 1994.

Van den Wijngaert, Mark et al. *België tijdens Wereldoorlog II.* Standaard Uitgeverij, 2004.

De Wilde Maurice *De Nieuwe Orde.* Series on BRT (Flemish television), 1981.

Willequet, Jacques *La Belgique sous la Botte.* Résistances et Collaborations, Editions
universitaires Begedis: Paris, 1986.

Williams, Charles *Pétain.* Little Brown: London, 2005.

Chapter 6. Resistance

Bernard, Henri *Un Géant de la Résistance: Walthère Dewé.* La Renaissance du Livre:
Brussels, 1971.

Bles, Mark *Child at War: The true Story of Hortense Daman.* Warner Books: London, 1989.

Caballero Jurado, Carlos (Paul Hannon, Illus.) *Resistance Warfare 1940–45.* Men at
Arms Series 169, Osprey, 1985.

Chauffrein, E. *La Résistance en Belgique.* In Memo 2–80.

Debruyne, Emmanuel *La Guerre secrete des Espions belges 1940–44.* Racine: Brussels,
2008.

Deneckere, K. (Transl.) *Gewapende Joodse Partizanen van België (Getuigenissen)*. Foreword by Marek Halter. Published by The Children of Armed Jewish Partisans of Belgium, 1997.

Despy-Meyer, Andrée et al. *25.11.1941 L'Université Libre de Bruxelles ferme ses Portes*. Archives de l'ULB, Brussels.

Le Fort de Huy. Office du Tourisme de Huy.

Galle, Hubert and Yannis Thanassekos *La Résistance en Belgique*. J.M. Collet, 1979.

Hogkinson, Terry *'Frederick' (La Mission oubliée)*. Larsen Grove Press: London, 2007.

Van den Kerchove, Gerda *Et cependant. . .je veux vivre ! (Souvenirs de captivité de Saint Gilles, Gommern, Ravensbrück)* Editions libres: Brussels, 1946.

Pauly, Albert *Du Perron à Piccadilly 1940–1945*. Editions J.M. Collet: Brussels, 1988.

Rely, Achiel 'The notorious Fort Breendonk', *After the Battle* 51, 1986.

Sadi Kirschen, G. *Six Amis viendront ce Soir*. Nicholson & Watson: London/Brussels, 1946.

Strubbe, Fernand *De geheime Oorlog 40/45: De Inlichting en Actie diensten in België*. Lannoo: Tielt, 1992.

D'Udekem d'Acoz, Marie-Pierre *Pour le Roi et la Patrie (La Noblesse belge dans la Résistance)*. Racine: Brussels, 2002.

Ugeux, William *Histoire de Résistants Cette Armée de l'Ombre qui a forcé la Victoire*. Duculot: Paris, 1979.

www.resistances.be (Resistance in Belgium.)

D'Ydewalle, Pierre *Mémoires II 1940–1945*. Racine: Brussels, 1997.

Chapter 7. Collaboration

Carrein, Kristof *De Vlaamse Oostfronters: Sociaal Profiel en Wervingsverloop, November 1941, Augustus 1944* in: BEG-CHTP –N° 6/1999.

Conway, Martin *Collaboration in Belgium (Leon Degrelle and the Rexist Movement)*. Yale University Press: London, 1993.

Conway, Martin *Léon Degrelle: The Years of Collaboration*. Oxford, 1993.

Degrelle, Léon *La Campagne de Russie 1941–1945*. Le Cheval Ailé: Paris, 1949.

Van Everbroeck, Christine *August Borms (Zijn Leven, zijn Oorlogen, zijn Dood)*. Manteau: Antwerp, 200.

Hermans, Theo et al. *The Flemish Movement 1780–1990*. The Athlone Press: London/Atlantic Heights, N.J., 1992.

'Les Feuilles de Chêne de Léon Degrelle', *39–45* (Magazine) February, 2006.

Littell, Jonathan *Le Sec et l'Humide*. Gallimard, 2008.

Plisnier, Flore 'Op alle Fronten in het nauw(België-Collaboratie in Wallonië)', *Knack*, 20 February 2008.

Plisnier, Flore *Ils ont pris les Armes pour Hitler*. Luc Pire: Brussels, 2008.

'Roger Mannaert – La Guerre à 17 ans' *39–45* (Magazine), November 2012.

Ruys, Manu *De Vlamingen (Een Volk in Beweging, Een natie in Wording)*. Lannoo: Tielt, 1972.

De Schaepdrijver, Sophie *De Groote Oorlog: Het Koninkrijk België tijdens de Eerste Wereldoorlog*. Olympus/Atlas, 1997.

Sint-Maartensfonds, V. S. *Vlamingen aan het Oostfront*. De Krijger Etnika: Antwerp, 1973.

Timmermans, Dries *De Fabriekswacht: Vlamingen in ' die Lufwaffe'*. De Krijger: Erpe, 2005.

Trigg, Jonathan *Hitler's Flemish Lions (The History of the 27th SS Freiwilligen Grenadier Division Langemarck-Flämische Nr1)*. Spellmount, 2007.
Waffen SS, een synopsis in: Nieuwe Orde http://www.nieuweorde.be/

Chapter 8. A tale of two trains
1940–1944 Les Années ténèbre. (Déportation et Résistances des Juifs en Belgique). Collection Musée Juif de Belgique, 1992.
Bloch, (Baron) Jean *Epreuves et combats*. Didier Devillez Institut d'Etudes du Judaïsme, 2002.
Brachfeld, Sylvain *Les Relations entre la Belgique et Israël*. Institut de Recherche sur le Judaïsme Belge: Herzliya, 1994.
Brachfeld, Sylvain *Geschonken Jaren*. S.B. Publishing: Herzlia, 2000.
Brachfeld, Sylvain *Ils ont survécu (Le sauvetage des Juifs en Belgique occupée)*. Editions Racine: Brussels, 2001.
Brachfeld, Sylvain *A Gift of Life (The Deportation and Rescue of the Jews in occupied Belgium 1940–1944)*. Institute for the Research on Belgian Judaism: Beth Shemesh, 2007.
Brachfeld, Sylvain *Merci de nous avoir sauvés (Témoignages d'Enfants Juifs cachés)*. Institut de Recherche sur le Judaïsme belge: Herzliya, 2007.
Coquio, Catherine and Aurélia Kalisky *L'Enfant et le Génocide (Témoignages sur l'Enfance pendant la Shoah)*. Laffont: Paris, 2007.
Van Doorslaer, R., Debruyne, E., Seberechts, F. and N. Wouters *La Belgique docile: Les Autorités belges et la Persécution des Juifs en Belgique durant la Seconde Guerre mondiale*. Editions Luc Pire: Brussels, 2007.
Gérard, J. *Ces Juifs qui firent la Belgique*. J.M. Collet: Braine l'Alleud, 1990.
Gutterman, Bella and Avner Shalev *To Bear Witness (Holocaust Remembrance at Yad Vashem)*. Yad Vashem: Jerusalem, 2005.
Marrus, Michaël R. and Robert O. Paxton *Vichy et les Juifs*. Calmann-Lévy: Paris, 1981.
Michman, Dan (ed.) *Belgium and the Holocaust (Jews, Belgians, Germans)*. Yad Vashem: Jerusalem, 1998.
Michman, Dan (ed.) *The Encyclopedia of the Righteous among the Nations (Rescuers of Jews during the Holocaust): Belgium*. Yad Vashem: Jerusalem, 2005.
Nowak, Herman *Cyrille Berger, Enfant caché (Un Enfant juif et des Justes parmi les Nations)*. La Longue Vue, 2000.
Prowizur-Szyper, Claire *Conte à Rebours (Une Résistante juive sous l'Occupation)*. Louis Musin: Brussels, 1979.
Prowizur-Szyper, Claire *Instantanés d'ici et d'ailleurs*. Louis Musin: Brussels, 1982.
Saerens, Lieven *Vreemdelingen in een Wereldstad: Een Geschiedenis van Antwerpen en zijn Joodse Bevolking*. Lannoo Uitgeverij: Tielt, 2000.
Schreiber Jean-Philippe and Rudi Van Doorslaer *Les Curateurs du Ghetto: L'Association des Juifs en Belgique sous l'Occupation nazie*. Labor, 1994.
Schreiber, Marion *Rebelles silencieux (L'Attaque du 20ème Convoi pour Auschwitz)*. Racine: Brussels, 2000.

Chapter 9. Liberation
Dewandre, Lt Gén. Robert *Au Galop de nos Blindés*. Editions J.M. Collet: Braine l'Alleud, 1991.

Edsel, Robert *Monuments Men: Allied Heroes, Nazi Thieves and the Greatest Treasure Hunt in History*. Arrow, 2010.

Engels, (Lt Col.) Emile *La Campagne des Ardennes*. Racine: Brussels, 2004.

Fana de l'Aviation HS 28 (La dernière Année de la Luftwaffe). Les opérations de la Luftwaffe en Belgique en 1944.

Gheysens, Roger *La Libération du Port d'Anvers par la Résistance belge*. In Memo 8–82.

Holt, Major and Mrs *Battlefield Guide to the Normandy D-Day Landing Beaches*. Pen & Sword: Barnsley, 1999.

Rely, Achiel 'Disaster at Antwerp – April 5, 1943' *After the Battle* 42, 1983.

Taghon, Peter *België 44 – De Bevrijding*. Lannoo: Tielt, 1993.

Reynolds, Michael *The Devil's Adjutant: Jochen Peiper, Panzer Leader*. Pen & Sword: Barnsley, 2009.

Ryan, Cornelius *A Bridge Too Far*. Popular Library: Terre Haute, Indiana USA, 1974.

Toland, John *Bastogne*. Calmann-Lévy: Paris, 1962 (Original title: *Battle*).

Chapter 10. Aftermath

Behell, (Lord) Nicholas *The Last Secret (Forcible Rapatriation to Russia 1944–1947)* (With an introduction by Hugh Trevor Roper). Penguin Books: London, 1995.

Close, (Général) Robert *Léopold III les 'non-dits'*. Ligne Claire: Brussels, 2001.

Fralon, José-Alain *Baudouin (L'Homme qui ne voulait pas être Roi)*. Fayard: Paris, 2001.

Keyes, Roger *Leopold III (Complot tegen de Koning. Deel 2 1940–1951)*. Lannoo: Tielt, 1988.

Léopold III *Pour l'Histoire (Sur quelques épisodes de mon règne)*. Racine: Brussels, 2001.

De Staercke, André *Mémoires sur la Régence et la Question royale*. Racine: Brussels, 2003.

Index